The Miracle du jour

The Miracle du jour

Terryl Warnock

MoonLit Press
Nonfiction

Williams   Doney Park   San Jose

First Published Summer Solstice 02017

The Miracle du jour
by
Terryl Warnock

Front cover photo by Eric Eliason with permission
Element of Water photo by Lisa Williams with permission.
All other interior photos by Terryl Warnock.

Cover and Book Design by Al Brown
mailto:al.brown@WebDustWorld.com
in cooperation with:
Web Dust World: Designing, Developing and Delivering Usable and
Sustainable Tools, Techniques and Technologies

Edited by Lynn Natal Hartman

"The Bat is Dead" was published in
the *Arizona Literary Magazine 2017*
and is reprinted here with permission of the Arizona Author's Association.

"Pursuit of Demons" was published in the
Northern Arizona Authors Association Collected Works Volume 2
and is reprinted here with permission of MoonLit Press

"'Tis the Season" previewed in *From Spark to Fire*
by the Sacred Circle Writers
and is reprinted here with permission of MoonLit Press

Published by:
MoonLit Press LLC
P. O. Box 126
Williams, Arizona 86046

http://MoonLitPress.com/

ISBN-13: 978-0-9894698-5-2
ISBN-ebook: 978-0-9894698-6-9

Library of Congress Control Number: 2017903551

For Bob,
once in a lifetime

and for all my teachers, great and small

Contents

Elemental

Teachers and Tuition

The Spiral of the Year

Conclusion

For the Interested Reader

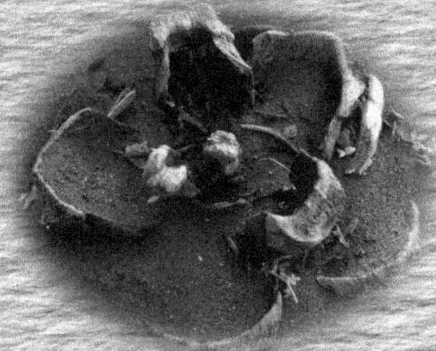

Introduction

Dear Reader;

When I'm getting to know someone new and the subject of spirituality comes up, people will often ask me what it means to be pagan. The short answer is Mother Nature is God Herself to me. The long answer follows. I am not sharing these experiences and the inspiration I gained from them with you to proselytize. I am not trying to convince anyone to convert. I hope everyone reading this is happy and fulfilled on their own spiritual path and in their own religious community. I am sharing these intimate stories and insight with you because these experiences have helped me be happier living in my own skin and in the world I do. I hope they might do the same for you.

The Miracle du jour hopes to resonate with people who are spiritual, people who are religious, and people who are both. *Miracle* seeks to take nothing away, only to add to. It wants to point out the common ground—environmental, spiritual, religious, and otherwise—all of us who inhabit Mother Earth share. *The Miracle du jour* would like only to inspire you to notice the sacred that surrounds you in whatever ways it does. The essays, fables, yarns, and spells here are some of the ways I notice and celebrate the sacred that surrounds me and I offer them to you *only* by way of example. These are the occurrences and encounters in my life that have filled my heart with happiness, my spirit with joy, and my mind with insight. I tend to find the miraculous not in the *super*-natural, but in the natural, and in small ways and places that can be easily overlooked. I contend here that a miracle does not need to be super-natural to incite wonder and save the world; that the Sacred, capital S, with all the redemption and salvation it entails, can be encountered in small-m miracles in each of our ordinary days.

Pagan is a much perjured and misunderstood term even still. It is a word loaded with stereotypical assumptions and has been burdened with bad press for millennia. The word in its most basic and historic sense, and as I use it here, means only "people from the country." Mine is not the propitiatory Mediterranean paganism of antiquity that required blood sacrifice and which was so maligned in early Christian teachings. My spirituality's lineage flows from Northern European strands of ancient nature worship, but the provenance of the spirituality I share with you in *The Miracle du jour* is not the point. Pagan as I use it here speaks of people who have not lost their connections with the natural world as sacred space; people who accept, maybe even privilege, intuitive and imaginative ways of knowing as valid; people who live the Spiral of the Year with keen apprehension and appreciation of the elemental and spiritual powers that surround them.

The larger point is that the world is very much worth saving and that it will be these small-p pagans—no matter what other political, religious, or community identities they might hold dear—who will save it.

There are a multitude of growing religious movements and institutions today that identify themselves as "pagan" or "neopagan." It is not for me to say what paganism is, writ large. What follows in *The Miracle du jour* are the epiphanies and insights of one animist, polytheistic pagan living in an enchanted world. I do not speak for all pagans and anyone who says they do should be regarded with deep suspicion. Pagan voices and their affiliations in the world today are as diverse as the stars in the night sky. There is no clear, overarching theological metanarrative in contemporary paganism; no definitive ancient canon; no dogma. Contemporary paganism is consequently both burdened with chaos and liberated with incredible lightness of religious freedom. Freedom that liberates pagan folk to write their own mythology, as I am sharing some of my mythology with you here.

I suspect *The Miracle du jour* will probably strike the pagan reader as stating the obvious in many ways. For them I hope only to have said it well. In fact the pagan reader may well find some comic relief in these pages because trying to force a cyclic, subtle pagan experience into the linear sequence and clear articulation required of a book has been torturous and distinctly un-natural. Un-pagan as I live paganism. As though the spring of the year could be distinct in some way from the winter that births it. Should a Spring Cleaning ritual go in Element of Water or the Spiral of the Year? Flip of the coin and it goes in Element of Water. It has been like trying to uncoil a spring. Although you might think *Roadside Puddles* would necessarily land in Element of Water, the larger point to the essay is the migratory birds who light on the puddles, so it ended up in Element of Air. Ridiculous.

Pagan readers will already know that sunwise, or deosil, is clockwise, and the direction to move when you want to do things, add things, and pray for spiritual increase. They will likewise already know that widdershins is counterclockwise, and the direction to move when you want to undo things in a spiritual sense. For instance, wind the Christmas lights around the tree deosil and take them off widdershins; stir the soup sunwise and scrub the pot widdershins. I have included such basic information here for the non-pagan reader.

Pagan readers will already understand that all of life's teachers don't work in schools and that time is cyclic. They know we are only tricked into thinking time is linear because our *experience* of it feels *linear*. But really, the story has no beginning, middle or end, only endless cycles of renewal. Non-pagans for whom this is an inconsistent or strangely new notion might pause for a moment to consider the fundamental design of the calendar and clock. Both must come back to where they started and start over at regular intervals to be intelligible. If time was linear the months and hours would just stack up on top of each other indefinitely and we can only imagine what time it might be now; how large the number would be or how complicated the name of the month.

The Miracle du jour is a pilgrimage. The journey is the point much more than the destination. Because the experiences I share with you here have not readily lent themselves to the kind of front-to-back sequence a book yearns for, *The Miracle du jour* wanders. Pagan and non-pagan reader alike will perhaps get more out of *The Miracle du jour* by reading it at random, letting it fall open where it will, than they will from reading it cover-to-cover.

Neither does *The Miracle du jour* fit neatly into any particular literary genre. Since everything I've written about here was either something I did, something that happened to me, something I trust,or something that happened close enough to me (with the one exception noted below) I gained happiness and peace of mind from the experience, I have a clear conscience about placing this book in the creative nonfiction genre. There are fables here, to be sure, but bear in mind one of the dictionary definitions of a fable is "a narrative intended to enforce a useful truth." These are my truths and I have written some of my small-m miracles as fables because I, I, I, me, me, me can get so very tiresome for both writer and reader alike.

More to the point, the miracle, the real gift in these small-m miracles is the realization that it's not all about me. That moment of recognition, the experience of beauty and peace, the thrill of excitement when I suck the air across my teeth and *get it* as epiphany is the same moment I feel myself in the presence of things of greater importance than myself. I am liberated in my insignificance, freed in my smallness. You will see this theme many times and in many ways in the ensuing pages. Such liberation, however, does not relieve me of my responsibilities as a member of the community in this wide, diverse, animated world. The realization, in fact, is that no matter how small I am, I am nonetheless part of a profoundly interconnected web. I must hold up my corner and trust others to hold up theirs. They are relying on me as I rely on them. No one goes it alone.

Take the miracles you find here or leave them as you will.

Another beneficial pause before we set out will be to consider the distinction between fact and truth. It is a more subtle distinction than may be readily apparent to us in a world that prefers to view itself in terms of polar opposites.

The perceived difference between scientific and religious understanding has been the wellspring of the internecine war between the two that has spanned centuries now. Each claims sole access to the inerrant, universal truth (=fact), but it is increasingly apparent (corroborated now even by the hardest of hard sciences, physics) that to think of facts as hard and universal is to draw an ambiguous and arbitrary line in the sand between what is considered fact and what is dismissed as fiction. Fact is, facts change. Fact is they always have and probably always will.

Time we started realizing there may be few universal, objective truths out there, religious or scientific for us to discover; facts writ large that are the same for everyone everywhere under all conditions. We are conscious beings and our consciousness shapes our understanding of our own realities (=facts=truths). Consciousness is the ocean we swim in all our lives and to use a tired metaphor, trying to explain consciousness to a conscious being is like trying to explain water to a fish. Consciousness infuses and suffuses the world, everyone's world, and one conscious being's definition and experience of reality may not be the same as that of another conscious being. That doesn't make it untrue.

For instance if *The Rock People* should be one of the fables you choose to read, you will discover my truth is that rocks are living things. I have taken much ribbing about this over the years but it doesn't bother me because I *know* the rock people are alive. My conviction is unshakable because my *experience* of them is experience with fellow, living, wise, sentient beings. That experience is based in the fact (!) that they talk to me. They have always talked to me and in a voice as real as yours or mine. My point in *The Rock People* is that we don't live long enough to say with any kind of scientific certainty they're *not* alive. Lack of proof is not proof of lack. The rock people, if there are such, will measure their lives in millions and billions of years —in time on a geologic and galactic scale we can scarcely conceive of from the perspective of the century or so we get to live if we're lucky. Even the two hundred thousand or so years since our species came to be distinct from our hominid ancestors would be merely a fleeting episode in their lives. All of human history would be only a flash in the pan from their perspective.

I was raised and educated to think I had to pick; I could be either rational or religious, but probably not both. I rejected that conditioning as too narrow long ago. Mythology is important self-defining truth; contextualized truth. It tells us who we are, where we came from, what matters to us and how we shall behave, whoever the "we" might be. Mythology is truth. It is our truth. Whether it might boil down to fact in the laboratory is beside the point. Mythology defines what we understand as real, what is important to us. My experience of these small epiphanies I share with you here were experiences of The Sacred, capital T, capital S. Best I can tell, that makes it as true as true gets and as real as real gets. I share them with you in case you might find some truth (small t) here on your own quest for capital-T Truth.

The only outright fabrication you'll find in *The Miracle du jour* is the epilogue to *Mary the Yogini*. It is a speculative edit on my part, a rewrite of a section of the Bible. It seeks only to ask a question and illustrate a point, not to profane or blaspheme. Its intent is not iconoclasm, but to challenge, perhaps recraft in some tiny way, the patriarchy's long-entrenched ideas about women; their power and their proper place. For those of you who hold the Bible dear and sacred and inerrant, I beg your forgiveness particularly. *The Miracle du jour* endeavors to be inclusive of all religions and spiritualities, harming none and alienating none.

I would argue that it is not only appropriate, but essential to bring our intellectual acumen and critical thinking abilities to bear in consideration of what we—as individuals and as a species—will hold sacred and, equally importantly, what we will consider profane. We stand on the brink of ecocide. If there is an overarching point to this pilgrimage it is that, as conscious beings, we can determine—**decide**—what we will hold sacred. I'm sharing *The Miracle du jour* with you to advocate we choose, together, to hold nature, the Mother Nature that birthed us and sustains us, Sacred (capital S).

§

These are cynical times. We must look to our own happiness and peace of mind. I suffer from what I call the Chicken Little disease. Among the things I like about myself is that I am sensitive and empathetic. It is my nature. It is also my fatal flaw. I take everything too seriously. I've tried to care less, but I can't. I can feel the pain of others. Because I ask "What is it like to be you?" of the world around me, and attend carefully to the answer, I pick up grief that is beyond both my responsibility and ability to carry. I become so overwhelmed with the ills of living in the modern world I run around in panicky circles flapping my wings (or mouth), convinced that "the sky is falling!! The sky is falling!! It's the end of the world as we know it!!" You know the type. Unfortunately, they (we) abound in this late modern (postmodern if you prefer), dysfunctional, and incredibly unfair world. Still, (back of hand to forehead) martyred as I am with things beyond my control, from whales choking on plastic in the ocean to the obscene social injustice human beings visit on one another, I have a happy heart. I have a happy heart because I look for a little miracle (small m) in each of my days—something positive and uplifting—and when I can put all the drama and pain of my disease aside long enough to look I always find one; the positive, the magical, the miraculous. When I need them most, when I am bruised and despairing, the world speaks messages of comfort to me in a simple pagan tongue if only I will pause long enough to listen. Because I look for it I can always find something to be happy about.

What's wrong with the world—my world, anyway—is rude and intrusive. The ills of the world butt into my life through the news and at the post office and over the internet and in a million other ways. They leave me either laid low with depression or running in Chicken Little circles. Looking for a miracle *du jour* in each of my days is a meditation, a mental health exercise that has saved me from stabbing myself in the heart. I share these little miracles and insights with you in case you suffer likewise.

The world can be a good place. There is beauty and love and connectedness and a thousand other blessings in every day and for myself, I feel *so* much better and so much more energetic and empowered to work toward solving all those other ills of the world when I pause and look for what is beautiful, what is right, what is interesting, what is worth saving—what is capital-S Sacred right in front of me.

Introduction

And last, a couple of housekeeping caveats before we embark on our pilgrimage:

Please be careful with opening yourself up to the Sacred (capital S), especially to the Other Side. The Sacred is powerful.

Consider power. Typically when we think of something as "powerful" what we're really thinking is something stronger than us. Power in a Sacred (capital S) context is frequently thought of as the territory occupied by the omniscient, omnipotent God (capital G); a super-natural God who has power over nature and death the rest of us must surrender to. That is not the God I'm generally writing about here. I'm writing about the god (small g and one of many), who surrenders to nature and to death.

Don't be foolish about it. The Sacred should not be toyed with or approached with a cavalier attitude. Scholars of religion observe that the Sacred has consistently manifested itself in ways that have been both intensely positive and horribly negative. There is no single experience of unqualified goodness. All of the Elements, for instance, explored in the first section of *The Miracle du jour* are powerful beyond human ken, so they can be perceived (from the smallness of a human perspective) as both beneficial and destructive. Element of Earth can be the rich, black, fecund soil that grows the food we live on, or it can be the city-leveling earthquake. Element of Air can be either the cooling, welcome summer breeze or the howling and violently destructive typhoon. Element of Water can be a cool, restorative drink of water on a hot summer's day or Noah's world-renewing flood.

Small-g gods and goddesses encourage us to accept responsibility for what we do so please do be sure to approach the power of the Sacred, whether Elemental in this world, or Otherworldly in the next, with humility and respect. Human life and psychological well-being can be small and powerless, fragile and vulnerable. Power can be brute. Be smart.

The Miracle du jour aims to share gratitude and wonder and to encourage readers to look for divine power *as well* in smaller, more unassuming places than the parting of seas or stone tablets inscribed by the hand of capital-G God. Sacred power can be delicate and subtle, too. For instance, the power to move a cold heart. How many of us have smiled in genuine joy at the giggle of a baby, even from the depths of despair? Or felt tears of gratitude prickling at the corners of our eyes to encounter a birdsong when we were sad?

Seek mentors and teachers you trust who will show you how to be safe and sensible and who will be there with you, at your side, while you gather and marshal your own strength and savvy.

Also be careful with bath salts (the bathing kind, avoid the drug kind entirely) and especially essential oils. Most essential oils should not be applied without dilution directly to your skin. Seek the guidance of a qualified herbalist or aromatherapist. One is recommended in the *For the Interested Reader* section, but I'm certain there is someone in your hometown too.

And if you should feel inspired to share a little miracle of your own I welcome your correspondence at **terryl@moonlitpress.com**. We can collaborate on sequels to this book. Regional and urban versions would be wonderful! I've written about the rural Southwest because it's all I know, but focusing on the specificity of the spot also evades the point. The basic premise here is that the miraculous and spiritually uplifting are everywhere, pervading Planet Earth and the human experience in a million different, small ways if only we can, and will, see it as such.

In humility, kinship and hope I remain
Very truly yours,
Terryl Warnock
Winter Solstice 02016

Elemental

EARTH, AIR, FIRE, WATER AND SPIRIT

Home is as much a consciousness as it is a place; it is abstract and concrete at the same time. Home is a huge word that carries tremendous weight. We toss it about cavalierly, as though we're all talking about the same thing, but we're not. The enormity of the notion differs for each of us.

For some, who stick to one place and can't imagine breathing the air anywhere else, home is rooted. It is generations of ancestors buried in the family plot out at the cemetery; a geographical point on Planet Earth. It is one place, our place. We don't make sense anywhere else. Although we are abandoned time and again by those who don't stick like we do, still we stay. We stubbornly plant our feet and refuse to let issues or people drive us away from the place we're anchored.

For the worldlier among us, home is expansive; it is through exploration these pilgrims learn who they are and where they belong. The people and environments they discover in their journeys are home to them, more than a particular spot. Where they came from and the horizons they are on their way to explore, more than where they originated, defines where they belong. Home encompasses the whole of Planet Earth.

Whether we are earthlings who adventure far afield to experience cultures different from our own, or earthlings who are deeply rooted in a singular place and wander only by offering hospitality to the peripatetic, Mother Earth knows us by our footprint. Earth is a synergistic cooperative of Earth, Air, Fire Water and Spirit, united in common kinship. Earth is home. Earth is haven.

§

If there were an iconic symbol of contemporary nature spirituality, one that believers wore around their necks, it might be a pentacle—a five-pointed star enclosed in a circle. The points of the star signify the elements whence all we are and all we can ever know originate: earth, air, fire, water and spirit; embraced by the circle of kinship within which we are all related. **All** of us.

The circle around the star symbolizes more than just the obvious fact that all human beings are related to one another, it speaks also to the delicate and complex interrelatedness of the totality of the natural world: humans, animals, plants, rocks, trees, mountains, rivers, wind, clouds, sunrises, sunsets, oceans, waves, the stars in the night sky, all are connected in a symbiotic net of mutual interdependence. We are each a miniscule part of an unimaginably vast whole. Native people of the Plains have a wonderful and all-encompassing term for this: *Mitakuye Oyasin*. All my relations.

Delineating divisions between the elements, say, for chapters in a book, is unnatural and awkward. Spirit and kinship suffuse all that we know and experience in the world. We all breathe the same Air and carry the Waters of Mother Ocean in our blood. We tread the same Earth and the same spark of cosmic Fire beats in all our breasts. None of the elements exist in isolation. None of us exist in isolation. Element of Fire must have Elements of Air, Earth, and Water (which comprise its fuel) to burn. Element of Earth must have Elements of Air, Fire and Water to grow and thrive. Element of Water must have Element of Earth to move (gravity) and purify itself, Element of Fire to be warm enough to remain liquid, and Element of Air to be gaseous enough to bring rain. The interconnections go on infinitely.

ঔ৹ও৹

Element of Earth: Home

We face North to honor and contemplate Element of Earth, Home, Mother to us all; the very ground beneath our feet. The powers of Element of Earth are receptive; the source of stability and prosperity. Mother Earth is The Source, our foundation, and each of us suckles at Her breast our life long. There are many restorative, simple pleasures granted by Element of Earth: eating when you're really hungry, finding shade when it's hot, and rolling in the dirt to name but a few. Watch your pet or your child enjoy just getting dirty; it's more than merely forbidden hedonistic pleasure, it is communing with the Mother Herself in an essential, personal way.

Spontaneous outbursts of reverence for Element of Earth dot the landscape—urban, rural and wild—in the form of cairns, those whimsical stacks of rocks that are at once elegant and spiritual. Cairns orient and ground us, they are a delightful surprise wherever they are encountered, and making one is not only fun, it's a meditation on balancing the irregular, an apt metaphor for a human life.

§

The pentacle also symbolizes Element of Earth, particularly. Mother Nature loves pentacles. She makes them everywhere. They're especially evident in the plant world; in the cross-section of an apple, for instance, and in a million different varieties of wildflowers. The pentacle represents beauty and sustenance, prosperity, and even money. Element of Earth is endurance and continuity.

Element of Earth teaches us Southwesterners to look for rock shade when it's really hot. Rock shade is different than any other kind of shade. It's not the dancing, lacy, lambent shade offered by the tree people. Rock shade is a solid, tangible thing. Stepping into it transforms air so hot your lungs grapple and suck at it to get a breath into a deep, satisfying sigh of relief. Rock shade is cooler, darker, more restorative and more refreshing than any other shadow we might seek for respite from the fiery gaze of the sun.

Element of Earth here in the Southwest is bold and apparent— striking and stark. Our notion of the sacred character of Element of Earth is different than that of people elsewhere. My Midwestern friends tell me tales of an Element of Earth we hardly know here. The Element of Earth they worship is black, loamy and fertile; you can't even find a rock to chock the car with if you should get a flat. It's different here, but no less sacred. Us Southwesterners are largely unaccustomed to the interference of vegetation between us and our Element of Earth.

Element of Earth is the ancient wisdom of rocks (*The Rock People*). Element of Earth here in the desert southwest is horizon, it is often vertical and far-flung (think Monument Valley or the Grand Canyon) and frequently reluctant to grow much for lack of water and organic material. While we yearn for gardens lush with flowers, herbs, and vegetables, we must often settle for rock gardens.

Element of Earth is both grave and germination. As we age, Element of Earth inexorably draws us back in, ever downward to our graves, to the ashes that are the inevitable end of a fleeting transitive lifetime, and on toward the new beginning that is rebirth. Element of Earth is gravity, it stoops our backs and pulls us back down into its bosom after the exuberant antigravity of youthful nadir (*Perched: Observations by a 21st-Century Gargoyle*).

The cosmos does not waste material and that of which we are all made *will* be recrafted into something else after we're done with it. Reincarnation is fact. It would serve us well not to worry so much about whether our precious egos will survive the transition. It's not all about us. The knowledge we will go on to something, someone else after we die can be liberating; it casts our puny existence as individuals into the endless tides of the cosmos. Feeling the pull of Earth as we age renders us a mote in the infinity of all that is, and in that smallness our individual cares and worries can vanish into insignificance.

And if letting go isn't your longest suit (it certainly isn't mine), consider this: consciousness is one of the organizing principles of the universe. Scientific and spiritual realms alike are coming into agreement that consciousness is background material woven into all of creation. That which was special and unique about each of us in our individual lifetimes may well endure after our death to go on to some greater cosmic adventure in the same way the ashes of our physical selves will. Let us be open to death as another leg in the grand adventure, but not worry so much about it till we get there. The best any of us can do is live a good life harming none, die a good death, and remain open to whatever comes next. These are the blessings of Element of Earth.

⁖⚯⚮⁖

THE ROCK PEOPLE

"Bumblebees and bristlecone pines inhabit temporal planes that barely intersect our own."

James Gleick, *Faster*

"There is a prejudice imposed on us by our brief window of consciousness; things that move are alive, things that don't are dead."

Robert Charles Wilson, *Spin*

The little boy with the happy heart skipped home from school with his book tucked under his arm. He loved to read and was lost in Mary Stewart's, *The Crystal Cave.* He lingered in it, savoring each page. Sometimes he got into trouble at school because, although the textbook he was supposed to be studying was open on top of the desk, he was really reading the Merlin book, open in his lap.

Today was special; he could hardly wait to get home so he could read from it to his best friends. He'd just gotten to the part where the old enchanter had introduced Merlin to the little crystal cave where the light played and danced in rainbows amongst the faceted faces of the crystals, and where the wind made Aeolian music on the harp without the interference of human hands. The boy often talked to his rock friends, and read them stories from good books, but now, for the first time the story was about them and he couldn't wait to share it with them!

The geode had been his very best rock friend since his Uncle Marvin had given it to him way back when he was just a baby, not even in kindergarten yet. Aunt Janet and Uncle Marvin were rock hounds and they wore the title proudly, restlessly. They were always adventuring hither, thither and yon on expeditions long and short in search of gems and minerals; rocks both spectacular and ordinary. Uncle Marvin was a lapidary as well and had cut the magical geode in half to expose the crystal caves in its heart. The boy with the happy heart had spent many captivated hours staring into the crystal depths in the stone as he cupped them lovingly in his little hands. He watched the light play and dance in millions of rainbows amongst the faceted faces of the crystals and they had gone on many fanciful imaginary journeys together. The boy had whispered many secrets into the crystalline ears, and they kept his confidences.

He had used to talk to them outright, when he was still just a baby, but when his parents heard him they became concerned. They made him put the geode back in the silver tray on his nightstand and go outside to play with human and dog friends like other little kids. His parents had even bought him a new teddy bear, but when they tried to take his geode friends away he cried and pouted until they put them back in the silver tray on the nightstand. The boy made sure he never talked to his geode friends when his parents were listening after that. Both halves of the magical rock assured the boy it was alright to have a part of himself he never let anyone else know about. After all, they said, they were half, but whole. Nobody else ever needed to know about the friendship between the boy and the geode. The boy dried his eyes and said thank you and was very careful to pick up the teddy bear and ignore the geode when his parents were looking.

When he got home from school with his crystal cave story, he zipped his geode friends in his jacket pockets and took the book and went out to the Ditch, a dry riverbed overgrown with pussy willows behind his house. He clambered down the bank and made his way to his favorite fort in the pussy willows, which was packed down and padded with old leaves and overgrown enough he could hide there. Pussy willows make natural basket-shaped hollows at their centers; this one was only big enough for one boy, one book, and both halves of one geode. He took the geodes out of his pocket, propped them up just so, and read to them in a soft voice.

The advantage of his pussy willow fort was he'd visited it often enough that all the crunchies inside it were already crunched out. It was different outside the fort; the boy could hear someone coming through the Ditch long before they ever got to the fort. Sometimes, scenting him, dogs came by to visit, but people weren't very observant and all he had to do was be quiet and the people would walk right by without ever knowing he was there. That was another advantage of rock friends. They were quiet. They would never betray your presence any more than they would ever betray your secrets.

So the friends listened to stories of magic and crystal caves and dreamt the afternoon away with shared tales of kind teachers, the music of the spheres, and mystical journeys. When the boy came home he put his friends back in their silver dish like they were just rocks, washed his hands for dinner, and hugged the teddy bear like it was very special to him.

§

The boy with the happy heart stretched his long, lean legs and ran all the way home from school. He was coltish and lanky now, a bit clumsy in his rapidly growing body, and he had abundances of energy he just had to burn off sometimes. He often ran home from school just because he could, but today was special. He had to get home and ask his geode friends about something important and exciting.

When he was just a baby, way back in the second grade reading stories of ancient sorcerers, he'd loved his geode friends of course, but he hadn't known how old they were. Now that he was a big boy in the sixth grade, he was learning all sorts of wonderful stuff he could never have imagined before. The tattered teddy bear sat on his bed, as always, a co-conspirator. The teddy bear kept confidences too, and never once let on to the boy's parents that the boy's best friends were the enchanted rock people. That was another great thing about having rocks as friends; they never wore out or had to be put in the washing machine which, all agreed, just couldn't be a very pleasant experience for the teddy bear.

The boy zipped the geodes into his jacket pockets and went out into the Ditch. He'd had to find a new, bigger fort years ago because the first one had become too small for him to fold his long legs into. The boy had made some modifications on this one; he'd woven a wall of pussy willow branches on the southwest side to break the wind. It made a tolerable back rest and cast good, dark shade, too. He had hung some crystals and beads from the pussy willows arching naturally overhead. His woven wall provided camouflage so the glinting of the crystals from the odd sunbeam that found its way in every once in a while didn't divulge the secret hiding place. It was the boy's favorite place to sit and daydream the hours away. Sometimes he brought a flashlight and read in the dim light of the pussy willow fort, but usually he just watched the clouds drifting overhead in glimpses afforded by the small, swaying curvy gaps in the leafy pussy willow roof. The pussy willows whispered their secrets to him and he kept their confidences. Today he didn't even notice the brilliant white clouds against the dark blue high altitude sky.

"Millions of years!" he said to his rock friends, "Do you know it took you *millions* of years to make those crystals?!"

The geode said, a gentle, indulgent smile in its voice, "Of course we knew. Didn't you?"

"No! I never even thought about it!" the boy was so excited he could hardly sit still, but he forced himself to lie back against the pliant, woven willow wall and be quiet so he could listen carefully. "No wonder you know so much! You've been watching and listening a *long* time!" he said in a dreamy voice. As his eyes wandered to the patchy green and blue and white roof with the charcoal-colored stripes of the branches overhead, he listened as his rock friends told him about all the long eons they had known. How they had first journeyed up from the very core of the planet itself, through the hot, molten volcano and out into the air. How they were buried back again, into ground now cold and dark. It was mere chance, they told him, a stroke of luck, really, to have been buried with a bubble of air in their belly. There in the cold, dark ground, with infinite patience, they had precipitated mineral magic out of the water that found its way into the air pocket at the heart of the stone and turned that magic into millions of tiny, faceted crystals.

They'd never known about rainbows, though, they said, until Uncle Marvin cut them in half and let the light in. It gave them a new perspective and broadened their vision enough so they could see and talk to little boys. In the next heartbeat Uncle Marvin had lovingly placed them into hands so small they could barely hold the softball-sized stone without dropping it. Hands attached to a face, the geode said, that was remarkably like the boy's own only an instant ago.

"An instant ago?" said the boy. "That was *years* ago. I was just a baby then!"

"For us it was less than an instant ago. Our lifetimes can last billions of years."

"*Billions!!*" exclaimed the boy, "How many is a billion?"

"It's a thousand million," said the geode, "and for you, an unimaginably vast number. It's the number of stars in the sky. You couldn't count to a billion in a human lifetime if you started the day you were born and never slept."

§

"Oh, god," one of his colleagues in graduate school sighed, rolling his eyes, "here we go *again*."

"Really," insisted the young man with the happy heart, "how can you know? How can we be so certain *they* don't have consciousness? I submit to you, for your consideration, *again*, that we haven't the life span to make such determinations with any confidence whatsoever. We can't possibly know either way. The thing about human beings is that they're hubristic and delusional. Anyone who has studied history, particularly the history of science, as much as we have, *has* to know that.

"We think if something doesn't have a life cycle or consciousness *like ours* then it doesn't have a life cycle or consciousness at all. Because we are hubristic and delusional we never even stop to think there may be vantage points—temporal, physical and spiritual—other than our own. I mean, think about it. A human lifetime from the perspective of the rock people would be less than an eye blink. For them to see us would be like us trying to see an electron. Do we know electrons exist? Yes, barely, but only as an abstraction. It's not like we can see them or interact with them, they're too small and too fast."

He stopped speaking and took a deep breath, embarrassed. His face wasn't red because of the depth of his passions or the commitment of his beliefs, though, he was by nature a shy person, awkward and unaccustomed to being the center of attention.

"All right, all right," the professor said gently, "settle down." The titters and snorts around the seminar table quieted. "Contemporary philosophers, including Mesle and Whitehead, who we read for this week, are beginning to argue that consciousness, which humans previously thought theirs exclusively, is probably a much broader phenomenon than has been suspected.

"And a wider understanding of the phenomenon of consciousness is a notion that is gaining purchase in a number of disparate disciplines now too: among philosophers, certainly. Whitehead and Mesle argue that consciousness permeates the breadth and depth of the biosphere, although they do state with some confidence that consciousness stops short of the mineral realm because they say rocks have no individuality. They say they don't change, and they don't *experience* consciousness. So your colleague here brings up a good point. How *can* we know?" He nodded to the young man with the happy heart, "And philosophers are not alone. Other disciplines, even in the scientific community, from whom philosophers and the rest of the humanities have been so distantly divorced since the Enlightenment, are starting to consider consciousness in broader terms than just the human. Some say consciousness is one of the organizing principles of the universe; background material, if you will, that gets woven into everything. And quantum physicists are fairly sure now that conscious matter cannot arise from unconscious matter. That would equate to the *ex nihilo* creation of something from nothing and that is difficult to defend logically, scientifically or philosophically.

"Neither should we discount intuitive ways of knowing out of hand. Ancient cultures untainted by Western Civilization are much more attached to place than are the rootless, restless moderns. This empowers them to know the world that surrounds them in a way and with a depth we can't possibly achieve. These ancient cultures have held avidly to animistic beliefs for the length and breadth of human history. They assert with confidence that the conscious, animate, interactive world of agents far transcends just the human. Do not fall into the trap of dismissing as 'primitive' the wisdom of indigenous people in favor of privileging only empirical information. The scientific community is often the last to know—think, say, something like ley lines—and materialistic science is prone to disassembling things to the point of incoherence in any case..."

"So, dude," one of the students at the table butted in, leveling a piercing sneer at the young man with the happy heart, his voice dripping sarcasm, "what, do you, like, *talk* to rocks?"

The young man blushed furiously, dropping his gaze to his hands, and said in a soft voice "As a matter of fact, I do."

The table erupted in laughter again. "And what, exactly, do they say to you?" a derisive young woman squealed, loudly enough to be heard over the din.

The young man with the happy heart banged both fists on the table, loudly, and jumped to his feet, knocking his chair over. The room was stunned to silence. "They tell me," he said, glaring into the derisive young woman's eyes, "that they were present at Creation. That they brought every drop of water on Planet Earth here from space, and that it was from their bodies the primordial ocean leached and lapped many of the minerals the biosphere used in the construction of the human body. They tell me," he paused to look around the room, "that they gathered the iron that oxygenates your blood from the infinity of the cosmos and brought it here."

The young man with the happy heart stood his chair back up and walked calmly to the other side of the table, leaning down to face the sneering young man directly, nose-to-nose. "They laughed," he said, "loudly, when I told them that Mesle and Whitehead see them as unchanging. 'Have they never heard of plate tectonics?' they asked me, 'Or erosion? Have they never been to the Grand Canyon?'

"And as for individuality," the young man with the happy heart continued, as he walked back to his place at the table, unzipped his jacket pockets and held out a half-geode in each hand for all to see, "you could throw this geode on a pile of a million geodes the same size and shape, and I'd be able to pick it out from all the others."

He looked around the room at the slack-jawed faces, zipped his geode friends back in his pockets, gathered up his books and backpack and walked out of the silent room.

It was the only time anyone could ever remember him losing his temper.

§

"Did a glacier leave this boulder here?" the beautiful young woman asked in all innocence and earnestness.

The man with the happy heart laughed merrily at her question. He never laughed at her derisively, for he remembered very well how sharply it cut. She was new to the area and he delighted in taking charge of her Southwestern indoctrination. He was in love with her and they were out for a walk in nature's splendor. It was their favorite thing to do in each other's company. They cherished the freedom of thought and speech they had when they were out hiking together.

"Naw," he said, "this area is volcanic, we grow 'em right out of the ground here."

"Oh," she said, a little flustered, "we grow food out of the ground where I'm from."

"A much more practical and prudent arrangement!" he said. "We grow rocks and pine trees here because that's all we *can* grow. And, Love, if you call this a boulder people will surely know you're not from around here. Not that they would ever think that, not with that irresistible Midwestern twang of yours." He brushed her lips tenderly with his fingertips.

"It's not a boulder?"

"Oh, no," he said, gesturing at the beach-ball-sized rock, "we don't generally think boulder till they're the size of at least a car. When we get back from visiting your folks, we'll go to the Grand Canyon and I'll show you some impressive boulders. You could hide the university library behind one of them!"

They left the very next day on vacation. They were committed to each other and driving to visit her parents in Ohio so he could be properly introduced. They had a flat tire in Illinois and, since they were on a bit of an incline, the man with the happy heart asked his beloved to go get a rock to chock behind the remaining good tire on the rear of the car, while he worked on loosening the lug nuts on the other side. He was hot and sticky and plastered with sweat, struggling with the jack and the luggage it was buried under by the time she returned. They were both swatting and scratching at the stinging insects. He stood up with a smile and noted, "Wow, this is a different world, isn't it? The sky isn't quite the right color here."

"What do you mean?" she asked, "It's a beautiful, clear day."

"Yes," he said, "it is indeed. But the sky isn't deep blue and the air is so wet here! I feel like a fish trying to breathe this moist air and I don't think I've ever sweated this much in my life! Not even in Death Valley in the summer!" He reached out to smooth her hair back from her moist forehead. "Did you find a rock for the tire, Love?" he asked.

"Um," she stubbed a toe in the dirt, "I couldn't find one."

He threw his head back and laughed out loud then jammed his ancient, well-stuffed carpetbag behind the tire. The bag had suffered countless insults at his family's hands since his grandmother had found it in an antique shop when she was a young woman. It had passed to the man with the happy heart after her death, and a tire track up its back would just be one more story the battered old bag could tell when it finally fell apart, which looked to be any day.

They had a delightful visit with her delightful parents, who approved of him without reservation. Although the couple were very contented and dared, for the first time, with her parents' consent, to whisper the 'm' word, the man with the happy heart felt slightly ill-at-ease the whole time he was in what they jokingly called the "back east world." Although the sky was never all the way blue, the green was spectacular. It was vivid and relentless—nothing like the muted sage-y green spring back home—and he found himself feeling ever so slightly claustrophobic. The vegetation was thick everywhere it hadn't been hacked away, and it encroached at every opportunity. He felt he was in an enchanted fairy tale forest, but hungered for vistas. He could walk ten feet off the road and, enveloped in vegetation, no longer see or hear the road at all. He had never before been in a landscape so actively and chaotically *alive*.

The back east world expressed its exuberant aliveness most eloquently with rot. The desiccated carcasses so iconic in the Southwest would never be seen here, they would have been molded over and covered with dead leaves and well on their way to compost before the rancher even missed his cow. There were fields of sweet peas full of heady perfume. The loamy smell of compost permeated everything here. It was a smell he loved, but an elusive and rare one in his arid homeland. He felt as though he had been deposited on another planet, one he was unaccustomed to.

He was a stranger here. He saw new things he couldn't account for like people cursing as they pulled up flowering plants and tossed them aside. "Anything that doesn't grow where it's wanted is a weed," one of the neighbors blustered.

"Where I come from, anything that grows a flower is wanted, wherever it chooses to grow." he told the red-faced gardener.

His future in-laws had a spectacular yard with a quarter acre of garden and an acre of lawn. Lawn that just grew there by itself and that had to be mowed twice a week, they said, or they wouldn't be able to mow it. Her parents laughed themselves silly when the man with the happy heart told them the extraordinary lengths he and his father had gone to just to get a postage-stamp of green grass to start growing at home: months of diligent care and watering of the tender young plants, and keeping the kids and dogs off of it till it could take root. It was a privilege in his family, not a chore to mow it, he told them, and he and his dad often vied for the opportunity to do so by flipping a coin.

While in the back east world they ate from the bounteous garden and the man with the happy heart thought he'd never eaten so well in his life.

Still, when he got back home he felt as though a weight had been lifted from him. The sky was the right color again and his nose felt dry and crunchy again when he woke up in the morning. The water tasted right; it had the faint tang of having been in the company of minerals, rather than plants. The water in the back east world had the faintest whiff of algae to it which wasn't unpleasant, necessarily, just unfamiliar. Although returning to grocery store veggies was a disappointment, the horizon was far flung again and there were boulders and vertical rock walls and the man with the happy heart felt as though he had been freed. He took deep, gasping breaths of the crispy dry air, and was so happy to be home he didn't notice his love's shoulders sag a little under new weight.

He took her on expeditions to meet the rock people—Mother Earth writ large—at every opportunity. The Grand Canyon, Monument Valley, Bryce, Zion, Arches National Monument. In his exuberance he didn't notice she became a little more quiet with each outing.

Re-entry. They were on their way back to the real world again after a week-long trip to Death Valley where, at almost 300 feet below sea level, it was as though the Goddess's Cauldron had boiled dry. Bubbles of salt blistered the bottom. He told her that the whole valley, when kissed by the extremely infrequent rains, would become carpeted overnight with the tiniest, most delicate yellow flowers she could imagine. But she could not imagine it. Where his eyes saw elemental wonder, the splendor of geology unobscured by vegetation, she saw only desolation and unrelenting, unforgiving, savagery—dessication and death. He felt liberated there. She felt mummified there.

It was on the way home from the Death Valley trip, after she'd had to bare her ass and squat out in the middle of the God-forsaken Mojave to pee without so much as a blade of grass to hide behind, that she turned to him, with flushed, sunburned face, parched lips and glittering eyes, and said "I can't live here. This world isn't my world, there's no grass and the wide open spaces intimidate me. These far-flung horizons you thrive on so make me feel exposed. Naked and vulnerable. Even where the horizon is close its scary and vertical, like up at the Canyon. It's rock, not the soft, forgiving, waving gentleness of vegetation overhead."

Tears running down her cheeks, she gazed into his eyes and his heart melted. It always did. There was nothing he wouldn't do for her. There was a sinking feeling in the pit of his stomach, but without a heartbeat's hesitation he said, "We can live wherever you're comfortable, my love. I'm sorry, I didn't know you weren't—can't be—at home here. I would never make things uncomfortable for you intentionally."

"No," she sighed, resignation in her voice. "I watched you carefully while we were in the back east world, and you're as much an alien there as I am here."

§

The old man was frail and bent, but he had a happy heart. Although he was in constant pain from arthritic joints and a crooked back, joy was his companion every wobbly tentative step along the way. His skin hung from him now like the baggy, ill-fitting garments he'd always favored and breath wheezed in his chest. He had never married and had no children, but his little sister had, and there was a grandniece of whom he was exceedingly fond. The old man with the happy heart had recruited his grandniece to help with a confidential, special mission this early autumn day.

She parked by a dry river bed he called the Ditch and helped him out of the car. She put the ski poles the funny old geezer used in lieu of a cane firmly in his hands and said, "Unk, *please* let me come with you. I won't tell a soul. I promise. I told you I'd be a rock—your rock—for whatever you wanted me to help you with today, and you said that means not telling anyone. Ever. I get that. I promise I won't tell. *Pllleeeeeeaaaaasssseee*," she whined.

He caressed her cheek softly and with love in his eyes said, "I know you won't, my dear, but this is something I have to do myself. By myself. I have to say goodbye to some very dear, very old friends today. Just don't tell anyone you brought me here."

She eyed his bulging, zipped-tight jacket pockets and the garden trowel in his back pocket with suspicion. "But what if you fall? Look how steep that is! You're going to walk down that bank by yourself?! I'm scared for you, Unk!"

"Well, we all gotta go someday, right?" he said with the sparkle of a joke in his face.

Her face fell.

"Ok, ok," he said in a soft voice, "that wasn't very funny and I'm sorry. People my age have a different sense of humor about that kind of stuff than you young folk do. I'll be all right. I have the cell phone in my pocket, and I have my walking sticks with me. If I'm not back in two hours you have my permission to panic and come look for me. I'm going to be right down there." He waved a skinny arm toward a faint glint in the thick pussy willows in the bottom of the dry riverbed. "Until then, no freaking out."

She nodded her head. "Ok," she said with resignation.

"Don't worry about me."

She nodded again, pouting.

"Promise."

"I promise."

"My sweet girl," he said, gently cupping her chin in his hand and lifting her face to meet his eyes, "please don't be sad and please don't worry if you can help it. My Dearest One, if this is my time and place, if I should die out here, peacefully, in one of my favorite places, with you keeping watch, know I died happy. And don't you ever be burdened with it, not for an instant, either. I would consider it a privilege if you would keep watch, even if it is the last time.

"But," he said, as the girl's chin started to quiver in his palm, "I don't think this is my day."

"'K," she said, her voice choked.

"All right then, I'll see you in a couple of hours." The old man smiled at her, grabbed his ski poles firmly and started down the bank with miniscule but confident steps.

The grandniece sighed and as she cleared the tears from her throat thought *At that rate, it's going to take him his full two hours just to get down there.*

The tracks and paths through the pussy willow thickets in the bottom of the Ditch were overgrown and the clearance seemed much narrower for the intervening decades since he'd walked them last. Eventually the old man with the happy heart found what he thought might have been the fort once. The willow wall he'd woven would have long since rotted away to nothing, and although he allowed it might be nothing more than a particularly impressive spider web, he thought he caught the subtle glint of crystal overhead. He couldn't be sure in the dim, dappled light, but he was almost convinced he could see the edge of a big blue bead he'd once tied into the willow ceiling, poking up out of the duff. Even if not, it was close enough. He knelt, painfully, and took the rock people out of his pocket, arranging them carefully on their silver tray for the last time.

The geode was as beautiful and shiny and sparkly as the first day they'd met; it had been joined since by a rose-shaped garnet, a piece of rose quartz, a small amethyst cluster and a fire agate. That was another good thing about having rocks for friends. They didn't get old and die on you and leave you like so many of his human friends had.

"I've brought you here to say goodbye," he told them, holding the silver tray in the palms of his long, shaking hands.

"Why?" the geode said, "We've only just met! You could take us back to that cave and let the wind-kissed harp sing to us again. We liked that story."

"I'm sorry," the old man said, "my time here is nearly done. I know you're not immortal, you've told me so enough times. But compared to me you may as well be. I've brought you here to put you back in the Earth, to entrust you to the cold and dark again because, well, I just don't trust anyone else."

"Trust them. . . what do you mean?"

"Well," said the old man, "most of my people can't see you for who you are. I don't trust them to get it. They think that because you don't live your life on a human scale of time and agitation, you're not alive, that you don't have the consciousness they take for granted in themselves. They think humans are privileged, special. And every time some other living thing shows evidence of consciousness, from cetaceans to their dogs to ancient stands of trees, they're surprised. Unsettled. Shocked to have to realize they're not alone and that they're not gods.

"They think because you don't speak human language you have nothing to say. I always hoped they could hear if they'd only listen. . . If only I could *get* them to listen . . . " the old man's voice trailed off with his thoughts. "But mostly they think I'm crazy. They've always thought I was crazy. I'm putting you back in the earth because I don't want someone to pick you up and just think you're rocks."

"We *are* just rocks," they teased.

"Well, you may be 'just rocks'," he said, "but you're so much more than that to me. You are rock people. We have been good friends all my life and one of the few things I'm going to miss when I go is you to talk to. You have always shared a unique perspective with me. I can't stand the thought of you living with someone who doesn't hear you, someone who can't really see you for who you are."

He made a feeble attempt to dig a hole, but the hard-packed earth wasn't about to give way to his wimpy little garden trowel. He smiled to himself at what his grandniece would have thought had he lugged a shovel down here to "say goodbye to old friends." She had a vivid imagination, that one, and would probably have thought he had been a gangster in his youth. In the end he had to settle for scraping a shallow depression out of the leaves and caliche, and bringing some loose earth to it from the lip of an obliging gopher hole nearby. He scooped the dirt into his sweater and, crawling, dragged it to the depression. He sat the silver tray carefully in the depression with tears glinting in his eyes.

"You're sending the silver tray with us? It was your mother's. We thought it was important to you."

"It is important to me, but I want you to have it, to remind you of me. Besides," he smiled, "some human cultures hold that there's a ferry with a boatman to take people across to the Other Side when they die, and that the boatman expects to be paid. I can't know anything about that until I get there, of course. This tray is real silver and if that mythology should prove true, I expect you to throw my bail."

"Will do!" the rock people sparkled, "See you on the Other Side. Um, the *Other Side*? What do you mean?"

"This body," said the old man with the happy heart, "as I have known it and as you have known me for the duration of our long-for-me-short-for-you friendship, will soon stop functioning as it has."

"What happens then?" asked the rock people.

"Then they place me in the ground and Earth takes the old body apart and makes it into something new."

"Mmm...," they said, with the warmth of the Core in their voices, "it's much the same with us. Our end isn't so sudden. It's not an end at all, but a gradual transformation. Earth steadily wears us down with water and air and the spinning of the planet, grain by grain, and makes us over again into something else. Some of us go to the beach to be made into sandstone in the bottom of some future sea. Some of us will be compressed to granite and buckle up someday into a fantastic future mountain range. Maybe we'll even get another ride through a volcano. That was really something!"

"This way," said the old man with the happy heart, "you'll have each other to talk to while you make your own way to the other side as your people know it, in the infinity of time, and then on to your own rebirth, into whatever Mother Earth decides your next incarnation will be. I will hope to reconnect with you again in a future lifetime, my friends."

The bent old man smiled, tears sparkling in his eyes, and covered the tray with the gopher's dirt. He struggled back to his feet, brushed his sweater off as best he could, strapped the ski poles around his spindly old wrists, and started the painful journey back to the car. It was only about a quarter of a mile, but it felt like a very, very long way.

He reached the bottom of the bank and looked up to see his grandniece's anxious face peering down.

"Oh! Thank God, Unk! You only had about five more minutes and I was coming to look for you! I've been worried sick!"

"Now, now," he said, "we talked about this. You didn't have permission to start worrying for two hours."

"Well, it's been two hours and besides, I can't help it."

"Ok," he said, "fair enough. I don't suppose you'd be willing to scramble on down here and give an old man a hand up this bank, would you?"

"You bet I would!" she said, her face lighting up. She bounded down the steep bank like a puppy loosed from a leash.

The old man with the happy heart gratefully surrendered one of his ski poles to put his hand on his grandniece's strong, supple young shoulder and let her do the lion's share of the work getting them both back up to the car. He was pale and sweating, grubby, scratched and bleeding. He was not the dignified, immaculate old man the girl was accustomed to. He was shaking more than usual by the time they got up to the car at last. He had a look of sad peace on his face as he sank into the car seat, exhausted.

Three months later, near the winter solstice, he had a massive stroke. His devoted grandniece never left his side. The old man with the happy heart only regained consciousness once, briefly. He slipped into death two days later as quietly and gently as a grain of sand washing up on a beach. By then the rest of his family had gathered around his bedside. "What was the last thing he said to you?" asked the old man's sister.

With tears streaming down her face, the young woman said "That he was ready to go and that he didn't have anyone to talk to any more."

§

When he came to the ferry on the beach of the broad, black river, he couldn't tell if it had been seconds or eons. The ferryman held out his hand to help the boy with the happy heart aboard and, nodding to a little silver tray sitting on his bench, assured him the fare had already been paid. The tray was polished and sparkling as if it were brand new, and the boy heaved a happy, contented sigh as he stepped aboard, ready for a new adventure.

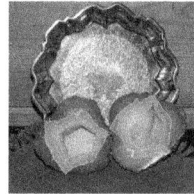

PERCHED: OBSERVATIONS BY A 21ST-CENTURY GARGOYLE

What scares you most? Being different, or being the same?

Me? Being different, hands down.

I'd rather take a sucker punch than be the center of attention. God save me from the pain of parties in my honor. Please just let me leave the job or pass the anniversary or my birthday in peace, and without fuss.

§

I have become a gargoyle slowly over the course of these past two decades. When I was 30, I was tall and straight. Gravity was my friend then; we liked to play together, climbing mountains and skiing downhill. Now, in my 50s gravity is pulling me back down into the Earth. I have become crooked and hideous. A real witch. I scare myself sometimes when I inadvertently pass a full-length mirror. All I need is a pointy hat and some warts and I'll be all set for Halloween.

I don't mind this crooked back so much, it has been an incredible learning experience and a blessing on many levels. Physically it has been a painful process, to be sure, but on an emotional and spiritual level it has been most instructive and illuminating. I always admired the Halloween witch. Obviously she isn't enslaved by the culture of cosmetics and hair care products. She doesn't care what she looks like and she doesn't care what other people think about the way she looks. It has to be liberating. She is among my feminist heroines.

§

On the physical, mundane level, Western medicine says it can fix me. The spinal surgeon tells me, without the least glint of humor in his eye or sarcasm in his voice, that all he'll have to do is break my back in 22 places, insert rods and pins along the length of it, and stand me back up straight again. Oh, and by the way, he says, there's no drug known to humankind that can touch the pain you'll be living in for the first few months, and getting out of it without an opiate addiction in the long run is highly unlikely. You'll require live-in help in the beginning, you won't be able to so much as wipe your own ass for the first few weeks.

I gawp at him like an idiot. Again I search his face for any indication he's trying to be funny, but no. No sparkle in his eye, not so much as a softening at the corners of his mouth. He's serious.

This spine is a genetic defect that runs through my family like a plague on our house. Three generations of us now have started out as tall, straight people who turn into question marks as we age. We're born with too much soft tissue in our joints, including our spines, and from there it is merely a matter of time and compression. Gravity pulls us back to the bosom of Mother Earth before our time, before we're dead. Element of Earth is the realm of both sprout and compost, whence we came and whither we are bound, both womb and grave. I pray I am the last of my line to carry Quasimodo's mark, but the physical, mundane level is the least of it.

§

Spiritually, the process has empowered me to consider demonology and invisibility in a way inaccessible to the straight and beautiful; to ponder that gray area between where things are known and where they are unknown. I can't help but mull the notion of good demons that chase bad demons away. Non-Christians are often fascinated by the ambivalent contradiction of Christian demonology. It's that old problem of theodicy that the benevolent monotheisms worldwide struggle with: if everything that is and happens is controlled by a single omnipotent, omnipresent, and benevolent God, how can the existence of evil in the world be accounted for? By a devil with demon helpers, who, since their powers vie with those of God Himself, are very scary indeed.

Our societal fears about the devil and death, and our terrified ignorance of what lies beyond death, become particularly obvious around Halloween when we take them out of our closets and our nightmares and parade them about so they can be mocked. It's just good fun, right? We ridicule our fears at Halloween so we can feel powerful over them; so we can reassure ourselves the demons can't really hurt us and that death isn't really the end because God is on our side. At Halloween we know it's just a costume. We know it's fake, a put-on, a farcical reversal of order. Carnivale. But for the rest of the year we're rather more comfortable if our demons remain invisible.

Consider the gargoyle. There they were, carved in stone, leering at people as they entered sacred precincts. Their architectural function was to gutter; to divert the water that might compromise the permanence of the stone façades of Christian sanctuaries; and although water spouts around the world and across millennia and diverse cultures have been crafted in ways that were beautiful, elegant, and even regal, medieval cathedral builders chose to give their gutters a frightening appearance.

Although it is a guess, because cathedral builders left no written explanations to posterity, we guess that the gargoyle's intent is to illustrate the ugliness of evil to worshipers. They serve to mock and terrify, perhaps even to weed out the unworthy: if appearance alone were enough to turn someone away from the saving grace of the Church, that coward would surely be considered undeserving of entry.

Some opine that gargoyles stand as protectors of the faithful and are scary because they scare evildoers away (the bad demons). It makes good sense. If you're going to do battle with demons you're probably well-advised to to go in wearing your fiercest visage. Leave all your beauty behind, put on your ugly scary gargoyle face—your baddest badass—gird your loins, and go forth.

Gargoyles have always appealed to me, even before my earthward turn. Their vantage point—alone, elevated and scary—gives them the opportunity to observe human nature about things humanity is too uncomfortable and too polite to express openly on the ground.

Things like loneliness. People are social creatures by nature, or at least so I've been told. I wouldn't know anything about it, being reclusive and introverted by nature. I'm fine perched up here by myself out of everyone's way; it is exhausting emotional work for me to be out amongst people. I hate to tell them I'd rather spend Thanksgiving home alone with a good book and a turkey TV dinner, so I go to the big, raucous gatherings and suffer. But the truth is I'd rather be home alone with a good book and a turkey TV dinner.

I can't imagine sharing the perspective of people who are socially "normal." I was too tall before I wasn't, and was derided for it, along with being too bookish and too ugly and too awkward. I stood a full head above everyone till this family Quasimodo thing overtook me, and I was teased mercilessly about it. "How's the air up there?" they'd sneer. I never did learn to dance as an adolescent when my peers were learning to do so. At that extra-awkward period of life I was two full heads taller than everyone else and the boys' faces were buried in my developing chest. They didn't mind it but I sure as hell did.

It's not that I wanted to be short. My friends, of course, were always shorter than me and shared things about their perspective I would have never guessed from my perch. One complained about her face being in everyone's sweaty armpits at crowded social events and another mentioned being forced to look up people's nostrils all the time; contemplating them through their nose hair and boogers. So although I did not want to be short, I did want to not be so conspicuously tall. I did not want to be the sore thumb that stuck out all the time. I didn't want to be so painfully, obviously, glaringly different.

§

I had a few good-looking years in my 20s and early 30s (during the time of life Ursula le Guin says beauty comes free with hormones), but even then I was striking rather than beautiful. I was tall, thin and athletic. I moved with powerful grace. I turned heads. People noticed, but my difference was different then. My best girlfriend, always overweight, was rendered invisible in my presence. She was able to observe much about the humanities from the vantage of her invisibility. I was the conspicuous center of attention and painfully self-conscious. I envied my heavy friend her invisibility.

And then I wasn't. As I started my earthward turn, I faded into welcome, delicious, comfortable invisibility—anonymity—through my 30s and early 40s. Then I, too, got to participate from a distance; make observations about myself and my fellows from a safe, anonymous place. For the first time I wasn't perched above everybody else, but one of them. I was "us" rather than "other." But my welcome respite in invisibility and anonymity seems to be over now.

§

The culture of narcissism has conditioned us to think we will never age. People get cosmetic surgery to look 20 years younger than they are, whatever their age. The culture of narcissism has conditioned us to think we will never die. People (encouraged by the for-profit medical business) cling to life at all costs, sometimes suffering horribly, for as long as they can hold out at the end.

I am now the Halloween Witch, a gargoyle perched on high, the demon to chase away all your insecure feelings about how you look. A monster to make you feel lucky about your body no matter how far afield of the fashion model ideal you might stray. Gargoyles serve to remind you of things you'd rather forget, and in turn, from the vantage point of this painful visibility I display again now, I am able to observe firsthand a fair spectrum of human vulnerabilities.

From my perch I see fear. There is shock and repugnance; the beautiful young faces speak eloquently of not wanting to get too close, not wanting to be contaminated; of wanting to get away so they don't have to think about it. The cosmetic culture of superficial beauty values us only by how we look; it is a culture that would rather not be reminded of ugliness by a gargoyle encountered in unexpected times and places. Kindly confine yourself to Halloween, will you?

From my perch I see dismissal. People are inclined to back away from gargoyles, happy to be past them. Some try to hide their revulsion as they hurry past or turn away, but perched on high as I am I can see the initial unguarded and honest reaction before they can cover it up. Women my age search, intently, for resonance. They are openly relieved when they find none and when they do see their future in me, I see despair. I smile at them as brilliantly as I possibly can to allay their fears.

Worst of all I see pity, that most loathsome of human emotions. I'd rather be despised than pitied. Pity would render me a victim and a martyr, and I am neither. Do they think I care about how I look? Would I be out in public leering down at the masses without a priest to save them from me if I did? I am the Halloween Witch and I wasn't vain when I was pretty, I sure as hell am not vain now. I wear what I'm comfortable in. It doesn't matter how it looks. Makeup? Hair? Why bother. Aside from some physical pain which is part of everyone's aging process, it's pretty wonderful being a gargoyle. It's as liberating as I always imagined it would be.

§

Ambivalence is encountered at the borderline where things are, by definition, unclear, where things are unknown. Borders challenge us to understand what's on either side of them. Gargoyles defend and define the borderline between good and evil. Ugliness in our culture is equated with evil. Good thing we have cosmetics and hair products so we can hide it.

What is evil? Is it something ambient in the world? Something outside of us that catches us and takes control somehow? A communicable disease? Or is it deeper than that? Something inside? A propensity we're born with? An inherent flaw in character?

Gargoyles confront us with these questions in ways both frightening and reassuring. If the origin of evil is external, gargoyles have the power to scare us back into our interior world, back into the sacred precincts where we are safe from evil, where we are immune from the disease. They face outward and protect the threshold of sanctuary, they keep the evil from getting too close.

If evil is something inside, some element of who we are, gargoyles resonate as kindred spirits, drawing us in. They empower us to bully. A beautiful young woman once stood on something in a crowded lobby back when the worst of my grotesqueness was just being too tall. She did so to make herself a head taller than everyone else in the lobby except me so she and her friends could mock and laugh.

It was harm with intent to harm. Ostensibly everyone in the crowd was an adult, but it felt like being in the sixth grade all over again. She and her friends squealed with delight in their sameness at the expense of my differentness as the heads at normal height in the lobby goggled back and forth between us. Was she cruel by nature or was she just confronted by a gargoyle she didn't want to be defiled by? She was uncomfortable with difference and felt safer being the same. Can't say as I blame her, really, it's something I've always longed for but there's no need to be cruel about it. It's all right, I'm comfortable being different now. I've become accustomed to it and have learned to live in the skin I'm in. By now people's fear and derision reflects off me and doesn't make me uglier. I seek neither to subvert nor contradict the powers of God. This body has been my home these many years and I am comfortable here at last. I submit me to the powers of God and to the pull of Mother Earth.

§

But this isn't about me, it's about demonology. What do you see when you look into the eyes of your nightmare? Do you find you're at home in your body? Have you been allowed to be at peace behind the face God gave you? Have you been able to take sanctuary in your nature, or has your quest been to become something, someone else? Someone who is different, or someone who is the same?

There is no lying to a gargoyle. When you meet the gaze of your nightmare, does it reassure and protect you? Chase all your insecure demons away? Or does it make you run in fear from what you see?

So, what scares you most? What's outside or what's inside?

§

"I'm not talking about Epiphany, I am talking about catharsis, a connection less magical and delicate, but a good deal more practical. There is nothing pretty about real catharsis. It is a painful meeting in which a human

being is emotionally overwhelmed, but emerges better
for that invasion. [Gargoyles] are dark throats, dark
drains from which accumulated muck may spew and
thus be dissipated. Look closely, because we rarely see
these ominous lares of the human psyche."

Stephen King
in the introduction to
Nightmares in the Sky, a photo essay by f-stop Fitzgerald

⚬⚭⚬

Element of Air: Spirit

We face the sunrise to honor Element of Air and know it is life itself for us and all our relations. *Mitakuye Oyasin.* We encounter Element of Air in the East, in the Sunrise, in the Beginning. Air is free. In Element of Air we find the sweet scents of flowers and incense unfurling on the breeze. The power of Element of Air is projective. Air brings the forces of freshness, thought, creativity, intelligence, play, the power of suspension, curiosity, the gift of instruction, and the blessings of freedom and recovery. Some of the sweetest things we know as humans we find in the East; Element of Air whispers and sings with the powerfully evocative languages of music, dance and speech. The lonely Aeolian music of the wind in the wire can elicit a chill on the warmest of days. This chill lets us know in no uncertain terms Element of Air does not confine itself to physical boundaries and sensations as we do. It has tremendous physical, mental, and spiritual power; Element of Air can howl or serenade, lullaby or holler. The most captivating works of literature are the merest whisper of the intellectual power of Air. I pray here in the East, now, in this moment, that the Goddess might make me a hollow reed from which Her voice may sing in these pages.

§

I was delighted and charmed, on a trip to Hawaii once, to hear people introduce themselves as being from "Windward Oahu." It was like catching hold of a kite on a string. It connected me with them and told me so much about their place, their home. They offered me their identity by means of their place and their Element. So, by way of introduction in kind, I am from Alpine Arizona. I grew up in the endless whispering pine forest, under the trees that rarely pause for breath as they murmur their ancient collective wisdom. Theirs is a comforting, yet unfathomable presence, always overhead. Like Windward Oahu, Alpine Arizona has shaped who I am in ways both profound and subtle.

Some people are blessed with balance. They stand firm in the crosshairs and manage all of the multiple and conflicting demands so inherent to human existence in the modern world with grace and good humor. They are like the circus performers who manage to keep all the plates spinning and aloft on all those long flexible poles; they dance nimbly and cheerfully from one pole to the next to give each one just the right amount of attention and energy to keep everything up and going well. It looks like it comes naturally and easily to them.

Then there are the rest of us.

The Indian people of Asia have been contemplating the deepest meanings of life for many long millennia, and Ayurvedic thought is among the many deeply insightful ways of knowing they have developed through their long years of observation. Ayurveda understands that the physical, emotional and spiritual aspects of a person are Elemental; constituted of Earth, Air, Fire and Water. Ayurveda considers the effects the interplay of these elemental constituents—the harmonies, strengths, weaknesses and relationships —have on the person as a whole.

We are all made of Earth, Air, Fire and Water of course but, aside from those fortunate few who stand so balanced near the center of the circle, keeping all their plates aloft and spinning at just the right speed effortlessly like they do, most of the rest of us are skewed, a little off balance. These elemental imbalances are called doshas and are categorized into Element of Air (vata), Element of Fire (pitta), and Element of Earth (kapha), each of which is further characterized wet or dry (Element of Water).

There is nothing to contain Element of Air, so vatas can be a little chaotic; they are creative and vulnerable to distraction by too much information. People listing a little to the Element of Fire, pittas, are the movers and shakers of our world; they are warriors whether it be in business, relationships, politics or war. People who lean more toward Element of Earth, kaphas, are grounded and deliberate; they are our teachers and storytellers. They are calm and safeguard legacy.

In extremely broad strokes, vatas notice things, pittas do things, and kaphas ponder. Vatas tend to notice things pittas might miss because they're busy doing, and things that kaphas might miss because they're thinking so deeply.

Sound and smell are particularly and powerfully evocative for vatas. Music is more than just enjoyment; it touches us in the very core of our being. I speak from experience when I tell you we tend to spend way too much money on music, and that some elder vatas like me have purchased their favorite music multiple times now as the technology of music has progressed: first on vinyl, then on tape, then on CD, and finally as an mp3 download. Some people's singing or speaking voices don't enter our awareness through our ears so much as they enter us bodily, through the solar plexus. Music can evoke memory of a place and time in the past so completely and so vividly we can taste it and smell it and re-experience the feelings we had then; live the loves and aspirations and disappointments all over again.

Then there is the power in those other, nonhuman voices. The return of the meadowlarks, with their exuberant song, to the prairie is a big event in the Spiral of the Year. The song is a powerful harbinger of the rebirth of spring; rebirth for the prairie and rebirth for me. The first time I hear that magical call every spring it fills up my heart so full tears of gratitude spill out of my eyes. The unbounded joy in the song stops me in my tracks. The gleeful, tumbling cascade of a canyon wren's song is only one of many compelling reasons to hike canyon country. Nobody I know can hear it without laughing along. The elk singing to their girlfriends in the fall can make human hearts swell with the power of the passing season.

There are other, less pleasant sounds that haunt vata nightmares and we wish we could forget ever having heard them: the basso, sputtering buzz of a dying beehive, or the empty plastic jar sound of the chickens pecking open the back of the unfortunate at the bottom of the pecking order. Vatas are particularly sensitive to tone of voice, too so neither sarcasm nor sincerity is lost on us. If you're going to lie to us, you must do it extremely well or we'll know.

Vatas are also sensitive to aromas both subtle and powerful. I have hyperventilated nearly to the point of fainting on the sweet yet tangy smell of the pine forest after a rain, and have been known to fill the house with so much incense in the winter when it's stale and closed up we all cough and wheeze.

It is from the East and in the Element of Air our intellectual capacity to overcome our baser instincts can be discovered. It is in the sunrise, then, that we are most civilized, where we can foster cooperation with those who are "other" than ourselves, where we can make peace with ourselves and the world around us. It is also from the

East whence blows our wanderlust, our restless, rootless impulse to travel and explore, to migrate in favor of that ever elusive greener grass (*Roadside Puddles*).

Element of Air is also where we encounter the imaginative journeys and adventures of bookishness; love of learning, reading, writing, and other such abstractions of consciousness. The epilogue to *Mary the Yogini* is the only outright fabrication, the only purely speculative yarn, in *The Miracle du jour*. *Mary the Yogini* dallies with the imaginative question of "what if?" and does not intend to insult anyone's religion. If the powerful thinkers of our age are correct, and if consciousness does shape reality, is a different world only so far away as altering—editing—key texts? I cannot help but ask these questions and I pray for your indulgence. I intend no harm. I intend only to stir imagination and call to your attention that the Bible is a book that (past tense) has been edited and rewritten many times. I would not want to be the one to tackle rewriting it. I am not Christian so it would not be appropriate. The epilogue to *Mary the Yogini* is a tease designed only to point out that the Bible is a book, a human artifact. The words had to pass from the mouth of God through human hands, minds, and consciousnesses to get on paper.

Most religious people seek the same, each in our own way. All religions can be sources of wisdom and peace. In religious community, as members of a larger whole, we pray we find the grace to welcome into our hearts, homes, and lives, persons of all faiths.

Science and religion love to point at each other across an impassable imaginary chasm and hurl insults. Each adamantly considers the other the disease of humanity. Both are absolutely certain of their own accuracy and inerrancy and of the absolute inaccuracy and folly of the other. Science and religion have spoken mutually incomprehensible languages; science has demanded scientific proof of religion and religion has demanded uncritical acceptance of canon. With the weighty and far-reaching questions we lay at the feet of both science and religion, we are trying to understand and articulate something so vast from our ephemeral human smallness we can barely grasp the questions, much less come up with a single, definitive answer. We are like those proverbial blind men and the elephant, trying to articulate Truth, whether in scientific or religious terms. None of the blind men were wrong about the elephant, but none could perceive the whole of it either.

Perhaps is is because the sound of the wind in the wire is so lonely and so chill it may be too easy, too simple, to equate Element of Air with cold and distance, with aloofness. Many people think first of a cold wind when they contemplate Element of Air, but warmth, animation and joy reside in the East as well; think blowing kisses or blowing on your hands when it's cold. Curiosity and the energy to pursue it are the blessings of Element of Air.

∽✢∾

ROADSIDE PUDDLES

Hummingbirds are among the most awesome of Mother Nature's many awesome creations, so small, fast and beautiful they hardly seem real. I muse sometimes that they might be an alien life form come to visit us, trying to establish communication, but we're too slow and thick to get it. A nickel outweighs the average hummingbird, yet they're fearless and voracious. Ostensibly they're fragile, vulnerable little birds—they must slow their metabolisms at night to keep from starving to death. Yet they're bold enough to undertake migrations on a planetary scale; summering in North America and wintering in Central and South America. They're fast enough and smart enough they're not afraid of much of anything. The fierce Aztec people of Mesoamerica recognized in the small but unintimidated hummingbird people the incarnation of their war god—Huitzilopochtli.

§

The dictionary definition of literature is something that "has excellence of form and expresses ideas of permanent or universal interest." Literature points beyond itself to something much larger, to more important truths. On the surface of it, Herman Melville's *Moby Dick* is just a story about a man with an obsessive hatred of a whale. But it is literature because it is so very much more than that; the story imparts important lessons to us, in a meaningful way, deep in the gut. Lessons through which we might know the futility of trying to take revenge on nature; and the all-important lesson that obsessive hatred is the ultimate lose/lose enterprise. It is the demise of those who offer the hate as much as it is the undoing of those who receive it.

Although literature is generally taken to mean something written, I offer here for your consideration that there are things and events surrounding us all the time that point beyond themselves to larger lessons, that speak eloquently of something more important, something of "permanent and universal interest." Literature can be something as humble as a hummingbird's nest, something so small we can barely discern the weight of it in our hand, that is at the same time as big as the cosmos. It can encompass all of everything that is.

After those first truly blustery fall storms, when we shiver with wind and cold forgotten since last winter, hummingbird's nests can sometimes be found on the ground here in the pine forests of Northern Arizona. The occupants and their parents are long gone; they're already basking in the sun on the beach in Mexico, sipping the nectar of tropical flowers.

The cutting fall winds sever the anchors of these architectural wonders, blowing them out of their secluded sanctuaries. These tiny nests are one of Mother Nature's most truly magical constructions. They're carefully made to be elastic and spongy; they bounce when they hit the ground.

Hummingbirds, like bees, seek out the magical and the miraculous that surround us all the time and gather it together in tiny little bits. Bees make honey from miniscule drops of nectar in uncounted flowers and weave an incredibly complicated social world into their nests (hives). Hummingbirds seek intimacy with each flower likewise and weave awe-inspiring little nests as well.

I found a hummingbird nest close to my home one fall I have treasured as a miracle *du jour* ever since. The hummingbird had sought us out and woven our family into her nest. There was a long, bright red hair from the tail or mane of the horse that lives around the corner. I am allowed to bring Biskit apples and carrots sometimes and gaze into her intelligent, liquid eyes while she contentedly crunches the treats. Biskit's hair was long enough to go around the nest several times (a lucky find) and was used as foundational weft in the hummingbird's artful weave. Around Biskit she had used, as warp, pliant natural local grasses; some white, white hair from my cat, Luna; a few of my mousy brown ones (Luna and I clean our hairbrushes outside so the birds can have our hair for nest building purposes); a couple of red and white matted chunks (small ones) from my sister's Husky, Sashi, who comes to visit sometimes, and who blows her coat a couple of times a year; some wonderful crinkly red-blonde beard hairs from a friend who likes to sit on the porch and tug at his beard thoughtfully as we converse over a cuppa when he visits; and even a playful splash of color from the frayed end of an old terrycloth beach towel disintegrating on the clothesline in its afterlife as a rag for washing out the animals' water bowls.

The bird people can teach us about home: the hummingbird worked all of us into her home, that makes it our home too. It makes her our kin and her children our godchildren.

§

We can learn a lot from the bird people on a lot of levels. I am rarely reminded so acutely of my limited view and my plodding, pedestrian human intellect as I am when I'm caught in the quicksilver gaze of the bird people. Their bright eyes miss very, very little. When I'm walking in the woods with my faded red cap, hummingbirds occasionally rocket in for a closer inspection. They startle me by appearing inches from my face with only a split second's notice. In an instant of musical whir and a chirped warning, these small-g gods and goddesses assess the situation, decide I am neither friend nor foe nor interesting nor edible, and streak away before my delighted gasp at the encounter is fully drawn. They dismiss me in a heartbeat as slow. Too slow by far. Hummingbirds ain't scairt, even if they are small. They'll pick up and take off on a planetary journey with naught but the wings on their backs and Mother Nature's imperative in their souls.

Birds of all kinds sing in unabashed joy at the rising of the sun, and lift our hearts with them. The bird people teach us that there is beauty in strength and intelligence. The bird people teach us about consciousness and community. Studies have shown that those amazing flocks of birds who look like they're all turning at the exact same time are doing just that. They are turning far too quickly to be the result of command-and-response. It's not one boss bird saying "turn here," or "follow me," with the with the rest responding. They're all plugged in to each other; they are navigating as a single consciousness and turn as one.

§

The bird people can also teach us what's important right now. They're trying to teach us that the most precious thing on this planet is neither diamonds nor gold; it's not oil, real estate or political power. The most precious, the most limited, and the most vulnerable thing on this planet is water clean enough to drink and bathe in and, if it is the way of your people, to live in and raise your young. Birds will make do with the slimy water in the birdbath if that's all there is, but the best, most joyous bird baths and longest, most quenching drinks occur preferentially in puddles of freshly melted snow or freshly fallen rain. They revel in it and we would be wise to follow their lead.

Roadside puddles are literature. Migration is the heartbeat of this planet. As climate change proceeds, bodies of open, clean, natural water are disappearing, especially here in the desert southwest. If we notice them at all, we might pause a moment in our frenetic modern rat race, to grieve for the migratory people. Theirs is a mandate to move. They have no choice. If we would but notice the pitiful flocks of Canadian geese huddled miserably on a puddle between the interstate and the railroad tracks as they pass through we might learn something. If we could, we might spare a moment's compassion for the pair of mallards trying to nest on a muddy wet spot the size of a dining room table with traffic roaring past them at 75 miles an hour. She hides in plain sight with her cryptic coloring while her mate desperately tries to conceal his brilliance behind a tumbleweed as they struggle to survive long enough to rear their young. If we could only see these fellow travelers of ours, we might be able to muster a little more compassion for our own restless species, ever moving about looking for home.

Perhaps it is because our own migrations are so pointless, so chaotic and so un-natural that humans don't seem to feel much compassion for the other migratory people on this planet; the elk, moving from high ground to low as the seasons change, getting splattered on the roadways as they do, or the whales eating plastic floating in the ocean on their hemispheric migrations. The list goes on and on. Restless, rootless creatures that we are, it's no wonder we might miss the larger lesson of this literature. Migration is regular and patterned, it exists to ensure the survival of the species who migrate. There is no pattern to our movement, only chaos. If we would stop and nest, roost awhile and become a part of the world where we land, rather than apart from it, we might find ourselves home and at peace at last. Maybe then we might find it within ourselves to privilege clean drinking water over fracking and find some sympathy in our hearts for the displaced and disposessed among our own kind.

MARY THE YOGINI

My big brother is Christian. It isn't and wasn't a choice he ever made. He wasn't so much born again as he was born Christian in the first place. God crafted him out of Christian material. There are lots of ways you can tell. The way he prays is one. It doesn't matter whether he's at my house, politely praying to the Great Goddess, or whether he's honoring Krisha's conversation with Shiva in the Bhagavad Gita when he's praying with Hindus at a local community center, it always sounds like he's praying to Jesus and His Father.

My brother lovingly accepts religious plurality in the world and is quick to recognize that probably all the different cultural and religious ways we pray, all the "different" Gods and Goddesses we pray to, are more likely differences in ourselves than they are differences in the Gods and Goddesses themselves. God—however we might perceive Him, Her, It or Them—is too big, too all-encompassing to be perceived in totality by such a small and limited thing as a human being. We lack both the breadth and depth to be able to comprehend, so we find our way to God as best we can, harming none, and pray to Him, Her, It or Them in a way that makes sense to *us*. God gets it and I can't imagine He, She, It, or They much care *how* we make our way there, only that we do, and that we do so harming none.

Another way you can tell my big brother is a Christian is that he is a scholar. Monotheisms are centered around a book so, religiously, my brother requires one. He engages his religion with passion *and* intellect. Although he is scrupulously open-minded to people of other religions, he is adrift without a Bible. He requires the certainty of canon. He's perfectly prepared to read his book with a critical eye but it all starts and ends with the Bible for him.

§

Culturally, we of the West are the people of the book. We privilege the written word. It is our intellectual and religious heritage, brought to the New World by the white northern European colonists who so brutally colonized and conquered the Americas. The most important book in bequeathing to us this literate heritage is, of course, the Judeo-Christian Bible. It is a book that has profoundly shaped such notions as gender and manifest destiny in the modern world which notions have, in turn, profoundly shaped our understanding and treatment of ourselves, our lovers, our neighbors, and our environment. Michel Foucault, intellectual luminary, observed that history is narrative, textual, and genealogical but fragmentary and ruptured by power. In non-academic terms, he pointed out that as people who privilege the written word, we get to write our own history, whether in past, present or future tense. It matters what we say. It matters what we write. We Craft our own reality, our world, in doing so.

We are the people of the book, specifically, of the Bible.

The wonderful thing about books is that they can be edited. Canonization was the West's misstep.

Religious metanarratives (much like universal scientific theories) point to human yearning for an overarching Truth, for one capital A Answer that fits all, an answer that will simplify this incredibly complicated and contentious human experience of ours. We seek the comfort of certainty, but blind ourselves with it. As Nietzsche pointed out "There are no facts, only interpretations." Nowhere is this more apparent or important than in the exegesis of religious texts.

It falls to the scholars of religion to examine theological and philosophical pronouncements, from outside the faith; to look carefully and objectively [sic] at the texts. It may be that it falls to them to plant the seeds of the postmodern era and edit the texts for a better contemporary fit, too. Jeffrey Kripal, religious scholar extraordinaire, iconoclastically invites all who would study religion to allow personal experiences to inform their scholarship; to augment their intellect with gnostic imagination and intuition.

In that spirit, I'm departing now, completely, from even a pretense of nonfiction and entering an imaginative realm of experimentation and ambivalence.

§

Imagine how different our world might be if Western modernity were influenced by the feminine made sacred, not by her power to woo God, but by God's power to woo her. Imagine if Jesus had been born of not one, but two powerful parents.

Imagine . . .

§

Elizabeth I of England was a formidable woman whose considerable brass was forged in the flames of the religious Reformation that very nearly burnt Europe to the ground. Her tyrannical father set spark to the pyre, in part in order to secure her legitimacy to rule. It was the first rip in the fabric of a Christianity which would eventually tear itself to rags.

Elizabeth was a ruthless peace monger whose long and prosperous reign is still considered a golden age by her people. She steadfastly refused to marry, unwilling to share her legitimacy with, or surrender it to the patriarchy. When she died, James of Scotland took her throne.

In 1604, in an effort to clarify the elusive and violently contentious matter of definitive Christianity, James undertook to have the Christian Bible translated accurately into English (from Latin) and engaged forty-seven of Britain's most learned scholars for the task. Their work was published in 1611. These scholars were supervised by the Dean of Westminster who was, of course, an intimate and colleague of the Dean of Oxford, John Bridges.

In 1614 King James dispatched Sir Thomas Roe to India to make another attempt at establishing trade with the opulent and exotic Mughal Emperor, Jahangir. Sir Thomas succeeded with brash assertion where his predecessors had failed with cowering subservience, and established East India Company operations in India.

Thus I have heard: Astonishing documents have been discovered under a flagstone during a recent renovation of an ancient Oxford building which had once housed the workroom of John Bridges. Carefully tied in an oiled leather bookbinder's apron were a few fragile parchment pages which recount an extraordinary dinner conversation, and its aftermath, between John Bridges and his old friend Sir Thomas Roe, one winter's evening in 1617. John writes that he was cheered and grateful to retire by the fire with a cup of wine and his old friend since the light failed so early for scholarly work in midwinter. Sir Thomas regaled his friend with remarkable tales of his travels to the exotic south of Asia on his diplomatic errand for King James. The most remarkable among them for Bridges, however, were not the stories of fantastic alien emperors and their unimaginable wealth, but the tales Roe told of the fiery, terrifying Mother Goddess of India, her angels—called yoginis—and the men who worshiped them.

Sir Thomas' tale sent John Bridges scurrying through the archives and worktables at first light on the next day with a niggling memory. Bridges stood in the scholarly lineage and shadow of Erasmus, the incorrigible collector of New Testament manuscripts in their original Greek, 100 years his senior. The king's Bible project was done and dusted by now, of course, but during its course Bridges had set some of Erasmus' more obscure work aside not knowing at the time how or where or even if it might legitimately fit into the king's Bible.

One of these Erasmus had entitled "The Book of Mary," and prefaced his translation with the explanation that he had saved the book from a Greek document of great apparent antiquity; one that had lamentably crumbled to dust even as he labored over it. Erasmus' translation of the Book of Mary followed:

And in the sixth month to a virgin of the house of David whose name was Mary, came the angel Gabriel and said unto her, Hail, thou that art highly favored. The Lord is with thee: blessed art thou among women.

And when she saw him she was troubled, and cast in her mind what manner of salutation this should be.

And the angel said unto her, Fear not, Mary, for thou has found favor with God.

And behold, thou shalt conceive in thy womb and bring forth a son, and shalt call his name Jesus.

He shall be great and shall be called the Son of the Highest; and the Lord God shall give unto him the throne of his father David.

And he shall reign over the house of Jacob for ever; and of his kingdom there shall be no end.

Then said Mary unto the angel, How shall this be, seeing I know not a man?

And the angel answered and said unto her, The Holy Ghost shall come upon thee, and the power of the Highest shall overshadow thee; therefore also that holy thing which shall be born of thee shall be called the Son of God.

Mary cast her eyes demurely as she reached to take the white lily from Gabriel's shining hand, and said unto him; I will have whose child I choose and in my own time.

With her other hand she reached forth and ripped out the angel's throat. She twisted his head off and drank of the essence of Gabriel's body until it was dry.

The angel's essence was not blood, for angels are not of this earth, but like sexual fluids, pulsating with light and the promise, but not the fulfillment, of life.

And Mary sent the headless, empty husk back to the Lord God, flying crookedly with sightless wings. His skull she made into a basin in which to keep the flower.

And the Lord God fumed in indignation in his heaven, but no matter the destruction wrought in heaven by his terrible wrath, the smoke of his fury could not choke the earth.

And the Lord God sent unto Mary his angel Raphael, with the beauty of the sun in his face, to beguile her, that she might bear his son.

And Mary smiled into Raphael's beauty and accepted his kiss of friendship. And her kiss drained his body of its essence and light, every drop. She worked the husk of his body into the fertile earth and from Raphael's staff she crafted a fence for her garden.

The Lord God closed his mighty eyes and bellowed in rage, but no matter the darkness nor din in heaven, he could neither obscure nor deafen the earth.

And God sent unto Mary his angel Kafziel to appeal for her justice, benevolence and mercy.

And Kafziel said unto Mary, is it not fitting that the Lord God should become manifest in this world as he did so create it?

And Mary said, How did he so create the world to abandon it? He left it willingly and in anger. And Mary tore Kafziel's arm from his body as she accepted the offering cup from his hand. The offering she used to water her garden. His arm she drained of its essence and the husk she broke into tiny pieces, which she used for seed. She said unto armless Kafziel, Take you therefore this message unto your master: If the Lord God would be incarnate in this good earth through his son, he must petition the Great Goddess, for manifestation in this earthly realm is by Her grace alone.

And the Lord God wept, but no matter his grief in heaven, his tears could not wet the earth.

And God sent unto Mary his angel Ariel, to lighten her heart that she might relent and accept his troth.

And Mary basked in the warmth of Ariel as she tore out his heart and drank of his essence, every drop. Ariel's heart she set above her garden that it might have light and warmth to grow.

And God became chill, for he had sent his light and warmth to Mary, but no matter the coldness of his fury, he could not bring winter unto the earth.

And the Lord God bade his fallen angel Lucifer go unto Mary, to seduce her.

And Mary laughed, saying unto Lucifer, You and I live on this earth together, but you are not of it and cannot propitiate the Great Goddess on behalf of your master. Begone, you hold no sway here.

And at last the Lord God himself came to the gate of Mary's garden and knelt in supplication before her. Humbled, he bowed his head unto her and held up His own heart to her in offering.

Behold, Mary, I have nothing greater of myself to offer you, I can give no more.

And Mary said unto him, I will bring your petition to the Great Goddess, return to me at the dark of the moon.

And Mary went unto the Great Goddess holding the heart of the Lord God in her hand.

The Great Goddess said unto her, you are grown fat and sleek, Mary my servant.

And Mary said unto the Great Goddess, The Lord God would return to the world from which he is estranged. He wishes a son and has made many offerings.

And the Great Goddess asked of Mary, Do you find him worthy?

And Mary said unto Her, he is arrogant and willful, but I will ensure that the son is not for I shall raise him with mine own hand and feed him from the garden of wisdom and power I have planted.

And the Great Goddess saw that it was good.

And at the dark of the moon came unto Mary her servant Joseph and together they made a child of their bodies, and the Holy Ghost filled the child with the light of the Lord God, and Jesus the savior was born into the world.

꧁ ꧂

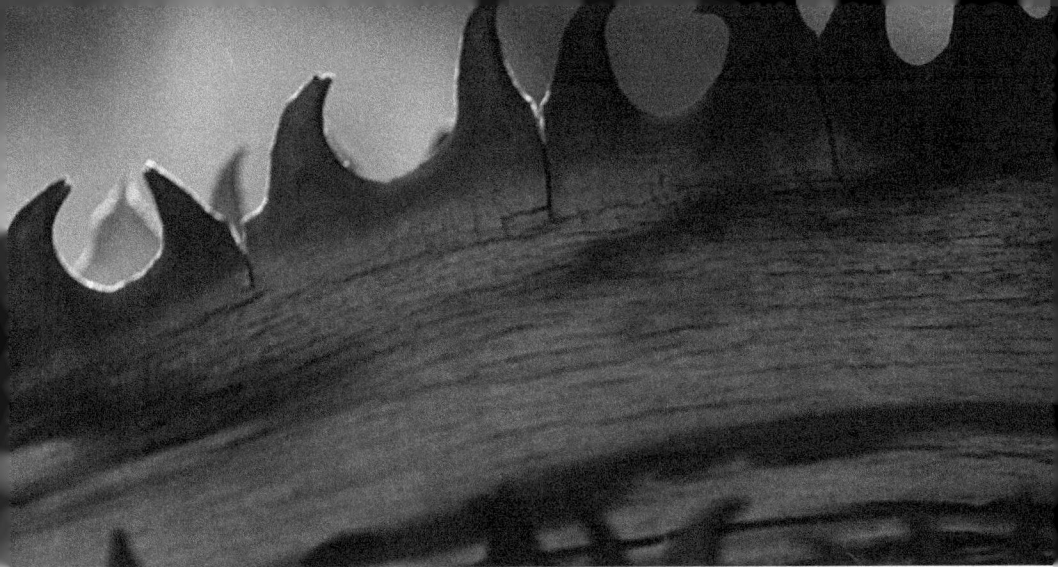

Element of Fire: Passion

We face South to honor and recognize the Element of Fire. The powers of Element of Fire are projective—radiant and transformative. Element of Fire makes us human. It is our oldest tool, our primal gathering place, our first Sacred Elemental kinship. It was huddled around the fire humans first found safety, warmth, and common purpose. It is where we discovered language and shared food. Element of Fire is where humanity formed interpersonal relationships and worked out social organization, where we first discovered ourselves as human, where we sang songs, and told stories of the dead. Element of Fire is the source of robust good health and physical energy, the hot blood of the body in motion; it is the source of courage and protection. Element of Fire is the heat of passionate love; both love of another person and of closely held beliefs with the worthy causes that attend them. Element of Fire brings the light and warmth of the stars to the black darkness of the cosmos in time. Element of Fire is with us in the dancing flame of each candle and each beat of our hearts.

§

The hearth fire is the center place, the axis around which we organize our lives. Whether symbolically or in fact, the centrality of the hearth in the consciousness of home is the same centrality occupied by the altar in other sacred precincts. Element of Fire is the pulsing heart of home. Although now largely symbolic in our contemporary houses, we do naturally still gravitate to the modern equivalent of the hearth fire, standing uncomfortably cramped and crowded in the kitchen at family parties while the comfortable chairs and couches of the "living room" go neglected. The safety and warmth of home is what drives the evils of fear, hunger and loneliness away. The hearth provides both spiritual and physical sustenance, it is a primal source of balanced energy, within and without.

It is a common and ancient mythological theme in old and new worlds alike that Fire was initially the exclusive property of the deities. It had been deemed a force too powerful for humans to use, and existed only in some place or time humans were either not allowed to go or could not reach. Element of Fire was taboo for it was divine power. Only First People, those extraordinarily bold and clever humans (such as Spider Woman and Prometheus) possessed the skills, ingenuity, and nerve to steal Fire from the Gods, bringing it to humans that we might reach our own lofty potential.

Perhaps because it is so awesomely powerful, it is in Element of Fire that we can see the full breadth and depth of the element's scope most clearly. Element of Fire can be either the gentle, sacred, primal hearth fire around which we all gather to eat and be safe in the arms of our family and tribe, or the howling war god, the holocaust, the all-consuming conflagration (*Icky Neighbors*).

And yet, the home fire is one of the things that bonds us together in the common experience of being human. Staring into a fire is hypnotic for us and in that simple contemplative, introspective act we are are united by a sense of our common humanity. As it dies, I often stare into the embers—the beating, pulsating heart of the Samhain fire, which is obscured by flames and fuel when the fire is young and busy—to commune with my dead and divine insight into my future path.

§

Many cultures in new and old world alike held a new-fire ceremony at significant intervals of time. In far Northern Europe, the interval was yearly, at Beltane in the spring, while in Mesoamerica it was at the beginning of each 52-year cycle of their long-count calendar. All fires throughout the land were ritually extinguished and relit from a newly-kindled ritual fire. Trusting in the regenerative power of the Sacred, this was nonetheless a dangerous time. If the new fire could not be drawn, in Mesoamerica it was thought that the sun would be destroyed forever and demons of darkness would descend to eat human beings. In Northern Europe the new fire was perceived of as protective; the virtues of its light protected people and livestock from poison and disease.

The power of Element of Fire is both receptive and banishing. It can be the gentle heat that cooks our food, or the banishing transformation of burning, for example, of an effigy or old love letters.

I lived with wood heat exclusively for decades and this experience gave me a close spiritual connection with Element of Fire. It is a lifestyle and I loved it. The autumn was filled with excursions into the forest with friends and family to get wood. We'd swap off—taking a load to my house this weekend and one to yours next. It was our primary weekend occupation September through November and every bit as much fun as a hike or bicycle ride. The work is too heavy and hot to do before the weather starts to cool but once it does, it is good clean fun to load up early and go out. Everybody comes home filthy and exhausted, but with a fire to warm their bones around during the dark and cold of the year. There is nothing quite as satisfying as watching your woodpile grow during the fall and shrink during the winter.

To live with the daily ritual of fire as necessity is to live with the Sacred. When I was home during the day, my own best (daily) new-fire ritual was to let the fire burn itself out completely around midday, when it was warmest outside. As the morning waned I'd split wood, make kindling (a special treat for those of us with a little OCD—the finer you shave it the better it works), and carry wood. When the fire was as cool as it was going to get it was time to shovel the ashes out of the woodstove (into a fireproof metal container with a good, tight lid on it, of course, to let any remaining embers cool), sweep the hearth and lay the fire. My aim was always to light the new fire with one match and no paper. There was nothing quite so spiritually rejuvenating in my entire world as sitting in the company of my new fire, feeding it larger and larger pieces of wood as it grew to warm the heart of my home. Sitting in attendance and blowing the little flame to life, offering the breath of my body, gave me a few moments to thank the tree and Mother Earth for bringing the warmth of the sun into my home to keep me warm. The flickering newborn flame would grow strong to stand watch against the cold, cold night.

This Elemental safety and warmth is the hearth fire, whether symbolic or real. Our human lives and the life of the hearth fire subsist in a reciprocal relationship. They participate in each other. The hearth requires tending. The fire must be fed and watched. It is not a building that makes a home, it is a shared fire. Element of Fire is the tie that binds. It is the tie that binds us to each other, to our families and our communities (*Born Pagan*). *Mitakuye Oyasin.*

The blessings of Element of Fire are passionate engagement, kinship, sanctuary and courage, and robust good health with the energy it imparts.

☙ ❧

ICKY NEIGHBORS

Memorial Day Day Weekend:

The little mottled brown and gray fuzzball explodes off the porch as if shot from a cannon, and streaks down the driveway to collapse in a wriggling heap, belly up, at my feet. "Nuuuuttttttmeeeeeeg, DAMMIT!" I hear the door to my neighbor's cabin in the woods slam open, and smile as I bend down to rub the belly of the four-pound bundle of exuberant joy. This is our Memorial Day Weekend ritual, Nutmeg and I, and we both look forward to it. Nutmeg is some kind of cute bottle-brush-nosed dog and he's a bright spot in anyone's day. His mission in life is to love and get love from everyone on the planet he encounters. It is impossible to be gloomy in his presence. Everybody should get to be as happy as Nutmeg at some point in their life. I like to woolgather about his world, how wonderful it must be to be him, being that joyful and loved all the time.

Nutmeg gathers his feet under him at the sound of his Dad's voice and starts to slink back up the driveway, still wagging uncontrollably (he has no tail to speak of so he just wags his whole body). My neighbor comes fuming down the driveway with his customary apologies. This is our ritual, too. We have one, sometimes two, conversations like this every year.

"I'm sorry," says my neighbor with an exasperated sigh. "He can't help himself. He knows the latch on that screen door won't hold when he sees someone coming down the road and gets excited. He'll tear the screen out someday."

"It's all right," I tell him (and mean it). "Nutmeg is a ray of sunshine in my day and I'm always happy to see him." Nutmeg collapses into another ecstatic heap at my feet and I kneel down this time to get a full-on two-handed belly rub. My neighbor and I talk for a few minutes about the weather and neighborhood gossip and how incorrigible Nutmeg is and then I'm on my way again, happier and more connected for the encounter. Nutmeg, now leashed, watches me go with wistful longing in his bright, black eyes. Nutmeg knows I adore him. His humans are in the majority of my sometimer neighbors, which is to say, exceedingly cool.

Most of my neighbors don't live here all the time. This is their second home, their weekend escape from the miserable heat of the desert where they live and work. I appreciate this about them. They get their cabin in the woods on weekends and I get to live in a quiet neighborhood the rest of the time. They come up to play with their kids in the snow, or run around on ATVs and dirt bikes, but they have lives and homes and jobs elsewhere. Most dream of retiring here and are entirely decent people.

§

The wind always blows here on the Mogollon Rim in the springtime. Just "The Rim," or "Rim Country," to locals, this immense landform—the edge of the Colorado Plateau—can be seen from space. Within an hour's drive from here the elevation drops a mile and a half as you travel south and southwest. It is country that lends itself to dramatic diversity of landscape; red rock canyon lands, forest, high desert, beautiful long vistas and changeable, unpredictable weather. One of very few meteorological constants around here is that the wind always blows in the spring on the Rim.

It is a gusty, moisture-sucking constant and although the pine forest ecosystem, in its natural state, thrived on fire, that was 140 years of mismanagement ago. The toxic combination of the greed of the timber barons who first robbed the forest of its protective overstory, with a policy of fire suppression since then, has resulted in an overgrown, unhealthy forest. Ponderosa pine saplings grow like grass without the benefit of the occasional fire to thin them out; they grow to choked, doghair thickets 20 feet tall and so dense sunlight cannot penetrate them.

In addition to being overgrown, the forest is parched now as almost 30 years of drought, here on the leading edge of climate change, can parch a forest. All it takes is one mistake, one match, one cigarette butt, one moment of inattention to start a catastrophic wildfire. Catastrophic fires here burn so hot they kill the soil. It's called moonscaping and although silviculturalists say forest ecologies can and will eventually recover after a moonscaping fire, it takes time for the soil to rebuild itself enough to support first bacterial and then plant and animal life.

Loss of a forest is a tragedy for generations in this arid place. Friends in the Pacific Northwest tell me tales of forests that thrive after a fire; forests that are lush with regrowth after only a few years. But not here. The face of the mountain that burned 40 years ago is just now starting to support some low plants and shrubs. No one now living will see mature trees there again in their lifetimes. The Southwestern forest is not something that can be replanted or rebuilt.

§

Nutmeg is not unlike other dogs. Dogs think the world belongs to them and their humans; they don't have any idea where they leave off and the rest of the world picks up. They think the entire world is theirs. Nutmeg's right to belly rubs from everyone he encounters is proprietary. Humanity has put much effort over the past 15,000 years or so into reinforcing this idea in the dog people. It is what makes the dog people good guardians and good friends. This is also why there are leash laws, and what makes it the responsibility of humans to set boundaries for them. The dog doesn't know his property, and his responsibility as guardian, ends at the driveway. It is up to his humans to delineate this boundary for him with a fence or a leash. In Nutmeg's case the cost of trespass is a belly rub. Other dogs aren't quite so charitable.

Likewise, Element of Fire does not respect arbitrary human boundaries, those lines we draw in the sand, say, between your property and mine. Although Element of Fire allows us the delusion of control (through things like fire departments and the forest service), open fires here in the deep woods, woods compromised by decades of drought and mismanagement, are terrifying. Hostile.

Everybody in the neighborhood, fulltimers and sometimers alike, dreads the arrival of my immediate neighbors to the south: the ignorant and impolite Icky Neighbors. They have no water system (we haul our water here) or septic system and, like dogs, do not respect boundaries or propriety.

The first thing the Ickies generally do when they get here of a Friday night is build a roaring fire outside no matter the time of year, how windy it is, or what the fire restrictions might be. They sit by their fire and drink beer and have a grand time and when their weekend is over, they leave it. They get in their cars and drive away. I can't count the number of fires they have left smoldering.

Living next door to the Icky Neighbors ain't pretty. Every time they leave, after I put the fire out, I heave a sigh of relief that the neighborhood and the forest it inhabits have survived another Icky weekend. I wonder at the self-absorption of these people. Do they not have any clue about where they are? Can it be that they don't understand the danger of wildfire? Or is it that they don't care?

§

Other of my sometimer neighbors usually here of a three-day weekend (working folk, obviously) seem to get it. They roll in with a passel of kids and dogs and grandparents. They stay up late, too, sitting around their campfire (but only when it's safe to have one). There are no fires on Memorial Day Weekend, because it's always dry and windy then, but there are many rolling adult laughs through the night, endless games of horse shoes, and much shrieking of happy children being allowed to play and romp and get dirty and sleep in sleeping bags. Their days here are filled with shinnying up trees and adventures in the woods. They keep their dogs on leashes, do not walk around with lit cigarettes, and put their fires all the way out when they leave. They're all happy to be here and more to the point, they seem to *understand* where they are. The Ickies do not.

Nutmeg's predictable annual petty larceny aside, most of my sometimer neighbors play by the rules. They rake up their pine needles and install water and septic systems. If they smoke they use an ash tray. They build their houses to code and are respectful of other people. The cool sometimer neighbors like to run their ATVs and dirtbikes around the clock, too, just like the Ickies do, but they do it on the dirt streets in the subdivision. The Ickies do it out in the woods, off-road, throwing trash, tearing up the forest and making roads where they will. Like their dogs, the Ickies don't seem to know where they leave off and the rest of the world picks up.

One fire season not so long ago was so scary and dry I did the cowardly thing and taped a note to the front of the Icky Neighbors' house before Memorial Day weekend, along with some forest service literature explaining that a fire isn't out until it is cold and wet.

What to my wondering eyes should appear at the close of the holiday weekend but the Icky Neighbors putting their fire out with a shovel and water. Wow! I wondered; can it really be possible they didn't know? Was it always as easy as just educating them?

Even if my parents hadn't taught me these things, before the Icky Neighbors I'd have thought it was obvious, that it wasn't difficult to figure out whether a fire was out or not. I now have to consider the possibility that the Icky Neighbors might not be malicious, just ignorant. Maybe they had never thought about it before. Seems the Icky neighbors might have something about neighbors to teach me as well.

I have to consider that my responsibility goes beyond merely putting their fires out for them when they leave. That is enabling. The Ickies may never learn to revere this place as Sacred without help, and I'm not helping them get it by excluding them from the community or begrudging them information.

§

Ponderosa Pine trees, in a healthy (=mature=old) forest, are practically immune to fire. They aren't usually killed by it and in fact, need it to sweep through every decade or so to clear all the dead needles and fallen branches from the ground underneath them. A mature stand of these magnificent trees is a wonder to experience. You can't see them, they're too big. One hundred fifty feet or more tall, and as big around as your living room. Being in the company of these immense and ancient beings is an experience that defies description. There's an overwhelming hugeness to their presence. They gently sway and creak in the wind and have thick, cracked orange and black bark. The green part (the crown) is so far off the ground it couldn't catch fire except under the most dire of circumstances.

But big timber is big business and fire disturbs human beings so the tall timber was cut and the doghair fires suppressed when the colonists hit Northern Arizona.

§

Four Ponderosas stand at the end of my driveway. While they aren't the stately matriarchs of an old growth forest (their crowns *are* close enough to the ground to catch fire), they are beautiful, healthy trees. Adolescents, probably, in the tree scheme of things, just a hundred years old or so. My friends stand sentinel at the entrance to my sacred space. They're like the spinster aunties who always seem to settle themselves at the doorway of a wedding reception. You can count on them not to let any questionable persons in. They interrogate arriving guests. Bride or groom? Who invited you? What is your connection?

I adore my driveway sentinels. They are old friends. They enjoy getting dressed up for Christmas with sparkling lights, and dumping snow down my collar when I'm shoveling out the cars after a snowstorm. They give me rough, scratchy kisses on the cheek when I hug them. And I fear for them.

I fear for them because they stand directly downwind of the Icky Neighbors and the fires they leave unattended. If it were just their own house and tree friends the Ickies would burn down it might be different, but Element of Fire doesn't work that way. So like it or not, like *them* or not, the Icky Neighbors and I are united in common community and common interests underneath this highly flammable canopy. No one goes it alone. We are all in this together.

There are experiences we share as humans that make us human; experiences that *define* us as human. Sitting around a fire in the dark and staring into the flames is one of them. It is primal; everyone is captivated by it. Whether it's a candle or a campfire, we can't help ourselves. We stare into it as we listen to the stories being told or just woolgather as we listen to it crackle and snap. Poke at it with our stick. Some yearn for this experience so badly they'll be stupid about it and put all of us at risk to get it.

§

"What's wrong with ya, ya damn rookie? I told you! You always—ALWAYS—keep the wind at your back!" my boss screamed at me, his voice finally piercing the roar of the fire and my intense focus on my work.

But I was too much of a dumbass rookie to have even noticed the shift of wind. I was busy saving the world. There I was, Woodsy Owl, with my helmet and my fireproof shirt out on my first forest fire, digging my line with all my heart like I'd been told to, where I'd been told to, making sure I got down into the dirt.

"Crown!! Crown!!" The rest of my crew were running off the line. I blinked for a second, uncomprehending. It was only for just a heartbeat or two. A 20-foot-tall spruce tree (roughly as tall as a two-story building), a Christmas tree with branches clear to the ground went up in front of me like a match. It exploded. When the fire is close it superheats the green part of the trees (the crown) and they detonate. The concussive wave shoved me like a straight-arm to the chest. I staggered back a step to catch my balance and could, at last, turn my feet of clay and run, one or two heartbeats too late. It was the most terrifying thing by far I have ever been close to in person.

Immediately when I reached safe distance, my boss grabbed me up by the scruff of the neck. "You left the shovel?"

"Hell yes I left the shovel! I damn near left the contents of my colon and bladder as well!" I babbled, crying, gasping for air in the searing heat of near fire, with my heart hammering in my ears. I couldn't tell if everything was swimming in front of my eyes from the heat and smoke or because I was about to pass out as waves of post-adrenaline nausea and exhaustion washed over me. Crushed me.

Before that experience I might have been tempted to think we've become numbed to the dangers of fire, what with all the catastrophic flame and explosions we see at the movies and in video games. But I can tell you with absolute conviction now, that's hogwash. I do not recommend getting up close and personal with a big, out of control fire—Element of Fire, capital E, capital F—to reconnect with the primal fear we might think we've risen above these days in our snug little homes, at safe technological remove from nature. It is an awful experience. These are not flames you stare into contentedly and contemplatively. These are flames you run in terror from.

Some of my best friends (and they seem like such reasonable people otherwise) just *love* fighting forest fires. They love that hazard pay and they love the adrenaline and volunteer for first response. No way. Not me. I'll get my adrenaline elsewhere, thank you, and take outhouse cleaning preferentially to fighting forest fires any day for my forest service paycheck. If it's threatening someone's house, I'm there in the spirit of community, but volunteer? Hike out into hell to confront Element of Fire in full fury? No thanks. It takes a brave soul, one with more guts than I have to do that kind of work. I am not made of the right stuff. I came home crying for my Mommy.

In much the same way disease sweeps catastrophically through overcrowded, squalid, starving human populations, doghair not only burns hot enough to kill the soil, but it provides ladder fuels that lift the fire up into the crowns of the trees. Once it's in the green, everybody's dead, all the trees and rookie (green) dumbass fire fighters who don't have the sense to pay attention to the wind.

Although the forest service is slowly and cautiously reintroducing fire to this ecosystem (and that's a good thing), 140 years of avarice and mismanagement after colonization we are left with only two choices best I can see as far as forest "management" goes here in the Southwest. Catastrophic fire or the back-breaking economic sinkhole of timber stand improvement. Trees are plants. They *get* thinning. The lesser evil here is clear. If we want our forests, in our lifetime, we need to be adults and take responsibility for the consequences of our past actions. We need to thin it, clean it, and then *leave it alone* to mature to the magnificent, fire-resistant old-growth stands of yore.

§

I'm paranoid about fire because I've been there and I know what it is like to confront that howling war god face-to-face. There is nothing meaningful me and my puny shovel are going to be able do about it. The wind always screams here on the Rim in the springtime. It's a gusty, moisture-sucking constant. We don't have any control of that whatsoever, or over which of the gazillion climate change tipping points we may have already passed, or over the transgressions of the past. The only thing we have control over is today. A confluence of factors has placed the forests of the Southwest in constant and grave danger of catastrophic fire and the only factor—the *only* one—any of us has any control over whatsoever now, is the fires we start.

Don't be a dog; understand where you leave off and the rest of the world picks up. Don't turn your neighbors into nagging witches with your ignorance. Try not to be an Icky neighbor. Bring your brain on vacation with you, wherever you might go. Strive to be the kind of tourist people enjoy sharing their community with. If you don't know, ask. Don't compromise the community and sacred space in which you are a stranger. Be aware that you enter a circle of friends when you're away from home, people (human and nonhuman) who have lived in each other's company for a long enough time that they trust each other; trust that none in the circle will endanger the rest unnecessarily. Here in the desert southwest, (as I hope it does everywhere) that circle of friends includes trees. Fire threatens the circle. You can probably figure out for yourself when it's too windy to burn and if a fire is all the way out if you give it a little consideration.

§

I offer you this in the spirit of paying it forward.

When you come to my community you become part of my circle, and when I come to your community I become part of yours. *Mitakuye Oyasin.* I offer you a local's perspective about fires and dogs here in in Northern Arizona in the hope you might be willing to help me likewise when I come to visit your circle. I don't have the first clue about how to survive in an urban environment, for example. I'm as much of a dumbass there as some people who start fires are here. I am helpless. I don't know what the dangers are there (to myself or others) or how to negotiate the landscape.

So I will endeavor to bring my brain with me, in turn, when I come to visit your community and your circle of friends, whoever that may include. I will attempt to be aware of my ignorance and will strive not to turn you into nags with it. My goal will be to not place you in danger. I will hope to be the kind of tourist you enjoy sharing your community and sacred space with. I will try not to take insult. Nobody likes to be confronted with their ignorance but I will try to play by the rules in your neck of the woods and if I don't know what the rules are, I'll ask. I will try to behave with common sense and respect. I will try very hard not to leave your world any worse off for my presence after I leave and ask in return only that you do the same when you come here.

§

I suspect there are Icky Neighbors in every neighborhood. There certainly have been in every neighborhood I've ever lived in. Let us cooperatively reach out and warm our hearts to these people. Let us continue to teach them how put out their fires and to rake their pine needles for them. Let us rescue their animals and children if need be, and teach them how and why to care. There is a difference between co-opting your neighbors and co-operating with them. Let's all drag each other *up* rather than down. Let us continue to teach them how and why to hold up their corner of the safety net we all rest in and rely on. Let us not think of them as them, but as us. Let us not abandon each other to uncaring. No one goes it alone.

How to Tell if
You Were Born Pagan

Looking back now, I realize I was born pagan, but like a lot of us, I didn't realize it till I was in my early 20s and flirting with finding my own identity. Back of my family's house in Northern Arizona was the "Rio" de Flag. We called it the Ditch, and the Ditch was a great place to just be a kid with no greater obligations than that. There were adventures aplenty to be had in the Ditch, new friends to be made, fantastic journeys of imagination to be taken, and forts to be built. The only price to be paid was that if you got really really dirty down there, Mom would hose you down in the backyard before she'd let you come into her clean house. But on a hot, dusty summer day, that was just as much fun as getting dirty, so it was a price gladly paid.

Owing to Northern Arizona's arid climate the Ditch was dry most of the time, but once in a very great while the Rio would actually have water in it. It was sluggish, brackish water, but it was natural water freely given by Mother Nature nonetheless, as opposed to the only other water we ever got to see outside past the end of the rain- or snowstorm proper, which came from a hose. Born and bred in this alpine desert, I never saw a body of water I couldn't swim across till I was in my teens, and didn't understand till much later even than that how many people had very different definitions of ponds, rivers and lakes than I did at the time. For those of us from the desert southwest, a pond can be a cow track that holds water for two summers running, and I've walked across "Lake" Mary many a time without getting wet much above the knees. We went to the Verde, a real river, on a picnic a couple of summers after these events, and even later yet I saw the Mississippi Ocean once. I still figure anything you can't see the other side of is an ocean. Although my understanding of what constitutes a Rio has changed a lot over the years, the Ditch was as much river as I'd ever known at the time.

The two or three times a year the Rio held water past the end of the rainstorm itself were a grand adventure in discovery for me, and most special among those discoveries were aquatic lifeforms. I met Boatmen. Shoot, walking on the water ain't no big deal for them. There were slimy, blooming algae, and fern-like plants who never stuck their heads up out of the water and into the air. There were frogs and tadpoles, but they were far too busy to dally and play with the likes of me. The water dogs, though, our own indigenous newts, they were different. They were so very special. They would gladly hang out and be the fire-breathing dragons in my mud castle moat all day long. Seems they had nothing better to do in the world than play in the mud with me, sit quietly and gently in my hand, or have a nice swim.

So when my Auntie and Uncle showed up at our house one hot summer afternoon with a whole tub full of water dogs in tow, I was particularly delighted. An especially special treat! Not only were my very best favorite Auntie and Uncle visiting, we were going to a real lake to play with our water dog friends the very next day! Auntie and Uncle were my favorites for lots of reasons. One of the best of those was that their black lab, Jezebel, was my best friend in the whole wide world. You couldn't ask for a more valiant and faithful friend, nor a better puddle-splashing buddy than Jez. I was beyond excited; a grand adventure was in the offing.

It was over dinner that night, though, that I began to get an inkling of what was to become of my friends in the tub in the garage. I came to suspect that they were to be spitted on a hook and eaten alive. I was even more horrified to fear that they might suffer this brutal sacrifice in order to entice a fish to swallow a razor-sharp hook, die a slow death, and end up in a frying pan! The adults were not overly concerned that I suddenly lost my appetite. Kids do, after all. They knew I'd be back around later for an apple or something, and they were much engaged besides in stimulating adult conversation. So I quietly excused myself and, as they sat over a second coffee, played cards, and caught up on old times, went out into the garage with Jez. A tear slipped down my cheek as I looked into her warm brown eyes and considered my quiet, gentle friends, trapped there in the tub of doom. I was too little by far to pick up the tub or even the smallest part of it, so I went out into the backyard and got my kid-sized bucket from the sandbox. I rinsed the sand out of it, filled it with clean water from the hose, and Jez and I started lugging two or three water dogs at a time clear through the backyard and down to the Ditch, way way out to the very last mud puddle I could find. We made trip after trip until I thought my stubby legs would give out, and until all my water dog friends were free. They never did have much get-up in their get-along, even in the most dire of emergencies, like this one. Although when you think about it, how much hustle does a fire-breathing dragon really need anyway? Still, I was scared for them as they ambled slowly off into the muck and algae in no particular hurry. "Run! Run you guys! Runaway!! Run for your lives!" I yelled after them.

§

"What in the world happened to you? I can see where you two have been, and I ought to tan your hide for going down there after dark, young lady, you know the rules. And so do you, Jez. We've been calling for you!"

My mother, voice angry and hands on her hips, loomed large in the back door, light spilling out from behind her. My lower lip trembled a little, and Jezzie's soft whimper spoke for both of us. Jez and I had already discussed that we might expect nothing better than the spanking and to bed with no dessert we had earned, being out after dark without letting her know where we'd gone and all, but our pitiful state must have softened her heart. We were covered with mud, head to toe and tail. My 4-year-old legs were scratched and trembling with exhaustion, the summer playdress tattered beyond repair. There were streaks left by tears down my sunburnt, dirty face. Jez was panting and her pink tongue was lolling out the side of her mouth

We got hosed down in the backyard, as usual, but with rather more parental gentleness than we expected under the circumstances. Mom actually smiled and gave me a kiss as she handed me my towel, and she scratched Jezzie's ears fondly as she rubbed her down. Dad, Auntie and Uncle all cooed and brought us treats when they saw us sopping and shivering, tired and hungry, standing there in the doorway. They put me in a warm bath and then my bed. As Mom turned out the light and walked out of the room, Jez gave me a kiss and a big smile, the kind of smile only dogs can give because they can smile with their whole bodies. She jumped up on the bed, curled her warm, solid self against my back, and we fell into an exhausted sleep together, smug, knowing that all was right in our world.

The next morning was quite a different story though, I'm sure you'll know. You can tell they're really mad when they use all three of your names and Jez is on her belly with her head down. We still got to go to the lake, but they didn't get to go fishing. They seemed really unhappy about it, too, which Jez and I couldn't figure out because there was so much fun to be had skipping stones and fetching sticks and squishing toes in the mud.

§

It was years later, when I first saw the magnificent fiery salamander, glowing there in the Sacred South, I instantly recognized as such the first pagan deity I had ever encountered. "I knew you could breathe fire, I just knew it!" I whispered as I knelt at the fire altar and offered my sincere and humble respects. I knew again the sustenance and warmth of steadfast friendship, the confidence imparted by mutual support, the nourishment of the hearth fire, and the enduring, loyal kinship of family. Looking back now I know it was the water dogs, Northern Arizona's own salamanders, who first taught me the true appreciation of these things. Looking back now, I know I was born pagan.

∽⊗ ⊗∾

Element of Water: Rebirth

We face sunset to honor Element of Water and know it is the stuff of life itself for us and all our relations, especially in these arid climes. The powers of Element of Water are receptive, restorative, germinative, and purifying. Element of Water is as joyous and sustaining as a hot drink on a cold winter's night; as elated as the gleeful abandon of a bird having a bath in a fresh puddle after a rainstorm. Honoring our Sacred Dead in the West warms us like one of Auntie's hugs whether she is on this side or the Other. Element of Water blesses with the healing, growth and kinship that is as the comingling of waters. Element of Water buoys our spirits and our bodies, brings us peaceful sleep, and joins us together in common experience.

§

The pine forest we inhabit here in Northern Arizona seems endless and this can be misleading. Those who hail from areas with more water will sometimes mistake the green, whispering forest that stretches to the horizon and beyond in so many directions for lushness. For wet. But those of us who have walked under these trees our life long, know that the forest lives precariously, with limited resources and in a very narrow range of tolerances. The dreaded bark beetles live in and with our Ponderosa Pine friends. They always have. The math is simple and brutal. If the trees get enough water, they are able make enough sap to pitch the beetles out. If the trees don't get water to pitch them out, the beetles bore into cambium (the delicate vascular system that lies underneath the protective bark and on top of the supporting wood) to rob them of their water and nutrients. To starve them. To kill them.

If we would, we could look to the ancient wisdom of these tree people to teach us an important lesson. Planet Earth, Mother Goddess, in the infinity of Father God's time, has a vast range of tolerances. We and all our family, the kin who sustain us from cradle to grave, from our parents to the immense forest, puny mortals that we are, have narrow tolerances. The most rare and precious thing on this whole, spinning water planet, is water clean enough to drink. All the water on Planet Earth was brought here from space at Creation. We should take care not to squander it.

Element of Water here in the Southwest is an extravagance, something to celebrate. Here in the desert, it's a partaaayyyy when there's enough rain for everybody. The trees around here like wet sex (just like everybody), and a generous summer monsoon season will inspire them to public displays of affection the following spring— profligate clouds of yellow pollen that coat everything from windshields to water bowls; and the following autumn as well— whirlybird seeds that swirl and dance their way to the ground on a blustery fall day.

Element of Water is the source of purification and renewal, humbling and liberating in the immensity and subtlety of its power. It is in the West, in Element of Water, we find healing and recovery from addiction, even gratitude for the pain that brought us to it. (*Gaiastorm and Spring Cleaning*).

Element of Water can cleanse us on more meaningful levels than just our sweaty skin, although I know you know the shower after the backpacking trip is every bit as wonderful as the hike itself. Element of Water is what all of us here on the water planet have most strongly in common, it washes us all together so that we may not remain ignorant of our kinship or untangle it. We all carry the oceans of this planet in our veins, and in the joining of our Waters it is impossible to separate ourselves from any other—*Mitakuye Oyasin*.

Element of Water is arguably the Element we are all most intimate with in all its subtleties. We know it well in gaseous, liquid, and crystalline forms. It is this intimacy, perhaps, that lends itself so well to the joyous abandon of play. Most of us have loved playing in the water, whether splashing in puddles, swimming, or skiing (*Love of Shoveling*).

§

As we face the sunset and Element of Water, we contemplate death, and the significance and duration of our place in the Spiral of time in the larger scheme of things (*Reincarnation*). Our culture conditions us to fear death. Perhaps because it represents such uncertainty; something none of us can know about till we go through it.

For those of us who believe in reincarnation, death is an inevitable crossing over into something, somewhere—someone—else. Something and somewhere and someone from which there's no coming back as the person we were before (save for brief spiritual visits at, say, Samhain), to be sure, but death is not an end in any kind of meaningful way. There is no uncertainty about it. Death is about continuance. It's a process. We are comforted by the continuity of being a small, small part of a greater whole we cannot begin to fathom, but to which we must surrender ourselves. We try to be brave and approach it in the spirit of adventure. We try not to cling. It's a little scary, but we take comfort in knowing its not the end. Death can be about connections, even with the severing of them (*Funeral for a Friend*).

§

Element of Water is famously feast or famine. Here on the leading edge of global climate change we feel its effects first and most acutely in Element of Water. Already some places are experiencing record flood levels and frequency. Even here in the desert we know it, even here we feel it.

When Element of Water gets hot it becomes gaseous. And when there's enough of it in Element of Air, it forms rain clouds and when there's so much the cloud can no longer hold it, it comes down again as rain. We have just had the wettest summer monsoon season we have had here in twenty years. I know this because I have lived here twenty years and for the first time ever since I've lived here, there were frogs in the yard! Little bright green tree frogs, about the size of a quarter. Amphibious people, who need wet skin to survive. Extraordinary.

The blessing of Element of Water is deep, healing sleep; the sleep that gives us the strength to get up and fight our way through another day like the one that left us crippled with exhaustion yesterday. The blessing of Element of Water is the capability and resiliency to get up and exercise again after being ill. Even though we're weak and wobbly it feels good to be on our feet again. It is Element of Water gives us help to flush toxic self-talk and banish unhealthy people and relationships from our lives, to start anew, to start better. It is Element of Water that buoys us up from the bottom of the abyss of grief, to make peace with our dead and with ourselves after crippling loss.

Element of Water gives us the tears to wash the wound that it might heal clean. In the blessings of Element of water we are reborn.

GAIASTORM

Mid-night:

Tonight my spirit soars.

Tonight I know the peace and fullness so painfully absent from my life these past years.

Tonight there are horizons and potential. Tonight there is hope.

Tonight I am grateful, tonight I live again.

Thank you, Gaia, for this night, for this storm, for my life.Thank you for the yellow crescent moon, hanging there over my left shoulder. The moon goddess is peeking through the frame in the clouds she has made. She has gilt it with her own pure, silver light and it is stunning. Achingly beautiful. Tonight I feel her eternal cycles in the very core of my being. Tonight I know that her beacon shines through my life, through the entirety of who I am and whoever I may grow to be. Tonight I know, for the first time, that I will survive.

Thank you for undershirts. Most of the time they're just a covering. Creature comfort for a body gone numb. Tonight though, this scant shirt allows me to feel the sensuous caress of the warm, wet breeze on my bare neck, too long missing a lover's touch. As I wend my way north towards my home and away from the heat of the desert, that moist caress turns chill. My nipples crinkle and harden, the lover's tender touch now become erotic.

Thank you for this magical, enchanted storm.

Thank you for the lightning. Gently flickering at first there in the north, it dances all around in the rounded woman-shapes of the clouds. It renders unto them exquisite and infinite shades of peach, charcoal, gray and purple, yet is itself never seen. Tears choke my throat as I am overwhelmed at the ethereal delicacy and majesty of your art in the sky this night.

Farther north the dance hastens, becomes urgent. Brilliant, piercing shafts of vibrant, pulsating light surround me, each finding its own unique and sometimes convoluted path between sky and Earth. Some unfurl gracefully, gossamer filaments unwinding as from a spool. They are threads of sacred power floating down towards the Earth. Others are lace, tat with the softest pinks, purples and whites in your weaving basket. Rippling gently and gracefully across the sky, swept along on waves of low rolling and rumbling, these choose never to touch Earth at all.

Some are bold and abrupt. These are close, loud, violent and frightening. Thrusting, crashing tridents that my eyes still see and my ears still hear even long after they have passed—lest I forget. These allow me to know my smallness, my powerlessness. I am blessed and freed in the knowing.

A landscape is revealed to me in the power of the lightning's illumination that is at once familiar and alien to me. In eyeblink glimpses I see a place that looks like home, I think, but I can't quite see long enough to tell for sure.

Thank you for the blues on the radio. Sometimes they're just inspirational music to clean house by, pleasing white noise to keep unwanted thoughts and feelings at bay. But tonight, here in this storm, the music stirs a place in me I thought long dead now, mournfully birthing anew feelings long forgotten. My heart aches but I am joyous.

Thank you for the rain, for the soft mist that moistens my upturned face. It nourishes Mother Earth and all her children. I, among them, am sustained and restored.

Thank you for the pounding, purifying deluge. It cleanses both my spirit and this landscape of obscuring pollution. Washed free of filth, of the blackness of fear and anger, I see clearly now a place clearly seen.

Thank you for the women. For the confidantes, allies, teachers, and partners in crime. Thank you for the life-giving nurturing of the mothers, for the healing wisdom of the crones, and for the bursting fecundity of the girls.

This web of women is a net for me now, it saves me from the peril I would seek. They are a knot in the end of a rope hanging over the abyss of despair. The chasm of the pit of a lifetime of "almosts," the emptiness of a life turned over and run empty—gone dry.

Tonight, surrounded by the power of the web and the sacred power of this storm, I stand at the center of the Spiral. Tonight I am the web and the web is me. I am filled with love for others and buoyed by their love for me. Tonight I am connected with all of the women, with all of life, with the Sacred. Tonight I am strong and whole.

§

Tomorrow I will be back in that other place. That artificially illuminated dayside landscape I know so well with its neuroses, work, worry, and the addictions which allow me to be almost enough, almost okay there. But tonight, here in this storm, I truly glimpse home; an unpolluted place of fullness and peace. A home rarely visited for the brevity of the illumination. Tonight I am filled with wonder at the power and beauty of the Sacred. Tonight I am cleansed and joyful. Here, tonight, in this storm, I really am enough.

For it is here tonight, in this place and in this storm, traveling my own unique and sometimes convoluted path, unfurling aimlessly from the spool of time, that I am at last, truly, and with every fiber of my being, grateful.

So thank you also, Gaia, for the pain, and for the foolish trust which led me to it. Otherwise I would not have known this joyful gratitude, the wonder of this night, or the sacred power of this storm.

∞

SPRING CLEANING

Mitakuye Oyasin, a ritual bath for all my relations:

Vernal Equinox is the time to play Goddess and exercise the power of transformation. It is a time to throw frugality to the wind (briefly) and Cast Element of Water with a lavish, perhaps even extravagant hand, even in this arid place, in the fine old, time honored tradition of spring cleaning. Get sweaty and sticky; even . . . muddy!

Muddy is not something we're very familiar with here in the desert, but on spring cleaning day, after you wash the cars and turn the garden and clean the shed and muck out the chicken coop and enjoy getting really dirty while you're getting everything else really clean, treat yourself—body, mind and spirit—to some spring cleaning as well.

Light a candle and sink into a steaming bath in a sparkling tub. Soak off your winter slumbers and bid farewell to any fear and negativity that may have been cooped up in the house with you all winter. Be polite, thank those fears and negativity for the blessing of the lessons they may have had to impart, and then watch them drain away at the end of your bath. The power of Element of Water is dilution and dispersion. Emotional pollutants that are heavy and crushing to us as puny, weak individuals, are diluted to insignificance by Element of Water and carried away to the vastness of Mother Earth's capacity to absorb. Ultimately these heavy burdens we all lug around with us, our insecurity, anger, confusion, and fear, can vanish into insignificance with a prayer. Pull the plug and speak gratitude for Element of Water and Mother Earth for carrying all this away and remaking it into something new and positive someday, somewhere. A seedling plant, or perhaps a rainbow, or maybe even a puddle for a child or a bird to splash and giggle in.

§

NEW MOON AND SEASON
BATH SALTS

Basic bath salts are three parts Epsom salts plus two parts baking soda plus one part table salt.

Add a few (!) drops of essential oils to invite their influences and resonances into your life for the coming turn. For the Spring of the year, try:

Grapefruit,

> for purification and to honor the ascendant power of the Sun.

Jasmine,

> just a whisper, in honor of the Moon Goddess.

Chamomile,

> for awareness, assistance in meditation, and to keep it sweet.

Ylang Ylang,

> for peace, sensuality, and love.

Geranium,

> for protection and to bring happiness.

Vetivert,

> for financial prosperity

Add a few yellow flower petals for intellect and intelligence, divination, eloquent communication, study and consciousness.

৩৫ ৩৫

LOVE OF SHOVELING

We finally got a snowstorm. A big one. We'd been salivating for one all winter. Praying for it. Putting out offerings and empty chalices in the hope Element of Water would fill them. Global climate change may very well be hammering the Eastern folk with colder, wetter winters, but climate change definitely translates to global warming here in the ever-desiccated American Southwest. Why, Flagstaff, Arizona, my home town, is among the top ten snowiest cities in the United States. Near the bottom, to be sure, but still it is a considerably snowy place. Or it was. When I was a kid we got a dozen or so significant snowstorms every winter with a doozy sprinkled in now and then. Now we're lucky if we get a couple of significant storms (say, six to twenty inches) in any given winter and, in recent years, if we get any winter moisture at all a lot of it has come in the form of rain.

The stock pond down the road speaks local truth eloquently. That truth is: we don't get to keep the water if it comes to us in the form of rain. Although rain makes things that enchant us desert rats, like rivulets and puddles big enough to romp in and get muddy, it is ephemeral. Element of Earth here is porous and volcanic; rain percolates down or runs off quickly. Snow hydrates better because it lingers.

I grieve those missing snowstorms of old like the old fuddy duddy I am now. I love everything about the snow, I always have. Even the work of it; putting the chains on the car, shoveling out, and helping people get their vehicles unstuck. I inherited love of this work from my Dad. He loved it too. We would get up early on snowy mornings to shovel out. Sure it needed doing, but we loved doing it. We especially loved doing it together. Scrape, pitch, repeat. He taught me how to use the right tool for the right job: the big grain scoop for volume and the little square-nose shovel for chopping and the corners. Oh, no, don't even blow off getting those corners. They get rounded and icy and treacherous. A guy could bust his ass. We'd work hard and laugh and joke and make snow angels and maybe he'd pull my sister and me around our cul-de-sac on the sled, and then we'd come in for a hot breakfast in a warm house before we got on with the mundane business of the day. Digging out is among my fondest childhood memories.

We got a monster doozy one year in the middle sixties—6 or 8 feet in just a few days—the banks at the sides of the driveway were so big even my 6'4" father couldn't throw it that high. Buildings were caving in all over town so everybody was shoveling their roofs. It was way fun for us kids. The snow was nearly up to the eaves, so Dad let us sled off the peak of the roof a bunch of times before we had to start helping with shoveling it off. We worked and played and were all exhausted by the end of the day. Although there was a rickety, icy aluminum ladder available, my sister and Dad and I had been jumping off the roof all day to get down. Mom didn't want to jump. She was shaking she was so tired but insisted she was going to get down by backing off of the roof onto that scary, slippery ladder on the front sidewalk. We all begged her to just jump into the safe, soft snow but she'd have none of it.

"All right, then," Dad said with a frown, "T, you get down and go hold the ladder." I did my last cannonball of the day and scrambled down to hold the ladder. My heart was hammering with a prayer that Mom wouldn't slip and fall to the cement I was standing on. As she turned around and started to inch sideways into position over the sidewalk and ladder, he pushed her. Just a little nudge. It wasn't playful or mean, you understand, it was for her own safety, while she was still out over the soft stuff. She screamed and fell, landing safely in snow up to her neck. We didn't dare none of us laugh. It was one of the few times I ever saw her really mad at him. Like really really mad—hot, seething, you're-sleeping-on-the-couch-and-forget-about-any-dinner kind of mad.

Shoveling snow is a meditation; a Zen kind of thing. Make a hole, clean it out. It's especially therapeutic for those of us who struggle with a little OCD. It's even better than the Zen of swimming laps, which is all about counting 'em off and watching the black stripe. But when you look behind you in the lap pool, the same 25 yards of water with the same black stripe are still there. When you look back at your shoveling meditation there are liberated vehicles and tidy, safe paths to walk.

Besides, shoveling snow is a great workout—cardio and otherwise. If I have a heart attack and die while I'm shoveling snow, know I died happy. I get to be outdoors in the aftermath of the storm, in the crystalline, magical world which, here in the Southwest, generally comes with brilliant sunshine and an achingly deep blue sky. Even when the temperatures are low, because we are at elevation and because there is so little sky to interfere between us and the sun, our cold is generally dry. By the time you've been shoveling for ten minutes or so, you're sweating and peeled down to your shirtsleeves. I'm told that the back East people will not understand this because their cold is damp and cutting and miserable and the thought of shoveling snow in a t-shirt in freezing weather will be appallingly alien to them.

The world sounds as wonderful and magical as it looks when the storm is fresh. It is muffled, sounds are deep and still. The world is softly reawakening with the sounds of trees and birds, the scraping of my shovel, and my own deep breathing. Shoveling snow is time to converse with the locals, all the other creatures who, like me, are out discovering the new-made world: my pine tree friends, the ravens and jays and squirrels who coach me so raucously, the human neighbors who are out either shoveling or pulling inner tubes up and down the street behind their ATVs having shrieking good fun, and my favorite, the occasional dog who has escaped his yard and is bounding through the snow with his tongue hanging out in ecstasy. They bring to my love of shoveling the joyous abandon the dog people are always so happy to share with us, if only we'll put the shovel down for a minute and throw a stick out in the deep stuff for them to find.

If one of the working definitions of a witch is an eccentric old woman living by herself on the outskirts of town with a houseful of cats, I am at last becoming the witch I was born to be. Finally growing into the role. I have a crooked back and a cabinet full of pain dope (no warts yet though, thankfully). "You should find a kid to do that for you," my friends tell me. "You should get a snowblower," my chiropractor says. "Here, let me get that for you," my kindly neighbor says as he tries to take the shovel from my hands. But I hold tight. There is a long, long list of chores I'd give up before I'd relinquish my snow shovel. Not once has anyone ever tried to take the scrub brush from my hand when I was on my hands and knees breaking my back trying to get the shower clean. They could have that one for the asking, but not my snow shovel.

§

The weather service said it was a large "complex" system that could leave us with anywhere between two and twenty-eight inches of snow.

I sniggered at this candyass safe-bet weather forecasting as simple cowardice and unwillingness to commit. But I looked at the weather map myself and it showed four low pressure systems all swirling and dancing around the edge of the massive Colorado Plateau, and allowed it might be hard to guess the outcome of such a chess game, even for educated meteorologists. Weather here on the Edge is difficult to forecast under the best of circumstances and multiple lows vying for power is hardly the best, or most predictable, of circumstances.

The eight inches or so on the ground the first morning was real Sierra Cement. At least that's what the Northern California powder hounds who transplanted themselves to Wolf Creek ski area when I was working there back in the day called it. They ate that heavy wet shit up. I didn't even bother putting my ski boots on. Skiing that wet heavy stuff is too much freakin' work! And besides, for those of us with glass knees, too freakin' dangerous as well. It doesn't give—you'll blow your knee long before you'll ever skid your turn. Those hardy souls said it was good for your skiing because it was carve or die, but I took their word for it and let 'em track it all up. I stayed in by the fire with a good book. I'd set an alarm even on my days off to get up and shovel out to get there early to help track it up if it was the light stuff, but they can have all of my part of the cement.

Back then I was just a spoiled brat, lazy and unwilling to ski in any but optimal conditions. It's one of the perks of working at a ski area known for its bottomless dry Southwestern fluff, but now, well, it's different. I had to get out in the Sierra Cement and shovel my way out to the chicken yard. Thank all the gods above and below for that cabinet full of pain dope. Sierra Cement is HEAVY. Oh, and may all the gods above and below pity you if you have to shovel someplace you've already walked on it. It turns to rock.

It was such very different snow than we usually get here. It sounded different. When the tree branches dump their load of the fluff we're accustomed to, there's a "poof" followed by the whispers of it gently cascading off the roof. Softly spoken as cold smoke. The Sierra Cement was breaking off branches that couldn't dump their load quickly enough and when they did offload it sounded like cannonballs dropping on the roof. Pow! Splat! It shook the house and made me and the cats jump. We're not accustomed to such violent snow.

It looked different, too. The puffy, light, Christmas card adornments the tree branches usually wear make them look proud and bold. Dressed up for a fairy tale party. Sometimes the tree people who line my driveway, the ones I've been shoveling under and around for decades now, titter when they manage to dump a load of fluff down my collar. In the past it's been all mischievous good fun for everyone. They couldn't hold the Sierra Cement, though. They quivered and looked sad and burdened and droopy. One of them smacked me down, without malice, with one of its cannonballs. As I got back to my feet, with those cartoon stars and tweety birds circling my head, I thought for a disoriented minute I was back in the second grade and Tobe Hubbard had beaned me with a slushball.

The forecasters were more sure of themselves by the second day of the storm, when the confluence of the four fronts was upon us, dancing overhead proper. It had rained all night and they called for 8 more inches of Sierra Cement during the daylight hours. I took some prophylactic pain dope, grabbed my shovel, and went forth. By the morning of the third day there were 8 inches of new cement on top of 4 inches of rained-down slush on top of apparently bottomless shoe-sucking mud. Now, how ya gonna shovel that?

It looked pristine and sparkling—the achingly blue skies and ravens and jays and bounding dog people were all there as usual—but it was truly ugly work to shovel. At best it slid off the shovel, if at all, with a smooth wet gush, like a cat finally throwing up after yakking forever. At worst it slid off the shovel, if at all, with a disturbing crunchy, slurping slap; the same awful wet grinding I hear in my back in the most agonizing of nights. It is a sound best left to slasher movies by my auditory esthetic.

I never thought I'd look back on my lift-operator/snow-shoveling days at Wolf Creek with such fondness. If Dad taught me the love of shoveling as a chore, working at Wolf Creek raised it to a professional art form. We moved it by hand by the ton. I learned the value of making a smooth surface, different textures and pitches, of course, for walking and skiing, and to craft a good ramp with the correct slope and bank. I learned to git 'er done late in the day so she sets up good at night. I learned to measure and cut a precision pit under the Borvig counterweight so it had the required clearance to drop, but most importantly I learned to call for help when I needed it. What I wouldn't have given for Mark Bean and his snowcat by that third morning, he could have had the Sierra Cement tidied up for me in about ten minutes. I was slinging slop and chipping ice for days.

My inner child was jumping up and down wanting to go out skinny skiing and wallowing and romping with the dogs. Woo hoo! Snow day! My outer adult, with her adult responsibilities and hinky back was bemoaning the fact it's such a long way, such a very long way, out to the chicken yard. Still, it's water falling out of the sky in the desert and that's a miracle *du jour* any way you look at it around here. I live off the grid, water-wise, and pay six and a half cents a gallon to have it trucked in. The stock pond and the pine forest slurped up and stowed away every drop they could and as for me, well, just one little snow angel was enough to get me back out there on the happy end of my snow shovel.

⋞℘ ℘⋟

REINCARNATION

I believe in reincarnation, but it's beyond belief, I know it. I know it with a cellular certainty that transcends the merely intellectual, the conscious trust. I know it with an understanding that casts my puny existence into the infinite tides of the cosmos and the vastness of time. Reincarnation renders me a mote in the unimaginable immensity of creation, an insignificant blink of the eye.

In the same way, I know there are intelligences in the universe so far superior to my own they might barely be able to perceive me and my kind as conscious beings. I know this when I look into the night sky, at that splash of infinity across the void that is the Milky Way. I know these intelligences exist in the same way I know my hands twitch at night when I dream. I don't need to see it, or experience or remember it on any kind of a conscious level. I know it happens. I know it in my gut in the same way I know other, ancient civilizations are out there.

Would they know I'm here? Me, an insignificant blink of the eye? That much is less certain.

Looking at my feet, I wonder.

Here in arid Northern Arizona, a walk in the rain is a rare treat, a confection to be savored. But I don't look around at the delighted trees, sipping at the bounteous nectar falling like manna from heaven, or even savor moistness on my skin and hair. I watch my feet and marvel at the teeming life roiling up out of the soil. Life I'm not even aware of most of the time.

They hide in the Dry, and only come out to play in the Wet, the earthworms, burrowing away in their chthonic busy-ness. With a kiss of Element of Water they surface, freed to explore a different dimension. They move across the dirt road where I walk with slow, deliberate purpose. Thoughtful purpose, perhaps, in their earthworm way so different from mine. Their tracks are straight and direct until they intersect another of their kind, then they glance off. What are they thinking? Where are they going? What is their mission on the surface, out in the Element of Air where they're such strangers?

Even when I finally get to see them because the moisture frees them from their subterranean nature, I can barely bring myself to perceive of them as conscious beings. They lift their tiny, blind heads and sway side to side, probing. Are they scenting? Exploring the strangeness of Air and light? Tasting the liberty to move their heads like that? Their earthy home must not allow such unimpeded freedom of movement. Do they lift their heads and wave around like that just because they can? Can they sense the road grader coming?

I try to imagine things from their perspective; their worm's eye view of the road. I ponder the depth of the wisdom I lack that they must surely have about soil. Things me and my kind will never—could never—know. Still, from my perspective and in my world of artifice, the world of dirt roads and the big machines that maintain them, they're dumbasses. So my half-hour walk today takes an hour and a half and leaves me with a backache because I stoop to pick so many of them out of the road and toss them back out under the trees where the road grader can't get 'em.

Invertebrate zoologists who study eye morphology say worm eyes are so simple they can sense light but not where it's coming from. Put your imaginary, wildly complex and perceptive human eye close to the ground for a worm's eye view, if you can. Try to imagine being able to differentiate up from down only. Try to draw your horizons in that close, that low to the ground. Try to imagine the unfathomable immensity, the roaring fury, the instantaneous genocide of the road grader. It would be Armageddon. Even at its most vengeful, the Bible has nothing to compare to it. The Flood was only a slow, creeping destruction rising over forty days and forty nights.

The birds like it, though. They don't seem to like flying around in the rain much. They light frequently to fluff and shake and complain, but they're out *en force* today because it's feast day. Easy pickin's.

§

If I should be reincarnated as a wormlike intelligence on one of those other, vastly more intelligent planets someday, and I'm dumb enough to crawl out on the road in front of the road grader, just because it's wet and it feels good, maybe someone will pause in the delight of their walk and throw me out under the trees where I can take my chances with the birds. Blessed Be.

⚜

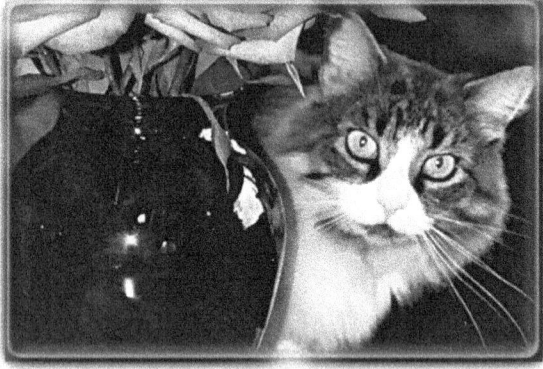

FUNERAL FOR A FRIEND

Father Time, Majestic Lord, I commend unto you the unique and precious spirit of my friend Piñon. I beg you, be kind to her.

Please help her know that she has taken a big chunk of my heart with her. Reassure her that my joyful love of her will always be with me, warming my soul, in each day, in every sweet dream, in every tender moment and in each bright season of my life, until the end of my days here. We will always be together. I must have confidence, this sad day, that the special connection between us will endure and that we will see each other again someday. I am comforted in this trust.

There was a tiny seedling growing here, where I dug your grave, Piñon. I will plant it in the scar that was last summer's forest fire, for hope's sake, for the future. Your parting gift to me was easy digging, and I thank you for it. I am grateful I didn't have to get your Uncle Layne over here to help. I'm grateful because I owe you this work and honor you with it. Some might find that strange somehow, perhaps even macabre, but I wanted to do it for you; you who never asked anything of me but a kind word, a warm lap, and the last teaspoon of milk in the cereal bowl. I owe myself this work.

I light the Sacred fire in your honor, this darkest night, my friend, that I might recall the brightness and warmth you have brought to my life. But do not tarry here, in the dance of light by this warm, bright fire for my sake. I resist the yearning to draw back your shroud for one last look at your dear face. Without those great, bright, green, questioning eyes looking back at me, it wouldn't be you in any case, and I will not dwell on the grave save for this one, long, dark, lonely night. Rather I will cherish the many sweet, joyful memories of you. Remember the time you tangled with that blue jay? You were just a little mite, and way in over your head. You were ever the puppy cat, following along in my cross-country ski tracks, always underfoot. Give my mom some of that quality laptime, purr and snuggle, when you get to the Other Side, and please tell her again that I miss her, too.

Know this and never forget it. You have been adored past all reason in this lifetime. I'm sorry for the unhappy times, but am grateful beyond words that we could share them.

I leave you now, my friend, with some food and water, and some herbs from the garden—you always did like to play jungle kitty there. I'm sending your favorite blankie and some real silver money with which to pay the boatman. You leave me with a very, very heavy heart. I am exhausted, and while you must on to your next grand adventure, I must on to mourn and to heal. Please do not feel badly about these tears, they are more for me than they are for you. I'm not sure how I'll get through the pain of losing you without you, for it was always you who would comfort my tears away. While the tears I shed this night will not fill my loneliness, nor dull the pain of this separation, they will wash the wound, that it might heal clean.

§

I leave you in the trusted keeping of the tree who, in our family, has become the sentinel between this world and the next. You are buried amongst Her roots and I know that you will sustain and nurture each other through this transition. I know I will see you again, that you will come back to me here, in this very place, maybe as a bright new branch on this old tree, maybe as a new sapling, maybe even a baby squirrel or blue jay nourished on the pine nuts the sentinel tree makes.

I will leave a single taper burning this night long on the altar to tonight light your way across. Godspeed you on your journey.

Gaia, Great Goddess, Mother Earth, on this night of autumn's first kiss, I commend into your loving, eternal embrace, the body of my friend, Piñon. Be kind to her.

ಀ಄ ಄ಀ

Teachers and Tuition

SYLLABUS:

Students are encouraged to come to class with an open mind, to recognize that life is a learning experience from start to finish, to think critically, and to be open to information from diverse internal and external sources including the imaginative, the spiritual, the intuitive, and the nonhuman.

Not all of the best teachers are the gentle, nurturing sages we encounter in our elders or at school or church. College is a good place to find lots of information—raw data—but coherence can remain stubbornly elusive. Sometimes the most important teachers in life are found in unexpected places and don't look at all like professors, grandmothers, or clergy. Teachers surround us all our lives in many different guises, and we can learn much from them if only we will use our capacity for critical thinking and pay attention to what they have to teach us. And just because they don't charge fees doesn't mean the lesson is free. There is almost always tuition to be paid. The best any of us can hope for is to learn without unnecessary pain.

Sometimes opportunities to learn something the easy way can get past us. The courses I am liable to sleep through are required to graduate, and the consequence of not paying attention is that the teacher, whoever or whatever it is, keeps turning the volume up. That is, the tuition keeps getting more expensive. If I fail or forget, I get to come back to repeat the lesson, over and over (insanity is doing the same thing over and over and expecting different results) until I get it. Until I pass.

There is much to recommend learning to live in the skin we're in. This states the obvious, I know, but I will confess I have wasted a great deal of time, energy and happiness wishing I was someone else. Wishing I was some how else. Wishing I was different than I am. Wishing I were thinner or heavier, or smarter or more ambitious or more socially skilled or could see better.

I see well enough, for instance, to appreciate the minutiae of the natural world, but not well enough to take the macro-zoom photographs I so perversely desire to take. This distortion also leads me—generally a non-materialistic person—to covet cameras I cannot afford and cannot see well enough to use. I ask myself why it isn't enough to revel in the intricacies of the natural world and admire the beautiful photographs other people take. I wonder why I can't be grateful that I am able to see at all, and well enough to perceive the minute world that fascinates me so. It is enough.

The camera and the minute world are among my teachers. The tuition they charge is disappointment. They have been trying to teach me to live in my own skin and be happy with it as is for a very long time now.

Objects can be teachers too. They can speak volumes and number among our teachers if only we perceive them as such and pay attention to the lessons they offer. A musical instrument, for instance, can teach us many things even if how to play isn't one of them. There can be as much gained through failure as through success in *The Piano*.

There are, of course, many important human professors too who wander in and out of our lives, although not all of them come to us from an educational institution. Teachers kind and brutal have important lessons to impart in the fable *The Extraordinary Thing*, and some human teachers teach by both example and contrast in *The Bat is Dead*.

Fear is an awesomely powerful and poignant teacher indeed. I seem to get the most meaningful lessons (that is, the lessons I am least eager to repeat and so, most motivated to remember) from my own fears, whether they're reasonable or not in *Pursuit of Demons* and *The Israeli*.

§

If we watch for them carefully enough, we might just find we are all surrounded by worthy and wise teachers all the time. They can make our lives easier or harder. If we pay attention to them, they will make us better and wiser people.

֍

THE PIANO

The child loved music to the depths of her soul. She was born that way. It was a love as deep and abiding as her heartbeat. At first it found requite in her parents' dueling stereos. Dad's classical and Mom's popular stuff would dance with one another like wave and beach. The child in her playpen was in ecstasy. Her parents weren't afraid to turn up the volume, either. The family would dance and sing to Tommy Edwards, and then clutch at their hearts, with tears glimmering in the corners of their eyes to Tchaikovsky. Mom didn't much care for Dad's opera, but she was a good sport about it because he was a good sport about her Tammy Wynette.

The child couldn't have been more than six when she got to sit on a piano bench and watch someone play.

By then the little girl was already a seasoned veteran of the symphony and opera. She knew how to sit still and be quiet in her patent leather shoes and ringlets and dressy dress and save her questions and observations and not shame her Dad in his shiny suit and special going-out-at-night tie. Not everybody knew when to applaud, but the little girl did. He taught her.

It was different though, sitting on that piano bench, It was as different to listening to music as walking is to flying, as smelling is to tasting, as dreaming is to the waking world. This was music making up close and personal. The little girl never could remember the face of the woman who let her sit on the bench next to her and watch her play, she only remembered the hands. The pianist's fingers wove their magic, effortlessly it seemed, coaxing the sound out of the awesome instrument. Tickling it. The child could feel the music vibrating in her gut and held her breath for fear of breaking the spell. Merely turning lead into gold or raising the dead would have been a poor, unimpressive second act. Looking back, the child couldn't remember what was played, only that it was happening right there, right in front of her, right next to her. She knew herself to be in the presence of the Sacred.

Her parents loved her. They watched her carefully all the time, so they knew. Her Dad asked her the very next day if she wanted piano lessons. She could hardly contain herself. "Yes! Yes! Yes! Yes, pleeeeeeaaaaaasse!" she bounced.

They were not a wealthy family. Her Dad made a deal to rescue the old piano from a dive bar down on Route 66 before the week was out. He rented a piano dolly—the professional tool that comes in two pieces with lifting leverage, fold-out handles and a ratcheting tie-down strap —and took the old Chevy pickup and four strapping manfriends with him (*fuerte hombres* he called them). Driving slow, he and the fuerte hombres and the old truck, squatting low, came home with the most godawful derelict eyesore anyone had ever seen. It was a black, heavy upright that had lived—hard—down at Joe's Place, maybe since the beginning of time. It smelled bad and sounded worse.

Mom was being a good sport about moving her car out to the driveway for the foreseeable future so the piano could inhabit the garage during its rehabilitation. The piano and the child were disappointed in each other from the first. Neither was what the other expected. The little girl who loved music was trying to be big about it, but this was clearly not what she had envisioned. The child's lip trembled a little and her Dad knelt down and put his arm around her and said "Don't worry, Tiger, we'll clean 'er up and get 'er tuned, You'll see, it'll be OK, she'll be good as new."

The child plinked a couple of keys even she could tell were sour and gave him a woeful look.

§

They started work that very night and worked on it every night for months on end. The little girl was expected to have her homework done by the time her Dad got home from work although it had previously been their family habit to have a little relaxation time and put your feet up and unplug from the day before dinner. After the ugly old black piano took over the garage, Mom put dinner on the table as soon as Dad walked through the door, and as soon as they were done eating, although it had previously been their family habit to have a little relaxation time and put your feet up and read or watch the tube after dinner, the child and her father would put on their grubbies and go out to the garage to work on the piano.

He was the stripping and sanding expert, the little girl the stainer and varnisher. They took everything off that would come off and stripped it, sanded it with the finest grit, stained it and varnished it. When they took off the front, a terrible, reeking cascade of old beer cans, confetti and cigarette butts came pouring out. Mom laughed until she cried. The pieces that wouldn't come off they carefully masked, stripped, sanded, stained and varnished where they stood.

They exposed exquisitely beautiful wood obscured by eons of smoke grime, cigarette burns, black paint and spilled drinks. The wood was the color of lit embers, with yellow grain that made it look as though it was on fire. Mahogany, maybe, they thought, what with the weight of the thing and all. No one was more surprised than the child that her new piano was so beautiful.

When it was finished, Dad had his fuerte hombres over for barbecued burgers and a six-pack and they moved the beautiful piano inside. The tuner came the very next day and the week following that, the little girl started her long-anticipated piano lessons.

§

Mrs. Swingler was a sweet, skinny ancient woman with translucent skin and purple hair who lived in a house full of cats and African violets. She would give the little girl African violets when she did well at a recital or learned a piece particularly well. The child and her mother always killed them. Inadvertently, you understand! They're very finicky, delicate plants. The girl told her mother she would have rather had a cat but her Mom said that probably wasn't going to happen.

Mrs. Swingler was never mean to the child and never gave her more than she could handle, but still the little girl discovered she would rather take a beating than perform in front of people at recitals. By then the next big disappointment between the beautiful old piano and the little girl who loved music had become painfully apparent. No matter how much her Mom made her practice, she was no great talent. She would never be more than an inadequate mimic. The child was nimble-fingered, and bright enough to understand music theory, but she had no sense of time. She was a stump; one of those people at concerts that can't clap with everyone else for very long. Even with a metronome and a piece of music she knew inside out, upside down and backwards, the child had to concentrate to keep the rhythm. She could never just relax and play. It was work. Hard work. As she struggled and floundered the child wondered at people who could keep time. Could they hear their heartbeats? Connect with it in some way she could not? As she was straining to keep time while she practiced, she would reach for that steady thump thump thump in her chest, only to falter and stumble with her piece. Her heart would start to race and she would lose her place and she would have to start over. It was dreary drudgery, far from the soaring, inspired enchantments she'd dreamed of.

As for the piano, the magnificent hardwood antique, although it had suffered many physical insults throughout its years in the bar, was accustomed to be played, and played well. There was a hole nearly worn in the sustaining pedal, and the ivory was worn through on many of the keys. The reverberation of the hardwood sounding board could lift the instrument's voice and make itself heard over the most raucous barroom. This timid, halting, inept child was an irritation.

By the time the child was twelve or so she had discovered the easy joy of her own stereo—technology that let her soar with the music she loved so dearly. Playing the piano was work and she was less and less willing to do it.

Fighting with her mother about practicing the piano became a daily affair that exhausted mother and daughter both. Mom finally relented and let her little stump quit lessons with Mrs. Swingler. Oh, the child, a young woman now, would plink at it every now and then, playing the same old tunes she'd worked so very hard to acquire with Mrs. Swingler, and her little sister just had to have her "Little Drummer Boy" every Christmas, but the dream was fading to hopelessness.

§

As the decades passed the child who loved music retreated further and further from the fantasy of music made into the lazy delight of music experienced. She grew up and moved on. She spent several fortunes buying first LPs, then 8-tracks, then cassettes, then CDs, then digital downloads, along with the increasingly sophisticated hardware required to play them. Car stereos improved dramatically much to her delight and the detriment of her hearing. She continued to harbor the secret, dwindling dream, though, to learn to play. Sheet music accumulated by the ream. She thought it might goad her to practice, but it got stacked in the piano bench and ignored along with all the old dog-eared pieces from Mrs. Swingler.

The child moved the piano into her own home, eventually, much to her mother's relief, and she even took lessons a couple of times in the ensuing years hoping against lost hope she would learn to play now that she was a determined adult. But it was a waste of time and money—still. She was still not talented, still could not keep rhythm, and was still unwilling to do the work. The piano became a large, expensive knick-knack shelf, a great place to display the Christmas village, but little more. She'd plink at it every now and then, playing the same old tunes and Christmas carols, but the piano was just a dust catcher. Every time she polished the beautiful old fiery wood, it was as though the dream of playing became a bit more distant, a bit more tarnished.

§

So she decided it was time to let go, to let the dear old thing try to find a new home, one that would appreciate it, one where it would be played, where it would fulfill the musical dreams and aspirations of someone more worthy than the child who loved music, now an old woman. She wanted it to go to someone deserving, so she chose to donate it rather than sell it. She chose a charity she trusted and played the beautiful old piano in the weeks between making the decision and pickup day more than she had in the previous ten years. She grieved the thought of letting it go. She sagged under the burden of pulling the plug at last on the lingering lifetime dream of learning to play music.

She wrote to the charity a dozen times in those intervening weeks about how precious it was—and how heavy. You need to bring four—FOUR—strong backs, she told them, **fuerte** hombres, and a real piano dolly.

She woke with a start on pickup day, heart pounding. At first she couldn't remember why. When it came back to her a pall settled over the bright, sparkling Northern Arizona spring day. Still, she told herself for the thousandth time; it was the right thing to do. She had known it was the right thing to do for a very long time. She steeled herself with a cuppa strong coffee and prepared herself for a sweet, wistful, appreciative goodbye to her dear old friend and nemesis as it went off to a brighter, more promising future.

Then Bozo and Bozo Inc. showed up with a flimsy wooden dolly, and a couple of guys, to move the massive instrument. The sweet, wistful, respectful goodbye she had dreamt of turned into a grotesque waking nightmare. Their "piano dolly," which was more closely akin to a mechanic's creeper than a tool to lift and move something as heavy as a solid mahogany piano, and the two strong backs they brought were not adequate by half. It was like watching an elephant trying to balance on a roller skate; tragic, unnecessary, dangerous, pointless and foolhardy. It was awful—they almost dropped it twice, and had bent one of the pedals before they finally got it in the truck. They had no emotional investment in the beautiful old thing; they didn't care if they were rough with it. It's true what they say: people don't appreciate what they're given for free. The little girl who loved music was weeping by the time they left; sobbing with the kind of deep grief that accompanies loss of a living, beloved being. A lifetime of not doing right by the magnificent old instrument was not enough. There had to be one more insult, one more disappointment. One last tragedy between them.

§

I gave away a big chunk of my family history that day. I only pray that my parents, both on the Other Side now, and Mrs. Swingler, and most of all, the magnificent old mahogany piano, can forgive me my trespasses against them. I pray the glorious old piano does, somehow, against all odds, find someone worthy of it in all the ways I was not.

The little girl who loved music understands much better now that commandment about loving thine enemies. Against all odds, she found she had come to treasure her nemesis; it kept her humble, kept her in close touch with her shortcomings and to the very end, forced her to accept the things she could not change.

ಶಿ ಅ

THE EXTRAORDINARY THING

Once upon a time, there was a very, very ordinary little girl. Wait, now, don't you feel even one little bit sorry for her. She actually figured it a lucky break after all, because it looked to her like it was the extraordinary people who were those most burdened in the world. Hadn't the extraordinarily idealistic and extraordinarily handsome young president had to die too young, leaving his children fatherless and the nation bereft? What about the extraordinarily beautiful people in the TV and on film? They had to live out their lives in the white-hot scrutiny of round-the-clock public attention, after all; they never got so much as a private moment or thought to themselves. Some people had to live the agony of being extraordinarily rich, ever unable to trust if other people genuinely cared for them, or hoped only for personal gain. The extraordinarily brilliant were driven mad watching the stupid and ignorant puff out their chests and lead the world into stupid and ignorant and unnecessary disasters time and again. The extraordinarily spiritual became psychotic, living the hypocrisy of a world in moral and ethical decay, which at the same time touted itself as the pinnacle of moral and ethical maturity. The extraordinarily strong were mobbed by weak, grasping people who sucked their strength away like vampires. The extraordinarily gifted were heartbroken because the world valued its inherent ugliness more than it did their inspired creations. One even cut off his own ear, if you can imagine such a thing.

So the ordinary little girl was really quite happy. When her extraordinarily cruel playmates told her how boring and ordinary she was, she agreed, even while their taunts still hurt her feelings and made her cry. They said it was wrong to be so ordinary and that she should be more like them, that she should be extraordinary. It all became very confusing, for she was very little and these seemed extraordinarily big notions. So, extraordinary should be ordinary, then, or what? The little girl didn't want to be cruel like them in any case, so she would run and crawl up in Auntie's lap. Auntie would dry her tears and feed her cookies, and cherish her hurts away, and help her find happiness again in all of the ordinary places. Auntie was a decidedly extraordinary person.

For ever so long the little girl wondered if Auntie might not be exceptional, an extraordinary person who was not burdened with it. As she grew up, though, she recognized that her Auntie's extraordinary capacity to love burdened her with more broken hearts than anyone could, or should, ever have to bear. Her beautiful, loving Auntie with her wrinkly cheeks and sparkly eyes and stooped back eventually died a bitter, hateful old woman.

These were better times though, when the girl was still little and Auntie was still happy in her loving. One day when the little girl came skipping to Auntie for a good dose of treasured, Auntie lingered with her hug for so long that the little girl started to squirm, like little girls do.

Noticing a glint of . . . were those tears? . . . in her Auntie's eyes she cried "Auntie, Auntie, are you all right?!"

"Yes, of course, Dearest One," Auntie answered with that smile that warmed the little girl's entire world. "I have something special for you today. Something important. Something extraordinary."

Auntie went and rummaged in the deepest secret-eye, private-eye places of her considerably packed closet and came back after a time with a bundle, wrapped in one of uncle's old shirts.

"Now, little girl," Auntie said seriously and ceremoniously as she sat the bundle on the kitchen table between them where they would meet to explore the world, "this is yours and yours alone. I give it to you today because you're ready now. You must always keep it close and guard it carefully."

The little girl's eyes were wide and her heart was hammering in her chest as Auntie unwrapped the Thing, and when the last tattered sleeve fell away, the little girl's smile and her heart both rose like the morning sun for there, on her Auntie's kitchen table, was the most special and extraordinary Thing she'd ever seen. It was wonderful! It was spectacular!

It was extraordinarily beautiful, with swirling colors as brilliant and pure as Mother Nature's own. It was graceful and fluid and curving. It almost seemed to wave in the breeze, or tickle and tremble like the aspen leaves. No, no it moved more like water, a gently flowing streamlet laughing and bubbling and gurgling smoothly over the rocks. But in fact it hadn't left the kitchen table, right where Auntie had placed it. It sang to the little girl in a soft, happy voice, like a clarion bell of silver. It might have been a goblet or a cup of some kind, she guessed, but it was much too rich for that. It seemed heavy and substantial for all it had wafer thin walls and a stem. It had a curling, convoluted—was that, a smiling?—lip, never meant for drinking. It might have been a vase, but it was too brilliant for that, it shone with its own soft, special light, generated from within. She knew it could never hold another's death even if it was a beautiful one, like the death of a flower. It might have been made of glass, but was never so cold and unforgiving as glass would be. It was warm to the touch and while it wasn't soft, it wasn't really hard, either, which surprised the little girl when she touched it, for she expected her trembling fingers to meet something rigid and sterile.

"Ohhhh . . . Auntie . . .," she breathed softly, reverently "what is it?"

In all of her life it was the first question, of at least a million she'd asked Auntie without looking her in the eye, for Auntie's eyes often revealed at least as many answers as her words did. The little girl was spellbound though, captivated, and could not tear her gaze from the extraordinary Thing. She felt as though she were looking at something so much greater than herself that it must be from god's own hand, or even the other world maybe. She wasn't scared, though, because it was, in another way, not greater than herself. Was that . . . ? Were those . . . ? Could it be that the extraordinary colors were swirling and pulsing with her own heartbeat?

Auntie's firm grasp cupped the little girl's chin and gently turned her head away from the extraordinary Thing; started the little girl breathing again, living again. Her life was different now than it had been only a moment ago. Something extraordinary had happened to the little girl. Something extraordinary had entered her life.

"Dearest One," Auntie said, stroking the little girl's hair and gazing into her face, "I can't tell you what this is, for to do so would rob you of the learning of the Thing, and that I would not do even if I could, which I can't." Looking into Auntie's eyes at that moment was like looking into the infinity of the night sky for the little girl. It was comforting, somehow, to be such an integral part of something so vast, but a little scary, too, to be so very, very little and so very, very ordinary, and the little girl's chin in Auntie's calloused hand began to tremble and her eyes began to well.

"Don't be scared," Auntie cooed as she gathered the little girl to her bosom for a healing, reassuring hug. "This Thing is yours now, it always has been, it was only in my keeping until the time was right, until you were ready, and you must trust that you are ready. Now, how about we have a cookie and feed that poor starvin' cat?"

Auntie wrapped the extraordinary Thing back up in its old shirt and they two had warm cookies and purring cat. When it was time to go the little girl clutched the Thing to her bony little-girl chest and walked home very slowly, very carefully, protective of her extraordinary bundle. She spent the rest of the afternoon making a special secret-eye, private-eye place for the extraordinary Thing in a corner of the wooden toy box her Dad had made for her. For protection, she surrounded it first with the softest and most forgiving things she had. She carefully wrapped it in the blankie Auntie had made for her when she was a baby, and then strategically placed her stuffed animal friends around it for guardians. Then, around the outside, she made a fort to protect the extraordinary Thing with the strongest things she had, which were her books, full of grand adventures and brave heroes. The little girl felt a little lonely at the thought of not seeing her friends very much any more, her books, and her stuffed animals, and her blankie, but she figured it was much more important to protect the extraordinary Thing, and her friends were very much impressed indeed with the seriousness of their charge. They accepted their solemn duty proudly, valiantly.

She wondered about the lesson of the extraordinary Thing as she lay awake that night, unable to find sleep without her friends for the first time in her life. She wondered what, if anything, the extraordinary Thing might have to do with being such an ordinary little girl. Maybe it had to do with moving beyond that. It had something very much to do with the future, of that she was certain, for after all, what could an ordinary little girl like her do with such an extraordinary and precious Thing?

The little girl kept the extraordinary Thing carefully hidden away, for she was reckless and chaotic as little girls are, and she eventually learned to sleep without her blankie and her books and her stuffed animals. Sometimes she would close the door to her room at night and under a bedspread tent with a flashlight, breathlessly get the extraordinary Thing out of its secret-eye, private-eye place to wonder and marvel at it, but she never showed it to another soul in all those reckless and chaotic years, not even her beloved parents or her most trusted forever best friends.

§

When she was a young woman at last, there was one young man who was special because he had extraordinarily deep eyes, and he gave her permission to be ordinary, which she thought was an extraordinarily kind thing indeed. She was tempted to show him the extraordinary Thing because she thought perhaps he might have some understanding of what the extraordinary Thing was; what it meant, perhaps even what it was for. She thought better of it though, after all, in the realization that she was still chaotic and reckless, and the extraordinary young man with the deep eyes and the kind spirit faded into the background of her life along with the rest who were not nearly so special.

Although it took years to come to, one day she realized that she was no longer a reckless and chaotic little girl but a steady, mature woman. She held a responsible job and had a mortgage, after all, and lived her life as best she was able without harming anyone in any way. She was kind to animals and little children, adored the stories of the elderly, recycled, worked ethically, and was as nice as she could be to people even when they weren't necessarily nice to her and didn't necessarily deserve it. Now, surely, she thought, the secret lesson of the extraordinary Thing would be revealed. Now, surely she was ready.

So she took the extraordinary Thing out of its secret-eye, private-eye place and placed it proudly on display right in the front window where the peace lily usually lived. She gave Jules Verne and the Jungle Book and Pippi Longstockings to the little girl who lived down the street. She kissed each one of her dingy, tired, stuffed animal guardians on the nose, wrapped them in the blankie, and put them away in the attic with a heavy heart. She feared they might be lonely, after all that time in the company of such an extraordinary Thing, which made her happy, for their sake, that the attic was full of bats.

Oddly enough, the extraordinary Thing didn't need to be cleaned or polished even after all of its years in the secret-eye, private-eye hiding place. It sparkled and shone and sang and shimmered in its ownlight just as brightly as it had the day Auntie had given it to her. In fact, if anything, the Thing was even more extraordinary than ever, it danced and swirled even more brilliantly, more urgently than it had before. It was as though the extraordinary Thing sensed the girl's racing heartbeat, her quickening, her excitement at finally not being reckless and chaotic, at finally being responsible and grown-up enough to have the extraordinary Thing out and learn its lesson at last.

The extraordinary Thing caused quite a stir in the neighborhood too, I'm sure you'll know. The little girl down the street trampled the catnip in front of the living room window near to death, and covered the glass with grubby little girl face prints looking and marveling, and there were several near wrecks in the street with people craning their necks for a glimpse, for it was a very extraordinary Thing indeed.

She prudently let the peace lily have the front window back, and put the extraordinary Thing on a beautiful little round, antique table at the end of the piano on an old piece of Auntie's handmade lace. Although she went about living her ordinary life much as she had before, somehow she walked a little straighter, now the extraordinary Thing was liberated from its secret-eye, private-eye hiding place. She felt just a little bolder, just a little calmer, and a lot less scared. She felt ... extraordinary.

She wondered if that might not be the lesson of the extraordinary Thing after all—not to be scared of the lesson of the extraordinary Thing. She didn't have all that much time to ponder it though, because strangely enough she caught the eye of an extraordinarily beautiful and extraordinarily brilliant young man just then. At first she thought it exceedingly strange that, while he wasn't particularly impressed with the extraordinary Thing, he did seem to be particularly impressed with her, ordinary as she was. Imagine! But then, she figured the extra-ordinary Thing probably didn't seem all that extra-ordinary to him, after all, because he was so extraordinary in his own right. She had such extraordinary feelings whenever she was around him that she figured extraordinary must seem quite ordinary to him, just as her mean-spirited playmates had foretold so very long ago.

His beauty and brilliance smote her eyes and her mind and her body and made her heart leap and swirl and somehow the extraordinary Thing was no longer the most beautiful, nor even the most extraordinary, Thing in her life anymore. Its colors weren't quite so brilliant and its opalescent dance was a mite more sluggish now by contrast, in the shadow of the beauty and brilliance of the extraordinary young man.

She was a mote, dancing in the sunbeam of him, and when he would leave her she would fall, lifeless. Sometimes as she waited for his return, waited for the dawn which was both terrible and wonderful to come to her once again, she would gaze at the ceiling and wonder after her old companions there in the attic and how they were getting on with their bat friends and if they might not enjoy her company for a spell, but she never went for a visit.

As the extraordinarily beautiful and brilliant young man became a comfortable and proprietary part of her life, she became ordinary again. The realization was gradual and excruciating for the girl. She wasn't extraordinary at all, he had tricked her, cruelly and disdainfully. She was still reckless and chaotic after all and he was, of course, quite mad. He was extraordinarily brilliant and had to watch the stupid and ignorant puff out their chests and lead his world, now her world too, into stupid and ignorant and unnecessary disasters time and again. He withered and blistered and chafed under the white-hot scrutiny of his extraordinary beauty. He was so burdened with his own extraordinary beauty and brilliance that he looked to the ordinary for comfort, for the contrast he needed to revel in his extraordinariness. He came to despise the ordinary and condescend to it, as one would perhaps a mirror that didn't show what you wanted to see, like the one in that fairy tale. She waited there on the floor now, inert and lifeless with the rest of the dust bunnies and the cat hair, for the sunbeam that never came anymore.

The extraordinarily beautiful and brilliant man became so burdened with the madness of his extraordinary beauty and brilliance he found he could not possibly carry the whole of it, and he took to breaking it off into pieces and tossing them into the extraordinary Thing to lighten his load. While she hoped with all her heart that somehow he would be able to offload enough burden to become light that she might dance in him again, she was also appalled, terrified. With each grain of rage or disdain or anguish or delusion he tossed into the extraordinary Thing, it became just a tiny bit more opaque, a bit more still, a bit heavier, more dull. She begged him to stop over and over again, but he would not and, ordinary as she was, she had no means to make him or even a guess as to how she might. She grieved as she laid there with the rest of the dust, without the energy or moisture for tears, her heart near to bursting with fear, confusion and betrayal.

One day, the extraordinarily beautiful and brilliant man cast the tiniest, most insignificant injustice into the extraordinary Thing as he haughtily stormed past out into the world with all the lunacy and rage it held for him. He never looked back to the girl on the floor or the extraordinary Thing, so he did not notice or even care that there were more grains on one side than the other, that the extraordinary Thing was no longer balanced and delicate, but lopsided and heavy. It started to teeter and tip as he slammed the door. The girl was transfixed, horrified at the inevitable, riveted as she watched in unbearable, agonizing slow motion, the extraordinary Thing topple and fall, shattering into a bazillion smithereens, scattering grains to the four winds.

It was as though a boulder had landed on her chest. Her world reeled and spun drunkenly around her. Her eyes could not believe nor her brain comprehend what had just happened. The stillness in the wake of the ear-splitting impact was deafening, and when the boulder had lain on her chest so long as to nearly smother her to death, she at last drew a long, ragged breath which she exhaled after an eternity and as the longest and saddest of moans, disturbing the dust bunnies. She gathered herself to her knees without knowing how, and sobbed the day away as the peace lily followed the sun around the cosmos as if it were any other day. When twilight fell and the man returned he found her on her knees, still, picking up smithereens. She hardly noticed him.

She mixed up a big batch of glue and meticulously, painstakingly started gluing every single smithereen back together in exactly the right place until her eyes were hollow and her back stooped with her work. She would occasionally look up to notice that the peace lily was looking towards the morning, or that the man was storming out, but she was so absorbed in her work that she was largely unaware of the rest of the world. She became haggard and thin, for a smithereen is very small indeed, and there were a bazillion of them to find amongst the dust bunnies, and grains, and cat hair and when she finished her work at last she was bewildered, disoriented. She straightened as much as she was able but she was crooked and hunched now, inclined to be always looking towards the floor. She placed the Thing back on Auntie's lace on the antique table by the piano. The dust bunnies and the grains she left where they lay.

The Thing was quite different now, of course, its once graceful dance of light was now full of sharp, spastic angles and the rainbows it threw were no longer curved and graceful, but serrated and tattered. The clear, pure colors now bled into each other and were muddy. The soft, ringing voice of the Thing was now a half-step off key, discordant, and its once elegant lines were now jagged and sticky with glue. As she pondered the Thing the man arrived, and for the first time since the shattering she noticed the exhaustion in him; he was haggard and a bit bent himself and there was a hint of panic along with the madness in his eyes now. Was that a glint of silver at his temples? She wondered for the barest of moments at how much time had passed as she knelt and glued there amongst the smithereens, and grains, and cat hair, and dust bunnies, but as that bare moment passed the man began to offload the extraordinary burdens he had been acquiring and lugging for all the time she had labored over the smithereens. He cried out in rage and relief has he cast grain after grain, stone after stone into the Thing.

The Thing toppled and fell again, but this time it only broke into a few pieces because, after all, it was more glue than extraordinary now. She felt one lonely tear slide down her now wrinkled cheek, but she dashed it away impatiently and, although it pained her terribly, set to work with determination. The man and his things she took to the curb like so much trash. She heard his raging about the extraordinary injustice and insanity of it and how she done him wrong diminish gradually in the distance as the garbage truck drove away down the street. She glued the Thing back together and took it up to the attic.

She set up a little-girl's play tea table there with the blankie as a table cloth and Thing in the middle and her cherished old friends seated around it. The grains and dust bunnies she swept up and worked into the soil of a new crescent-moon shaped garden outside. She planted herbs in the garden in honor of her Auntie who had always smelled of lavender and who had served the little girl chamomile tea to calm her when she was reckless and chaotic. Every once and again she would go up and have a tea party with her friends and visit the only part of her that had ever been extraordinary, now covered in dust and bat guano, there in the attic. Although her back would be forever bent, she straightened out as much as she could, and went back to being happy in all the ordinary ways.

ঙ৹ৎ ৎ৹ঙ

THE BAT IS DEAD

We are gathered here today, standing on the dirt wherein the bones of our ancestors lie, and in the comforting embrace of our family, Lord, to bid our sacred dead Godspeed on her journey to the other side. We give over unto the keeping of Mother Earth the mortal remains of our beloved Bat, who lived a long and full life and who was blessed with a passing that was as easy and gentle as a grain of sand washing up on a beach. It is the best any of us can hope for. We pray You, Mother Earth, accept these ashes to recraft as You see fit. We pray You, Lord, will welcome the unique, quirky spirit of our Sweet Bat into Your loving arms and thence on to immortality in the infinite reaches of the infinite, spinning cosmos. She will never die for us. The Bat is dead, long live the Bat.

We don't name our Bats until after they're gone to the other side and then only to delineate their period of influence, one from the next. It's like naming a geological epoch or an art form—the Cenozoic Bat or the Oriental Bat. Stereotypes don't spontaneously generate, so we do understand that other families have the odd batty Auntie here and there, but in my family there is a long and distinguished, unbroken line of Bats; a streak of very strange, mostly childless women; a counter-Darwinist mutation that has run through our family for generations now. They are, to the woman, peculiar, eccentric and sometimes outright bizarre but they are also, to the woman, loving and generous creatures who adopt freely and cherish deeply. For us, the living, Bat is a term of endearment, a title of honor.

We love our Bats deeply; they are some of the strongest and most interesting women in our family, for they rarely know their limitations. They transgress both boundaries and propriety. They embarrass us all terribly, but they teach and entertain as they go. These Bats stretch our imaginations, our patience, and our hearts.

§

Grandma didn't have any children. She was my first Bat, the BattleBat. She adopted her second husband's small grandchildren as her own and was as generous to them with her money and her love as she was with her scathing criticism. Nobody, but nobody, crossed the BattleBat, especially not little kids. She freely admitted she wasn't good with children or pets and that she didn't particularly care for their company. When we went to Grandma's house we were on our best behavior. We wore our shiny patent-leather shoes and our starched dresses and our ringlets and sat on our hands and kept our mouths shut or by god, Mom said, there'd be hell to pay. The BattleBat was one of my heroes though; a role model to look up to. She was the most intelligent woman I ever knew and had the kind of vivid, contextualized recall of nearly a century of a life well-lived I can barely come up with from an hour ago. She could remember the dress someone had been wearing 65 years earlier when she'd first met them and every nuance of the stock market every day she'd played it. The BattleBat was a hard driving businesswoman; she owned and ran businesses in a man's world long before it was fashionable or acceptable for women to do so. The product of their times, a good number of men underestimated her in business owing to her gender. All came to regret it. She was fair but she was ruthless. The BattleBat was a force of nature; she loved traveling and ostentatious parties.

RedBat (Irish, not communist), like many Bats, was ambivalent; she could be mean and played favorites, but every child should be treasured by such a Bat. I was the chosen favorite and counted myself very lucky, for I was cherished beyond all reason. The RedBat was at once very feminine—she was always dressed to the nines and I never,

ever saw her without her hair "done"—and just one of the boys. She'd take those scrupulously manicured nails of hers to the ball field and smoke you with her fastball. She'd cram that meticulously curled and dyed hair under a cap to take the dogs and kids out to the lake to let them get wet and muddy and exhausted. RedBat let the kids light her cigarettes with her Zippo lighter. It was the only time we were allowed to play with fire and it never came without a lecture about the dangers of playing with fire. RedBat was a force of nature too, but in a much different way. She was fierce, like a mother bear protecting her cubs. She loved unconditionally and with intense focus.

By the end of her reign, it didn't matter to FunBat in the least that she could no longer see well enough to accurately aim a gun, or that she wasn't strong enough to pick up rocks any more; by god, if she said we were going shooting or rock hounding we were going shooting or rock hounding. We were, of course, more than willing to pick up the rocks she wanted and take them home for her and she had always been so careful with the guns that the shooting range wasn't as scary as you might think. FunBat was most like a cookie grandma of any of the Bats. She was loving and cuddly and let the little ones curl up on her lap. She let us take her treasured artifacts in our hands. She trusted us on an adult level and we loved her for it without reservation.

Legend has it the BattleBat wasn't as eccentric by half as her predecessor, my biological Grandma, who was the only one of the Bats in my direct line who had children of her own. GrannyBat was an OCD control freak to a fare-thee-well. She had three children, my father, my uncle and my Bat, now the SweetBat. Stories of GrannyBat's peculiarities were always whispered behind hands but, in keeping with the Bat tradition, with the greatest of respect and love. It was said that none of her three men—her husband and two sons—ever left the house without ironed clothes on, even down to their boxer shorts and socks. Unaccountably, GrannyBat wrapped each and every clean dish she put in the cupboard in clean paper towels each and every night after dinner. This may account for the innate nature of SweetBat's OCD tendencies and her excessive use of paper towels. I may never have to buy paper towels again after cleaning out the SweetBat's apartment following her death.

§

The "home" where the SweetBat lived at the end of her reign was one dedicated to the corporatization of aging. The manager told me in a very crisp, professional tone that turnover was important, that we were contractually obligated to pay rent for 30 days from "the expiration," and that we were required to vacate the premises within that period.

These are people who deal with death on a daily basis. The SweetBat was a client, not family. It was heart-wrenching to hear; the SweetBat's life and her death were immediately and heartlessly severed from more pressing business matters at hand. This was no ancient family homestead we could clean out at our leisure; this was a tiny one-bedroom apartment in a retirement community founded and organized for the purpose of dying; a place where the aging can go to enjoy or squander the rewards of a prosperous life; a place where people can pay for comfort and attention as they age. We had to put aside our outrage at the commodification of our SweetBat's death. We conscripted our crew, finally found a day everyone could make the trip (28 days from the expiration), showed up in the distant city with two pickup trucks, and took the SweetBat's life apart that day.

The other women in my family seem to have a magical ability to discern what to keep and what to jettison over the course of a human lifetime, but one of the consistently batty traits of the Bats is they don't quite seem to know what is treasure and what is detritus. The BattleBat dumped family pictures in the trash without the slightest twinge of conscience when she moved to her home, but agonized over which of the gazillion decks of cards to take with her. RedBat wasn't like some of us who stock several sizes of clothing to accommodate our fluctuating weight, she remained the same size her whole life but was disinclined to pass up a swanky department store clothing sale item whether it fit her or not. When we cleaned out her house after she died, her closets were crammed so tight with brand-new clothes you had to get an elbow in and throw your weight behind it to get the first measly hanger out. The few clothes that actually fit her only took up the first few inches of a miles long closet. And FunBat, who was always up for a walk in the woods with the kids and who would never, ever have told a child she couldn't bring an interesting and important rock home, had to be moved out of her ancestral home with a front-end loader and a dump truck.

Urgency bordering on panic nipped at our heels all day the day we had to move the SweetBat's things out of the home. There was no nostalgic lingering over the stuff, no time to mull or reminisce the importance or history of things. Split-second decisions had to be made about what to keep and what to throw away and we made them without regard to much of anything other than the clock and space in the trucks. We could not loiter to contemplate anyone we knew who would have appreciated her awesome art-deco-ish solid oak furniture, or how much fun a garage sale might have been. We had no time for fond memories. We clamped our teeth down firmly on our tears, swallowed the lumps in our throats, made the difficult choices, laughed at the easy ones, and kept the strong backs in our party busy the day long schlepping her stuff down the elevator on hand trucks. We took her life apart mercilessly that day, and dumped it by the truckload.

We laughed at our SweetBat's penchant for saving product boxes and shopping bags (I came home and surreptitiously recycled most of my own collection) and at some of the very strange articles of clothing. None of us could ever remember seeing her in the silver lamé zebra-striped ball cap, but there it was, like a flashlight in the darkness of her closet; a beacon shining out from among the more muted, tasteful colors she generally preferred to wear. We found some gems, though, among the detritus she'd saved; ancient newspaper clippings, and a letter from GrannyBat explaining to the SweetBat (who was just a sweet batling at the time—or is it a batlet?) how her brothers had gotten in a drunken fight—with each other—at a bar in Winslow; a fight that landed them first in jail and ultimately in the military. This had always been an apocryphal tale in my family, and to have it in GrannyBat's own hand—dismayed at the incorrigibility of her well-ironed boys—is a treasure.

A human lifetime transcends its accumulated stuff, of course, but we were after all under a rapidly expiring contractual obligation and we counted the truckloads off on our fingers: four to the Goodwill, one to the dump, two to bring home. We were proud we winnowed it down to two truckloads in just one day. We were sad and ashamed all that was left to mark the SweetBat's physical passage through this lifetime were an urn of ashes and two truckloads of stuff.

§

Retirement homes like the one the SweetBat preferred to any of the admittedly inadequate family options available to her, are ambivalent. They attract both hangers-on who are the kindest, most caring people on God's green Earth, people who offer genuine and compassionate care for the elderly; and hangers-on who are the vilest and most unethical vultures, people who are equally ready to fleece the vulnerable, the frightened, and the angry as they lose their independence.

I am The Bat ascendant now, an aging eccentric like the Bats before me, and I take great comfort knowing I will be spared the artificiality of the relationships the SweetBat surrounded herself with in her declining years. Whatever comfort I'm given in my turn will come from people with whom I share genuine caring and community, and not from paid caregivers and avaricious financial "advisers" who would like to convince me to make bad decisions in their best financial interests. I have proven myself perfectly capable of making my own bad financial decisions from the get-go and am consequently not wealthy enough by far to pop up on anyone's sucker radar. It is a blessing.

§

It has fallen to me to settle the estates of our sacred dead several times now. I suppose it's only fitting that I have become the death maven in my family since I do stand in the direct lineage of the BattleBat. Although I lack her awesome memory and ruthlessness, she did teach me how a frosty business bitch operates at a tender age. Easy way or hard way (their choice) I can get the job done.

It's heartbreaking to go through the SweetBat's affairs and watch her deterioration; to see that she became more and more vulnerable to manipulation and predation as she became more and more batty. From the unethical financial advisers to worthy causes, many were very successful parting her from her capital in her last years. She was frightened and they took advantage of that. And why wouldn't she be frightened? She was on every terrifying mailing list in the country. She was assaulted with graphic images of tortured animals, threats of losing her socialized income and medical care, and lurid political threats splashed garishly across the daily mountain of junk mail she read assiduously: "Which American city will Iran nuke first?" "Radical Islamic terrorists are infiltrating our refugee programs!" "Supreme

Court Justice Antonin Scalia was murdered IN COLD BLOOD!" "Are they coming for you next?"

How did we become so culturally invested in terrifying our elders? Why? We ought to be ashamed of ourselves.

§

The SweetBat made us all bat crap crazy. Since I was both closest to her in geographical proximity and furthest from her politically, she made me craziest of all because I was there for the downward spiral. It fell to me to wade in and perform triage when she was having a meltdown.

"I never took a dime from the taxpayers of this country in my whole life!!" she once yelled at me during one of several tax-related meltdowns.

"But Auntie, the taxpayers paid your paycheck for your entire career, and Social Security and Medicare are both taxpayer-funded programs."

"The taxpayers didn't pay my paycheck! I worked for the school district! And Social Security is like a savings account!"

"Um, school districts are generally funded by property taxes."

"They are NOT!!"

"Well, who do you think pays for education in this country?"

"The schools are just on their own, they pay for themselves."

"No, Auntie, I'm pretty sure school districts are funded through taxes on property owners in the district, with aid from state and federal programs."

She folded her arms across her chest and turned her back to me and huffed "I just won't believe it." I watched her intently for a few seconds, sure she would echolocate and take flight.

But now that she's gone all I can remember is how alike we are and always have been. I was born to be the eccentric old woman living by herself on the outskirts of town with a houseful of cats. I am a batty old lady, now, from a long, bizarre, distinguished line of batty old ladies. I have big shoes to fill, but I have studied my craft carefully and at the feet of the SweetBat, who was Mistress of the Art. Although I doubt I can attain her heights of eccentricity and outright weirdness, I do yearn for a strong finish. I'm every bit as OCD as the SweetBat was, but unlike her, I am aware of it, at least for now, and try to keep it in check.

While she would put cleaning the coffee maker on the calendar, and turn down theater tickets for that day in favor of the coffee maker I, at least so far, will take in the theater and clean the coffee maker another day. She kept detailed lists of her medical history; salt or fluid intake, say, where I keep detailed lists of my favorite harbingers—the first meadowlarks and prairie dogs of spring, the first hummingbirds of summer, and the first red leaves of autumn. I keep lists of who I've already gifted with my handmade crocheted Christmas trees. I don't want to inflict more than one on anyone—people do feel obligated to display them. My SweetBat and I both love animals as much as we do people and we both had pets, nieces, and nephews in lieu of children of our own. Like her I eventually just gave up on my hair. None of us Bats come from good hair people. RedBat's hair always looked good, but only because she tortured it weekly at the salon. For the rest of us, whether it's cut and styled or not it still looks like crap. Now I just leave it look like crap, same as SweetBat did. Maybe I should have kept the silver lamé zebra-striped cap.

Ascending to the position of Bat carries heavy responsibility in my family, but I am also finding it tremendously liberating. The Halloween witch is probably the Bat of her family, too. She's eccentric enough not to care what people think about how her hair her looks, either.

SweetBat and I are different in very fundamental ways, though, too. She was afraid of death in a way I can never be. She was not a spiritual person so she fought it. Hard. She had the kind of gold-plated retirement nobody but the one percent gets now, and used enough socialized medical care for a small country (while vehemently denying anyone else's right to such care). She's on the Other Side now and because she was so frightened of death, I'm grateful beyond words that her passing was quick. She was still bitching about politics in the ambulance. Three hours of happy drugs later she was gone.

I wonder how they will characterize my reign as Bat after I pass. I hope for something spiritual or scholarly, but it's not my place to say. I only aspire to serve well. I may be the first Bat to be proud of the title and self-aware of my status, the first one my family can call Bat to her face without fear of insult. I suspect my self-awareness will make gift-giving easy for my family from here on in. I want a Batmobile bumper sticker, and expect to receive bat-themed everything; t-shirts to Christmas decorations. I promise to be a loving and generous Bat as well as peculiar, eccentric, and even bizarre. I promise to embarrass my family terribly, to transgress boundaries and propriety, and to teach and entertain as I go.

§

I am the last Bat standing now, Lord, and by all that's right and holy, I'm next out. I am gathered here today in the warm and comforting embrace of my family, standing on the dirt wherein the bones of my ancestors lie, to bid my sacred dead Godspeed on her journey to the other side. I pray You, Lord, will welcome the erratic and unique spirit of the SweetBat into your loving embrace. I don't know why You, in your wisdom, have placed this line of strange, eccentric, mostly childless women in my family, but I am grateful for them beyond words; they are wonderful in their strangeness and ambivalence; they love freely and adopt readily and have enriched my life beyond measure. I am the Bat ascendant now and I can say what I want without filters, too. Like the SweetBat before me I shall endeavor not to be cruel. She could be hurtful, certainly, but transgression without hurtful intent is not malicious, just unfiltered. Please, Lord, I pray, let me be a good Bat in my turn. Let me drive my niece and nephew bat crap crazy as I endear myself to them while I—and my eccentricities with me—age and distill but please, Lord let me serve with dignity. I pray, never let me be as free and as loud in public with information about my bowel movements as was my predecessor.

THE BAT IS DEAD, LONG LIVE THE BAT

Arizona Literary Awards 2016 Essay Second Place

PURSUIT OF DEMONS

She was hard-pressed to account for the anxiety that prickled at the back of her neck out here tonight. This was usually one of the most peaceful places she knew. It was the perfect night. It was sparkling clear and crispy cold. The subzero temperature was holding the hero snow with just enough crust on it she didn't break through. Not too soft, not too hard. Goldilocks snow—just right.

It was still. There was not a whisper of wind. In the silence all she could hear was her own easy breath and the soft buzz of the fish scales on the bottom of her cross-country skis as they slid across the snow. And best of all, a glorious full winter moon lit the night so brilliantly that shadows were cast long. The few stars bright enough to pierce the moonshine burnt in the sky like living things. The pipeline was the best place to cross-country ski because it was flat and clear of trees and fences. Usually skiing out here was an experience that rejuvenated her, but tonight there was something wrong. It started as a vague, undefined foreboding, a small anxiety like you get when you leave for work and can't remember if you've turned off the coffee.

Most nights, after the long-ish hike from her house to the pipeline, she first skied west on it for a few miles, till just before it crossed the road, to warm up. Then she'd turn around and face east, toward the Sacred Mountain, and ski for miles on end with happy abandon and a spiritual awareness that bordered on ecstasy. Most nights, the rough figure eight on the pipeline she called the west and east loops restored her soul, her strength, and her sanity. But not tonight. As she made her way out the west loop this night, the foreboding became a niggling worry, gradually grew into outright fear, and by the time she was nearing the end of the west loop, where she'd have to turn back, she was skiing for all she was worth. She was terrified. Something was following her. Something was chasing her. She was running for her life.

She glanced behind her on the fly. The road was coming up fast and she realized with dread that she would have to make the turn soon and pass it—whatever it was—in close proximity. Her legs pumped harder and harder, but the nameless, formless terror was still flickering there, just over her shoulder, at the periphery of her vision. Sensed more than seen.

She made a panicked, abrupt one-eighty. It was the kind of maneuver that could cost you a knee on downhill gear and it was a none-too-smart move on skinnies either, but the desperation of pursuit had robbed her of any kind of pragmatic decision-making process. Run!! Her panic screamed at her, RUN!!

Her guts fell through the soles of her feet when she realized that it was the old terror; her nemesis, the demon that had been pursuing her all her life. Recognizing the familiarity made it more, not less, less scary.

Just as she made the unwise turn she thought she saw a filament fly past her head. It was a thread so fine she wasn't sure she'd actually seen it at all. Wild-eyed, she dismissed it as just a mean trick of the light. It probably wasn't really there. She choked back the tears as she faced the Sacred Mountain and started the long ski eastward. It was usually her favorite and most spiritual leg of the trek, but tonight it filled her with dread. She knew she could not afford to cry, it would only rob her of vital breath needed to keep up the frantic pace, to try to outrun it. She could not, would not, let the demon catch her. It was such a beautiful night. She grieved for the other nights, so many of them, out here skiing in the full moonlight when it was tears of gratitude and wonder that caught at her breath, rather than tears of terror and panic.

She wondered why the demon chose to pursue her here and now, in this sacred time and in this sacred space. She'd always felt so safe and so free out here. She'd run from the demon aplenty dayside and for many years now; snatching her ass through the door of her house, checking the closet before she could go to sleep, looking for monsters under the bed like some scared little kid, and always at the insistence of that vague flicker, the unnamed, unseen, over-whelming terror. Never before had she encountered it out here; never before in the sacred light of her cherished wintry full Moon Goddess.

Her chest and legs were on fire. She was drenched in sweat; exhausted, and utterly spent. She had skied as fast as she could for hours now, tasted blood in the back of her throat, and felt a wet stickiness in her boots that could only mean both heels were beyond blistered. She'd used up the last of her desperation and knew if she hadn't lost it yet the demon had her now, had her here. She looked back over her shoulder and cried out in anguish at the flicker there, hovering menacingly and effortlessly keeping pace.

She stopped. Her head sank to her heaving chest in resignation. Kicking out of her skis and dropping her poles she turned and fell to her knees in the crunchy snow, arms outstretched. Hysteria ripped an inhuman shriek from her throat like a rusty iron hinge forced open against its will. "What are you and why do you pursue me so!?" she screeched. "What evil is this?! What harm have I done you?!"

The only sounds in answer were the roaring of blood in her ears, the pounding of her heart and her anguished, rasping breath. The heat from her body billowed out in frosty, sparkling clouds. The inky night, the inscrutable Moon Goddess, the glittering stars, the snow with its incongruous night shadows, the Sacred Mountain observing dispassionately, even the demon—none had a voice for her.

She fell over onto her back, dramatically, and the tears started in earnest. "Just do as you will then!" she sobbed. By the time the tears were spent and her breaths were just steamy little puffs, her heart rate was down and her body temperature was plummeting. She realized her blood sugar was low and her body's fuel had been spent. She felt, for the first time this terror-stricken night, the intense cold of the mid-February, mid-night. She was miles from home and safety, it was ten or more below, and she was soaking wet. It might not be the demon that would kill her. She started to gather herself back together, thinking that if the demon wasn't going to do her in, she ought to give some thought to getting back. As she got to her knees, she thought she noticed a filament lying next to her in the snow.

It was barely discernible at first—not much more than a vague pattern in the glinting crystals of ice. She blinked, trying to clear her sight. It was no more significant than a spider web when she first slid her trembling, gloved fingers under it, but it seemed to gather substance as she let it slide across her hand, then across both hands. She gave it a cautious, curious tug, unaware of holding her breath. The thread seemed to go on forever. Hand over hand, slowly at first and then more rapidly she pulled at the thread, coiling it behind her. The line garnered heft along its length. It was heavier now, like a clothesline.

She got a momentary memory of her Dad, looming over her when she was little, telling her a story about curiosity and a cat, but dismissed it to concentrate on the task at hand. The line was heavier yet now; a rope heavy enough to moor a boat, and it was getting heavier with every span she pulled in. She was on her feet and pulling hard. There was something weighty at the other end and she was getting hot and sweaty again with the exertion, digging the heels of her boots into the icy snow now, for purchase to heave. The thought that she might be hypothermic and hallucinating flitted across her awareness like a butterfly, improbably lovely and fleeting. This couldn't really be happening. Right?

A shape inched towards her out of the surreal shadows of the full moon on the whiteness of the snow.

When she finally pulled it close, she walked around it, considering the odd thing. It was an old-timey trunk, like the pirates used for treasure. It was heavy and wooden, with a domed top and riveted steel bands running around it. It was wrapped in a heavy chain that was secured with an ancient, rusty lock. "What the. . .?" she muttered under her breath.

She almost jumped out of her skin when a muffled voice from inside the chest said, "Why don't you open it and find out?"

Indignant, her immediate response was, "Oh, HELL no," but then the terror of the demon returned. Too exhausted to run any further, she fell to her knees again, as though before the headsman's block and started to plead, "I . . I. . .d-d-don't have the key. I don't want to. I'm so . . . scared." Her voice quivered in confusion and fear.

"You have the key. You've always had the key, you just never knew it." The voice, muted by the chest, was kind and gentle, ringing vague, distant bells of welcome acquaintance in her heart. Not at all how she thought a demon might sound.

"Are you the demon?" she asked, her voice raspy and shrill, still edged with hysteria, "Why have you been chasing me out here tonight? Why would you harm me? Why would you intrude on my sanctuary? This is where I come to get away from the demons. This is where I come to get away from YOU." She had started to cry again, fatigue and cold overwhelming her, and when she hung her head in shame at her cowardice, to her astonishment, she found an ancient skeleton key in her shaking hand.

"I'm no demon, and I never was. At least I never intended to be, and I haven't been chasing you. I've been locked up in this box all along. It's you who have been dragging me all over creation with you. You have both the tether and the key."

"Say what? I don't. . . uh, . . would never!" She was starting to feel dizzy and disoriented. Looking behind her at the piles and coils of rope, she noticed for the first time that the spider web filament originated with her. It was tied around her chest, and tightly, too, constricting her breath. "Your voice sounds so familiar, somehow," she said, "like someone from the distant past, maybe from a different lifetime. It warms me a little, although the night is so cold. Do I know you?"

"You might have, once."

As the terror and panic began to pass once again, she started to be aware of the world around her. The moon had crossed the sky and was sinking toward the horizon. She began to wonder how long she'd been out here. She felt as though she were edging towards the brink of unconsciousness. She shook her head to clear her sight and thoughts. She had to focus, concentrate hard, to work the key and lock with numb, violently shaking hands. She finally got the lock open and unwrapped the chain from the massive old chest. Opening the lid and cautiously peeping inside, she whispered, "Is that you?"

There was nothing inside the chest but a small, conical, silver bell, reflecting the dazzling face of the full moon. It had a black ribbon, that might have been purple dayside, and a spiral worked down its argentine length. She sat back on her heels, perplexed.

"Ring the bell," the gentle voice urged, no longer muffled by the chest, but softly spoken still, "and exorcise the demons from this sacred place. Ring the bell."

She reached through a gathering, darkening, swirling fog for the point of achingly bright light. She was having trouble keeping her eyes open and her head up now. As she grasped the ribbon her shivering involuntarily rang the bell. The chest and the rope and the demon and the presence that had been the mysterious voice, all vanished into the moonlight.

She came to with a start and looked around, drawing a deep breath, now free of the constricting filament around her chest. She was alone again on the east loop and at peace, with the benevolent and reassuring smile of the Moon Goddess gazing down at her. Things were again as they always had been, as they always should be. There was no demon here, only the joy of the winter's night in the shadow of the Sacred Mountain. She smiled. She became aware of her body again; the agony in her feet, the fact that her hands were probably frostbitten by now, and that her core temperature was dangerously low. "I'd best get in," she thought, and staggered to her feet. She put her skis over her shoulder to start for home, hoofing it. No sense even trying to work the bindings with these frozen fingers, and anyway there were too many fences between here and the house. She stuffed the bell into a pocket, and with a passing regret about leaving the easy packed snow of the pipeline, set out, making post holes through the deep stuff. The few miles between her and home might as well have been a million that night. She almost hung herself on two of the fences, trying to climb over them reeling like a drunk. When she would stagger and fall, the bell in her pocket would give a muted chime, somehow giving her the resolve to get back on her feet and put one in front of the other again.

She was never so happy to see the lights of home. She flung her gear down in the yard and fell through the door. Although she knew she should eat and tend her feet and hands, she was just too tired and cold and weak to care anymore. She grabbed the quilt off the back of the couch, wrapped it around her, and fell into a deep, deep sleep on the hardwood floor in the warmth of the fire she'd left burning in the woodstove.

She dreamt of voices.

She would soften and smile in her sleep at the cheerful chatter from the little silver bell, brightly insisting that the demons be gone and stay gone, all of them. The mysterious voice from the chest reassured her through the night, like a kindly uncle or the dearest of old friends, as soothing as a hot drink on a bitter cold day. She dreamt of tender hands wrapping her frozen fingers around a hot mug of soup, bandaging her feet, and combing out her hair which, fleeing panic, had become wildly tangled and matted under her hat. She dreamt of someone lending a stout shoulder to help her gimp upstairs on crippled feet and into an already warm bed. She dreamt it odd that, although most of the tender hands and gentle voices that had tucked her in before had always said "Sweet Dreams," to her, this one said "Sweet Dreamlessness."

A tear slipped from underneath her sleeping lashes and dropped onto the cold and unforgiving hardwood floor.

Epilogue

She woke the next morning sore and dehydrated, disoriented and hung over, not daring to move at all for several minutes. Remembering, she was grateful to wake at all. Remembering, she wondered how much of it had been real and how much hypothermic hallucination. The demon had been chasing her for a lifetime now, and she hadn't been hypothermic when it started out after her last night, so that much, at least, had been real. For the rest of it though, well, surely it never happened. It never could have happened. She rubbed her gritty eyes and rolled over, moving cautiously, to stretch the kinks out of a body cramped from the hard surface on which it had slept.

There was a fresh wave of fire as the mess in her boots broke open and started to bleed again. She dragged herself to a kitchen chair and peeled the gloves off, none too eager to note her damaged hands, but only one nail blackening so far and very few blisters. Damn lucky. She'd keep all her fingers—this time. She was even less eager to start on her feet, the very thought nauseated her. She took a meditative breath and offered a prayer for the strength to face the pain and do what had to be done. As she did so, though, she glanced through the kitchen window and a glint from the tree in the front yard caught her eye. She grabbed the broom that stood beside the front door, to use as a makeshift crutch, and hobbled out onto the porch for a better look. There, to her wonder, hanging by a purple ribbon, was a little silver bell with a spiral pattern, catching the rising sun's face and reflecting it dazzlingly. The bell nattered brightly, keeping the demons at bay as the tree danced, tickled by the morning breeze and the birds in its branches.

Although hobbled up for the next week or so, she felt better than she had in years. She could move better and breathe more deeply. She smiled to herself often and, curiously, found her thoughts wandering in the direction of the demon. Her demon. Against all odds, after running from him in terror for the length and breadth of her days, she found herself wishing him well.

⟡

THE ISRAELI

My heart was dancing like a dust mote in a sunbeam as I crunched my way to work through six inches of new snow. Life just doesn't get any happier than that in my drought-ravaged homeland. Not even the discordant chorus of distressed electronics, which had obviously suffered some sort of electrical insult during the night, could dampen my singing spirit as I unlocked the auto parts shop. I eyed the customer who was waiting warily, though. Visitors here typically find our retro low-tech establishment either charming or utterly infuriating. Much to my relief this one was charmed and cheerfully perched himself on the counter stool with a cuppa (because when I'm opening shift, flipping the switch on that coffee pot comes first no matter what other disasters might be unfolding in the moment). We chatted as he waited patiently for me to get everything back on line and up and running.

He wanted some tire chains, he told me, for his journey north on treacherous Highway 64 to see the Grand Canyon in all its snow-covered splendor. Not much snow where he was from, he said, and he wanted to be careful with his nice car.

"Where's that?" I asked, as I agreed with the wisdom of his decision about the chains and complimented him on his resolve to go see the Canyon in spite of the snowy roads, assuring him that with a blanket of snow is as beautiful as it ever gets.

"Well, I live in L. A. now, but Israel is home." He beamed.

"Oh," my eyes and heart both plummeted to the vicinity of my grease-splattered work shoes "I'm so sorry."

"Why sorry?" he asked.

"Well, because it's so sad and violent there. I've quit listening to the radio in the morning because of it. It's just such a depressing way to start the day, hearing in grim detail how many Israelis and Palestinians died today. There seems no sense to it, or any answer. Any end."

His merry chuckle drew my perplexed gaze, if not my heart, from the floor.

"Let me tell you something." He said, "When I moved to Los Angeles from Israel, I was afraid to go outside my house for months on end. I was terrified that some gangsta was going to murder me for a pack of cigarettes at a convenience store, or that I would be shot by some crazy with a complaint about the post office or something.

"Israel gets its information about America from Hollywood. It paints a picture of cavalier and indiscriminate violence. You Americans get your information about Israel through the news, which also paints an incredibly violent scene. Neither picture is necessarily an accurate reflection of daily life in either country. Living in Israel is a very rich experience, spiritually and politically. Israelis are deeply *engaged* with each other and their politics in a way that might seem alien to a lot of Americans. The streets aren't any more dangerous than they are in L.A., the violence just has greater political implications. I can't wait to get back to Israel."

§

I thanked him most sincerely for his perspective and understanding, this jolly and adventuresome spirit, as I wrapped up our transaction at last. I was able to shed my pity, that most loathsome and despicable of human emotions, for the Israelis and Palestinians. In that instant they became "us" for me, rather than "them." I watched the news from my nearest big city over the next few days, taking careful note of the body count. While the Phoenix news may lack the macabre suicide bombers and the "body parts" the press feels the need to knife our guts with these days, more people died in Phoenix that week from senseless and pointless violence than died in the Israeli/Palestinian conflict.

This gentle Wandering Jew left profound gifts in his wake. One was gratitude for the outdated technology here in the hinterlands of Northern Arizona. I never before considered it anything greater than a monumental pain in the ass to complicate my workday and piss off my customers. It now afforded me an extra minute or two to listen and learn—learn that my customer is more than just a wallet. He is a human being with meaningful insight to offer.

The far more precious gift was the understanding that senseless and pointless violence is not a middle-Eastern problem, it's not "theirs." It is a human problem. It's ours. It belongs to us all, it scars and diminishes each one of us. Perhaps when enough of us can accept this in a meaningful, personal sense, if enough of us are lucky enough to encounter a teacher in an auto parts shop on a bright, brittle cold morning, we as a whole may also be able to see our way clear to rise above senseless and meaningless violence at last, everywhere it occurs.

ॐ

The Spiral of the Year

Introduction

Some things never seem to change.

It was the best of times, it was the worst of times.

Charles Dickens wrote those iconic and inspired words 150 years ago, but they still ring true. Life after the French Revolution was brutal. Life in the modern gristmill can be brutal as well. We'd like to think we're more civilized than our barbarian ancestors; that we are sophisticated, more noble and enlightened. In many ways we are. In many, many ways (by way of counting our blessings) these are the best of times. Our lives are better now, materially and spiritually, than they ever have been before; than they were in the dark ages that precede us.

We have the freedom to worship as we please now without fear of being burned at the stake. Or do we? Religion is still persecuted in today's world in many places and in many ways. Although nutritious, ethical food is more and more elusive, most of us get enough to eat. Or do we? Starvation amid plenty is still prevalent here and around the world. Most of us have a roof over our heads, and don't have to worry about getting cholera from our drinking water. Yet there are too many homeless people in every city in every country on Earth, and water clean enough to drink is the most rare and precious thing anywhere. In this age of miraculous medicine, few of us have to suffer hopeless physical pain, and many crippling or fatal diseases of yore can be cured completely. Still, inequitable access to health care is also still rampant in many places on Planet Earth, rich nation or poor. We think the terror after the French Revolution, when the streets of Paris ran with blood, was barbaric, but violence still touches far too many lives. The streets still run with blood.

It is still the best of times. It is still the worst of times.

Perhaps future generations will look back on these as the dark ages. I wonder, did the people living in the Medieval Dark Ages know they were living in dark ages? Aside from niggling suspicions, I think probably not. Our technologically harried lives can feel relentless; chaotic and disconnected. We work round the clock chasing enough money to live well; to buy that clean water and good food and a roof over our heads and sophisticated health care. We struggle to find the peace and time to enjoy our prosperous lives with our families. Deep, restorative sleep is elusive; as is carefree play and robust physical health. We're not sick, precisely, so much as we are just exhausted; worn thin by the chase. As we lie awake in our beds at night, staring at the ceiling we have a niggling suspicion that these might be the dark ages and that we weren't made or meant to live this way, not really.

Seeking invigoration and regeneration, we turn now to the Spiral of the Year and the rebirth, resurrection, restoration, and renewal it can hold for us in so many ways. There is life after death in the Spiral, on physical, spiritual, intellectual, and emotional levels. In the waxing and waning of the Spiral of time we can find reassurance that none of our problems—immense though they may be—are insurmountable. They need not be integral to our lives. They need not define us but are merely heavy burdens we carry. With eyes and heart open, and with rituals observed, we can rejuvenate ourselves and reconnect with what's important to us, with the way we feel we were really made and meant to live, even if needs must return on the morrow to the work-a-day chase.

One of the best ways to connect with the Spiral is to eat locally and seasonally. Doing so opens us to the rhythms of Mother Earth; it brings a sense of belonging and connectedness and invites the Sacred into our lives. It is healthy for us and our families and for the Earth as well.

Living the Spiral need not necessarily be a matter of reinventing the wheel and creating new rituals. We need only remember, and observe them with full consciousness. For instances abound: When we drag an evergreen tree into our homes near to the Winter Solstice and cover it with lights, it's more than just an altar for conspicuous consumerism and a staging area for the redistribution of wealth. Christmas trees symbolize the eternal nature of evergreens. They reassure us that there is life after death because they stand immortal through the season of death for the rest of the vegetative world. When we bring them into our homes and decorate them at the Winter Solstice they are prayers offered for the return of the light (Sun), and the rebirth it brings with it, during the darkest part of the year. This celebration of the natural cycles of light has been wedded to the celebration of the birth of the Son (Jesus) as savior into this, the mundane world. All religions that developed in areas with enough latitude that there is a significant difference in hours of light and dark, summer to winter, spiritually celebrate the standing still of Winter Solstice and the turn back to the light. The deeper meaning of humanity's various Winter Solstice rituals complement each other, they do not contradict.

Tossing a coin into water asks Element of Water to grant your wish and throwing a pinch of salt over your shoulder to avert bad luck asks Element of Earth to forgive the waste of the spilled salt. The veneration of the fertility symbols of eggs and rabbits at Easter rejoices in the resurrection of spring and celebrates the stable fecundity of continuance. There are many important seasonal rituals of renewal already surrounding us. We need only remember, and observe them with full consciousness; with the awareness that we are living in a living world, that we are a part of it rather than apart from it.

§

We begin our annual pilgrimage into the Spiral of the Year as the warm, golden, flickering light of autumn wanes brittle and harsh. By Halloween, Samhain, the light has become the unblinking glare that presages death. Samhain is the last and greatest of the three harvest festivals: Lughnasadh on August 2nd, Mabon at the Autumn Equinox and Samhain on November Eve. Pagan folk generally reckon that the year ends and begins at Samhain.

The stillness of Samhain after the dizzying pace of the fall harvest leaves us breathing hard. It's time to take a deep breath and let our heart rates slow down. Get a hot cuppa and sit on the porch of an early-dark evening to listen to the elk sing to their girlfriends (they're actually singing their challenge to other males, but I prefer to think of it as a serenade). Pause a moment to enjoy those last few loads of laundry dried outside in the wan sun and fresh air. Rummage in the sock drawer for the thick ones that have migrated to the bottom over the course of the summer, and get out that stack of yummy, fleecy, cuddly jammies. Get those heavy winter quilts out of the cedar-lined box at last and languish under the heaviness of winter's warm nest. Delight with the pinwheel seeds of the pine trees as they dance and spin their way to Earth on their journey to their next lifetime on a blustery day.

On November Eve we must accept at last that the wild abundance of the Sun at its full strength is over and that the vegetative world is dying. The Sun crosses over to the Otherworld and awaits rebirth and resurrection at the Winter Solstice. In the waning light of the year, if you open your imaginative heart and eye wide enough, you can feel the veil between this world and the next thinning, feel its permeability.

The word *witch*, like the word *pagan*, has been much perjured over a very long span of time. Many people outside the Craft still find it difficult not to think of a witch or a pagan without some inherent misgivings, horror movie negativity. You might think witchcraft and witches terribly complicated and mysterious, with all their potions and spells and the like, but most contemporary witches are just simple folk, trying to live a virtuous life without harming anyone.

There are not volumes and volumes of religious doctrine for a witch to memorize and adhere to. There are only two commandments for contemporary pagans. First is to harm none (intent matters). The second is that what you put out into the universe is what you get back, as so elegantly articulated by the Hindu notion of *karma*. The math is simple and written in stone. Any witch who would Cast those horror movie curses would be a magnet for bad luck, so witches are scrupulously careful to keep it clean. Ask what you ask for yourself in a pure, clean, positive way, harming none (*Practice Limited to White Magic*).

§

After Samhain winter settles in proper. Lots of people understandably suffer from lack of light and warmth during the dark, cold turn of the year. Winter Solstice for them is a glorious turning back toward the light. I love all of it, the dark of the year and the light. There's something about the darkness that makes me feel closest to the Sacred, though, that mysterious immensity I can sense but not fully understand. I love Christmas lights, the sympathetic magic most of us Cast to entice and strengthen the newly born Sun. I love snowy weather and settling by the fire with a good book. *A Sensual Season* celebrates cozying in with loved ones during the dark and cold of the year and leaving the oven open when you've finished baking to help warm the house.

By early February the darkest time of the year is passed. We feel ourselves begin to stir a little, drowsy from our long winter dreaming, with the fragile, thin increase in sunlight. The young god, born at the Winter Solstice, grows and strengthens. Pagan folk call this Imbolc and it's a great time to take down the Christmas lights.

Autumnal and Vernal Equinoxes are times of change, tipping points, fleeting moments in time to pray for balance (*The Sweet Spot*). It is at the Equinoxes that day and night meet. The elation we feel at crossing over that transitory line charges us with the spirit of moving on from the doldrums of the old season and into the exuberance of the next. Winter to summer or summer to winter as the case may be. We anticipate with exhilaration the peak of the next season; summer's blazing heat and light, or winter's cold and dark. Passing the Equinox, we feel gathering momentum.

The balance of the Equinox is ephemeral, and if the world begins to think of stirring to life at the Spring Equinox the growing strength of the now virile young god bursts forth with burgeoning fertility at Beltane, May Day. The vegetative world is gloriously reincarnated and joyously resurrected to new life, bringing us with it. The union of the Mother with the light and heat of the Father brings hope and the promise of eternity on that sacred spring day when the first, stubborn, tender little plant people start to poke their heads up out of the frozen, dead earth; through the desiccated corpses of their dead. The tenacity and strength of these tiny wonders is a marvel and I am always humbled by them. They are not so fragile as they might look, I think. Their dogged determination resurrects all that feels dead in me after the long winter, without fail, every time (*Blush*).

Summer and Winter Solstices are the extremes, powerful times to manifest change. Midsummer is a time for weddings and celebrations of transition. Cast your cares and troubles into the Summer Solstice to wane with the Sun (*A Summer Solstice Serenity Spell*), to let go of the past, of the outdated parts of our lives that no longer serve us. Cast your prayers and hopes for growth into the Winter Solstice to gather strength with the waxing of the season. Mother Earth is eternal, Her power is constant and steady. The power of the god is transformation.

There's a subtle change in the light early in each spring and fall. It's a magical day. The rational mind knows that the sun is arcing ever so slightly higher or lower in the sky but here, on the ground, the upshot is that the world is illuminated differently. It's the same world, but it doesn't taste or smell or look quite the same. The spider webs, invisible only yesterday, shimmer and dance with the breeze in gossamer ecstasy today. The light tastes just a little different, the world sparkles just a little more, and whether your heart is pounding because that subtle change in light tells you the long winter you've endured is almost over, or your blood is racing because the mornings will soon turn crisp and the end of the withering, exhausting summer draws nigh, there's a bounce in your step and a lightness in your heart that can only be accounted for by living the Spiral of the Year; by celebrating the change and riding the crest of elation that goes with it.

I am delighted and humbled on that first late summer (and early spring) day I can taste the difference and feel that subtle shift (*'Tis the Season*). In this recognition I become integrally linked in a tangible, physical, and emotional sense with the great cosmic Spiral of time. Making this connection I am rendered infinitesimally small. I am blessed and freed in knowing myself to be such a small part of something so much more immense than I in space and time. Suddenly my problems don't seem so overwhelming. They don't seem to matter as much anymore and they're not so heavy to carry by far.

Out here in the arid hinterlands we don't get much frost, the air is generally too dry. It must surely be different for people in moister climes where the phenomenon is neither so rare nor as welcome but here, the Autumnal Equinox is marked by a special morning; a morning after the night has been just cold enough, and the air has had just enough moisture that the whole world in the morning—every minute surface of it—is coated in dazzling ice crystals; a magical morning that robs the day of its dread, of every bit of negativity and fear it might have held. You walk out your door to go to work, your own black cloud of worry and anger firmly in tow and in an instant of recognition—poof!—it all vanishes with a sharp, indrawn breath of wonder at the glittering, sparkling beauty of the world. The morning is filled with uncounted little rainbows and you wonder what you were so worried and pissed off about a second ago. Those rainbows help me put down burdens that are not mine to carry. At the same time they give me the resolve and strength to change what I can, to carry what it is my responsibility to carry. It is in those tiny rainbows I always seem to be first able to recognize that the busy-ness of the fall season—harvest, by any other name—is upon us. Generally it is in full swing before I even realize it. The kids are back to school and the holiday season looms large. If you want to give handmade gifts, it's time to get a start on them. It's time to set by and put up for winter, get the wood in and fill the freezer (*Barbarians and the Politics of Place*).

§

It is the journey, not the destination that transforms the pilgrim. This pilgrimage through the Spiral of the Year returns to its point of departure, as all pilgrimages must, to the death at Samhain that presages rebirth. While death isn't something to look forward to, it's nothing to fear either. Today's Halloween is a caricature of ancient Samhain. The witches and goblins of Halloween, masquerade and trick-or-treat (although loads of fun) are cartoon remnants of the respectful rituals and veneration for the ancestors of yore on this sacred night. A prayer for Samhain and the death that must come before rebirth celebrates the dead and the end of the old year with *On Shadows.* Samhain, although a time for contemplating death and honoring those who have gone before us, is not—should not be—a sad, dreary or frightening time. I harvest herbs planted at Beltane (May Day) at Samahain and put some in the fire for my dead, as a prayer for their continuance and well-being. My offering lets them know I love them and am thinking of them. My message and prayers are carried to them—out into the heavens—in the fragrant smoke.

I don't feel afraid of my dead on this night when the separation between this world and the next is thin and arbitrary, but experience a loving connection with them. Their spirits flit through and light around me, almost imperceptibly. If I weren't paying such close attention I might miss their presence altogether. Their feather touch raises the hair on the back of my neck and I find myself talking to them. Talking to the long-dead roommate I loved enough to move in with, and with whom such a toxic relationship developed. I am able at last to explain myself and to ask for forgiveness. I commune with the spirits of my beloved pets on the other side. I find myself better able to understand my parents, to see the world through their eyes and understand them as the fallible and flawed human beings they were rather than the ideal, perfect godlike parents the child petulantly demanded they be. I am able to forgive myself, and them, for the character flaws I learned so eagerly at their feet. It's almost like talking to myself, but somehow, at Samhain, I know they hear me. Somehow I feel their forgiveness, too, for all of my human warts and failings and I am able to breathe more deeply and be more at peace with myself and with the dead than at any other time of the year. As you age, you accumulate dead, it's just the way things are. The Samhain flame is to light their way, so they can find their way across to this world and find their way back to the Other Side by morning. Every year the host of beloved spirits on the other side who come to visit me, drawn by the flicker of the Samhain flame, grows, and grows more dynamic. As my own years weigh heavier and I am forced to face the inevitable, as we all eventually must, my close connection with my dead comforts me. With each passing Samhain I can feel the loving arms of that community making ready to welcome me when I cross over in my own time.

⚬❊❊⚬

PRACTICE LIMITED TO
WHITE MAGIC

The bitter, acrid taste at the back of her mouth had settled there like a hibernating toad. It was a hairball stuck in her throat, gagging her with each breath. It had been an eternity. Although six months is a short span in a human life, she could no longer remember life without that faint taste of bile and decay on the back of her tongue. Everything she ate tasted like sawdust. Everything she drank tasted like piss.

Determined not to vomit the grief up on some unsuspecting stranger or innocent passerby, Nell clenched her jaws down around the stench with every breath she took, both conscious and unconscious. In the light of day this effort left her with a tight, angry face; mouth downturned and neck muscles rigid. By night it gave her terrible headaches. Her dentist said if she didn't quit clenching her teeth so hard at night she would break them. She didn't care.

People had once been drawn to her like moths to light. She had overheard herself described as "vivacious and engaging." Now they whispered behind their hands, groping for words like "listless and distant . . . cold." She wondered if moths avoided darkness, if they were pushed away by darkness as inexorably as they were drawn to the light. She didn't care about that either. She would have preferred the moths leave her alone anyway. She would have preferred everyone leave her alone.

Finally the dreadful year she'd lost her beloved father was turning to fall. He had died suddenly and unexpectedly in the early spring. Finally the world around her was dying with her and she didn't quite feel so out of sync. Finally she didn't have to be around happy

163

summertime people doing happy summertime stuff. Finally school had started and the children plodding to the bus stop in the morning with shoulders stooped under the burdens of their backpacks and gloom looked like she did. Felt like she felt. Nell's back was bent with her cares and gloom too.

Her Mother had become a needy stone around her neck, and Nell found herself unequal to the task of being the rock of the family for the first time in her life. She had to admit now she had probably never been the steady influence she'd always thought she was; that she wasn't the strong, independent woman she'd always preferred to see herself as.

Her Dad had been the rock. Her Dad had always been the rock, the very earth they all stood on. When he was taken so suddenly and unexpectedly, Nell felt like the earth itself had fallen away from under her feet. She had been in free fall for six months now, stomach plastered to the roof of her mouth, waiting to hit at the bottom. She hoped the impact would kill her but she never landed, just fell indefinitely. Freud might have said something about her closeness with her father, she supposed, but screw Freud. She and her Dad were close. They always had been close. Nell had idolized him as a child and they were friends as much as relations as adults. They enjoyed each other's company. They enjoyed doing the same things. There was nothing Freudian about it. Mom said they had been joined at the hip since the minute Nell had been born. People teased her father about Nell being his oldest son. Father and daughter smiled at this because it was so true. Nell was lost without him. Disoriented and confused. Adrift.

Family and friends had dragged her to every self-help group in town. Her Mother had insisted on a psychologist, and Rochelle, her best friend, had taken her to counselors and AA and naturopaths and massage therapists and Reiki treatments and acupuncture and even a drum circle. Nothing worked. Nell was despondent. Could barely draw her next puke-flavored breath. Thought she should have suffocated by now.

§

"A Witch??!!" Nell could hardly believe her ears. "Really??!! Surely you jest. What, does she, like, cast spells? Ride around on a broomstick? Worship the devil? Gimme a break, Ro. I'd rather get a bottle of whiskey and drink myself to death. Gawd, you're stretching now. Are you desperate, or what?"

Rochelle might just as well have lost her father, too, or Nell herself for that matter. Ro's sorrow at the loss of her happy, energetic friend knew no bounds. Yes, Ro thought, as a matter of fact, she was desperate. But out loud she said "No, really, Nell, this woman is good. I heard from a friend of a friend of a friend that she helped. That it was like, magic. She doesn't worship the devil. I spoke with her on the phone and she said for her there is no devil."

Nell groaned, rolled her eyes.

"Come on, please? Look, it's not like she charges money or anything. I'll go with you if you want. What could it hurt?"

"Ok, OK!" Nell snapped. "But you gotta make me a promise, Ro."

"I would do anything for you Nell, you know that. I just miss you, girl. I miss you like you used to be. You know, back when you weren't an asshole."

Nell's head jerked up, taking in Ro's raised eyebrows and mischievous smile. Her angry face softened. "I'm sorry, Ro, I guess I miss me too, like I used to be. I just can't seem to get back on my feet. I miss him so much. I've been slapped down so hard I don't know if I'll ever be able to get up again.

"People don't know how to be around me any more and I don't know how to be around them. They can feel my grief. It's like they want so badly to say something—anything—to make me feel better, that they say stupid and inappropriate things that really don't help.

"You know Ed, right? The vendor I work with? Well, he came in the shop last week for the first time since Dad died and he was shocked and dismayed at the news, like they all are. I had to tell him the story. I have to tell *all* of them the story, and when I finished, Ed said to me—swear to God—'You don't know how lucky you are to lose your Dad this way.'

"It was like he punched me in the gut. I could hardly breathe, Ro, my jaw was on the floor. Then Ed starts telling me this story about his mother's long, slow, suffering, hideous death from cancer. It lasted thirteen horrific years and he said they were all so relieved when it was over they felt guilty about it; said that I was lucky I didn't have to watch my Dad suffer like that; that I was lucky he was just snatched away.

"Now, Ed is a good guy, and he wasn't trying to be cruel or anything, he was just grasping for something to say, something to make it feel better. I finally had to tell him 'Shut the fuck up, Ed, you're *not* helping!!' Then he was the slapped one and tears started to gather in his eyes and, even though I didn't think it was possible, I felt even worse than I did before. There's no bottom to this thing, Ro. We concluded our business and both slunk away on our bellies, whining for mercy. It was awful."

Ro was the only person Nell would allow herself to cry around, and as she had done so many times over the past six months, she stepped closer, put her arms around Nell, and just let her cry. Ro never said anything, not 'there, there,' or 'He's in a better place,' or any of the other inane things people say to try and quell another person's grief. She just held her and let her cry. Crying on Ro's shoulder was the only time in months Nell could remember her fists and the knot in her gut unclenching even a little bit. And when Ro's shoulder was wet and Nell finally hiccuped her way back to the world that had so little regard for her as to take her Dad away, Ro said, "What?"

"What what?"

"You said you'd go see the witch if I made you a promise."

"Oh, yeah. You gotta promise me if this doesn't work you'll back off. Leave me to my misery. Just let this kill me. I don't mind dying. I don't want to live in this kind of misery anyway, and I'm tired of bringing the misery of it into other people's lives, too."

"Look, I've told you a gazillion times your Dad would not want you to suffer like this. He's gonna kick your ass when you get to the other side, whether sooner or later, and if I promised you something like that, he'd kick my ass too so I'll promise no such of a damned thing. Girl, there are times I just want to smack you."

"Sometimes I think it would do me good." said Nell with a faint, insincere smile. She sighed. They were standing outside her father's business, the one Nell had been forced to step in and buy after her Dad had died. A lot of her parents' money was tied up in it and her Mother was too much of an emotional cripple to pick it up and run with it.

Not for the first time, Nell thought what a blessing and a curse it was to be the spinster daughter, to be her father's eldest son. That's what made it both her privilege and burden to step up and bail her Mom out with the business. Nell was grateful she'd been at a place in her life where she'd been able to leave her career du jour to help out. It was the right thing to do and she was proud of making the right decision, of doing the right thing. This was an alright job. As alright as any of them had been.

Auto parts. Dealing with the customers was fine, it was the people who'd dealt with the business for eons, like Ed, that were hard to cope with. Vendors and bankers and old friends of her father's who hadn't heard yet. Six months in and she was still having to tell the story over and over and over to people who hadn't yet made their once-a-year business call. Although she usually loved Christmas, Nell was dreading it this year more than she cared to say. She was dreading Christmas cards; Christmas cards to and from friends and business associates she hadn't had an opportunity to notify yet. Then she'd have to write it over and over. It just kept getting worse.

Over and over and over again she'd had to tell the story, live it again and again. Her robustly healthy 68-year-old father had gone in for a minor, routine surgery. He developed a blood clot which, the night he was released from the hospital, had broken loose and clogged his pulmonary aorta. He was dead in ten minutes. He had been on the golf course three days before he died.

"I know Dad wouldn't want me to suffer like this. Ro, and in truth, I'm happy for him. He wouldn't have wanted it any other way and I wouldn't have wanted him to suffer either. I just wasn't ready. It's myself I feel sorry for, I can't seem to help it. Between running this f'in place," she gestured vaguely at the door of the shop, where an employee was hovering anxiously, obviously in need of her, "and trying to hold my Mom up so she doesn't fall to pieces, it just feels like there's nothing left of me. Of that me from before you and I and everyone else liked."

Ro glanced at the employee, briskly turned on her heel and walked away saying "I'm picking you up at seven. Be ready. No excuses."

Nell shrugged, put her sour face back on and went back to work.

§

At seven, as agreed, Nell was out of uniform, showered, fed, and ready. She hadn't been sleeping well and was so exhausted by the end of her work day she didn't think she could put one foot in front of the other. She started to whine about it immediately as soon as she got in the car.

"Never mind all of that, you candyass," said Ro, "You promised and besides, I talked to her on the phone and she said all you needed to do tonight was listen."

Nell slumped into the passenger seat of Ro's car. "Great, that I can do, I think."

"You better."

They drove for some time in an uncomfortable silence when Nell said, reaching to turn the radio on. "Jesus, where does she live, anyway? Over the river and through the woods? I feel like Gretel, you know, of Hansel and Gretel. Damn, and I didn't bring any breadcrumbs or anything."

"Har-dee-har. Very funny. I'm laughing so hard I can hardly stand it."

Nell turned up the volume and they listened to loud music, which eliminated the option of any more awkward or cranky conversation. Finally Ro pulled off the dirt road and parked. There was about a half moon, but otherwise it was pitch black. There was no house or lights in sight.

"What, does the coven meet in the deep dark woods? The sacrificial victim never heard from again? You know tomorrow is my outside sales day. I'll be missed."

"Oh," said Ro, "if I was going to have you killed, I'd have done it months ago, as a mercy. I'd have done it myself and I'd have done it at the shop. Put you out of your misery. It would be the kindest thing to do, really, but I'd make sure everyone knew, and knew why, first."

"Right," said Nell, "thanks, pal." as she followed Ro down a long-ish curved driveway.

"She told me to park at the top of the driveway at night because it's hard as hell to back out of here in the dark." Ro said as the glimmer of dimly lighted windows and a parked truck came into sight.

§

Ro knocked and as a middle-aged woman dressed in jeans and a flannel shirt opened her door warm, moist cinnamon and clove-scented air wafted out to greet the two younger women. It smelled like Halloween; candy apples and hot cider.

The witch's first thought was that they looked like nothing so much as a couple of puppies. Slightly disheveled and perhaps a little too easily distracted. Rochelle's energy was sparkling, delighted. If she *had* been a puppy, or maybe a little younger human, she would have been bouncing. The other, sadly, was like a puppy who had been beaten. Her stillness was forced and there was a terrible vacancy in her eyes. The kind of vacancy and exhaustion only the very tired, the very betrayed, and the very injured display. Her energy was muddy and stagnant, swampy and dull. There was a faint miasma about her. She was washed, to be sure, the smells of soap and shampoo clung to her skin and hair, and her clothes were clean, but there was something else, a tinge of curdled milk, perhaps, or maybe a sour dish cloth.

"Hello, Rochelle," the woman said, and sticking her hand out in Nell's direction, "you must be Nell. Please do come in."

Nell nodded a little too vigorously, gaping and stammering, "Uh, yes, I'm. . . uh, yes, I'm Nell. It's er . . . nice to meet you."

The woman's handshake was warm, dry and strong. She drew Nell into the fragrant candle-lit house saying "What, were you expecting warts? Black robes? A pointy hat? I have a pointy hat, actually, but I'm much more comfortable dressed as I am and I'm afraid I can't manage any warts on demand."

Nell dropped her eyes and mumbled "Sorry, I didn't mean to stare. I-I didn't know what to expect."

"Fair enough," said the witch, "neither did I. All Rochelle told me was that her friend was the walking wounded, staggering around under a burden of misery and grief and calling it a life. She wondered if I might be willing to help. I'm Laura. Would you like some tea?" she asked, gesturing to three chairs at the round dining room table which was set with table linens—quilted place mats and cloth napkins—polished silver teaspoons, and a bowl of apples in the center.

"Sure," Ro and Nell said simultaneously, as they kicked off their shoes and padded into the small, shabby-but-clean cabin. It was a comfy, lived-in place, decorated eclectically with stars, moons, dangling sparkly stuff, shelves and shelves of books, plants, comfortable chairs, and dark purple curtains. Nell felt at ease here at once. Well, as at ease as she ever felt any where in the world any more.

"Help yourself to an apple if you like," the witch called from the kitchen over the clangor of making tea, "they're homemade. The elk have left me a few, which was good of them."

As Nell settled into her chair a chubby white cat jumped into her lap as if it belonged there. It curled up, purring, and dozed off immediately. Nell was startled.

"Nell, this is Luna," said Laura, returning with the tea, "and she always seems to know who's in need of a purring kitty to pet. She's very generous that way. I've cried a river of tears into that fur and she never seems to mind."

"Mmmm..." Nell murmured, already lost in the sensual experience of stroking the long white vibrating back. The cat obviously enjoyed it and clearly expected it. Nell found herself willing to comply. Happy to. Strangely happy to. She took a deep breath and a sip of tea and looked up to find Laura and Ro looking at her expectantly.

"Oh, . . . er, what?" she said.

"Would you like to tell me your story?" asked Laura, "tell me why you're here tonight?"

"No, not particularly," said Nell, "and I'm here tonight because Ro made me come. Wouldn't take no for an answer."

"All right then," said Laura, "I'll start. Here's what Rochelle has told me. She's told me that you've lost someone very dear to you, and that you are devastated; so devastated you are having a hard time thinking of going on. So devastated you can't take care of yourself or anyone else counting on you including the business it falls to you to keep afloat. She tells me . . ." Laura paused and Nell looked back up sharply—her attention had wandered back to the purring cat—"that you're mean now when you never were before."

Nell glared at Ro, whose chin started to quiver as her eyes filled with tears.

Seeing the hurt in her friend's face and knowing she'd been the source of it was all it took. The last straw. Nell's jaws unclenched and she gasped for breath. The tears streamed down her face. Her eyes never lifted again from the cat in her lap, but, voice breaking, she told the story—yet again. This time, somehow, though, with the witch and the cat and Ro and the relaxing tea and the soft candlelight, she told it differently. She was able to put herself in it. To tell, not just of Dad and what happened to him, but to tell of her own hurt and disbelief. She was able to tell the *whole* story; of the awful adolescent years when she'd been alienated from her Dad and how much it hurt her but that she would have never let him see that then. Never. She was able to tell that it was many years later she and her Dad had been reconciled, that her Dad had been tremendously hurt by Nell's childish behavior, too, and that if anything, they were closer after reconciling than they'd ever been before. They were able to be close as adults, rather than as parent and child. She was able to tell the witch that her relationship with her father had evolved into one of mutual respect and support, and that she had come to rely on him emotionally, if anything, more than she had even as a child. Her Dad had been a god of some kind to her when she'd been a kid, he'd been refuge and warmth and the safety of unconditional love and bedtime stories and being a timer at the swim meets but that, as an adult, he'd been all of those things plus so much more. He'd become mentor, friend and loyal ally as well. She entrusted him with all her secrets, all her fears and insecure feelings. He was one of the few people who knew her well enough to know she'd always been her own worst enemy, and she didn't know, she told the witch, how she could possibly soldier on without him. How could she continue the fight without him there to help her figure out which battles to choose?

Sure enough, although her back was soaked with tears by now, the cat rolled over in her lap when Nell fell silent and stretched full out, belly up, with a loud, chirping cat-sigh. Nell looked up at the other women at the table at last. Ro's eyes were downcast, but the witch was looking at her. Really looking at her, with kindness and compassion and genuine concern in her eyes.

"Please don't say you know just how I feel," said Nell defensively, trying to reach for the handkerchief in her back pocket without disturbing the cat.

"No, I don't know how you feel. I didn't come from a loving family like you did and I wasn't that close with either of my parents, so I've never had anyone like your Dad in my life. No one I could count on like that. But I do know what it's like to lose someone precious to me and I didn't think I'd be able to draw my next breath without him."

"Well, thanks for that small kindness, at least. I hate it when people say that. They don't know. They can't know how I feel! It also pisses me off when they ask if there's anything they can do. What the fuck do they think they can *do*. If they can't bring him back from the dead then there's nothing they can do to help." Nell glared at the witch again, through tear-filled eyes.

The witch smiled. "Well," she said, "is there anything I can do?"

Nell blew. "What the fuck!?" she yelled, "I just told you there's *nothing you can do!!!*"

The witch looked at Ro and said, "You're right, she has completely lost any kind of a sense of humor." Turning to Nell she said, "And you're right, I can't bring your Dad back from the dead. You know nobody in the world of the living can do that. Tell me, do you believe in an afterlife?"

"Yeah, I guess." Nell replied.

"Good, that will be most helpful."

"Most helpful with what?"

"I would like to Craft two rituals of healing for you: one at the full moon and one at the new moon to help you make peace with your dead and with yourself."

"You can cure me with magic?" Nell asked, incredulous, hopeful.

"No," said the witch, "but you can cure yourself with magic. The rituals I will Craft for you will require your participation. There is little other people can do to help you, but there is an awful lot you can do to help yourself. I am willing to show you how if you're willing to be shown."

Surprised that her anger had not raised a likewise angry response from the witch, Nell said, guardedly, "OK, sure, I'll try anything."

"Will you?" asked the witch as she got up from the table. She poured another cup of tea. "You must prepare yourself between now and the next full moon. Your timing is fortunate. This is October and, with Halloween, of course it is a particularly auspicious time to seek connection and peace with your dead and the Other World. At the following new moon, which falls on Halloween night itself, we will have another ritual, one to help you make peace with yourself. Maybe going into Thanksgiving your holiday season can be happier than your year so far.

"The grief has a hold of you, Nell, and doesn't want to let you go. You are clinging to it with a death grip as well. Who knows why any of us do such things? Maybe you feel it's all of your father that's left to you. Return here on the night of Wednesday, the 15th. That's the next full moon. It's only nine days from now. The moon will rise at about 6 p.m. that night. Be here an hour before that, and spend some time thinking of what you want from your father out of this, what you'd like to say to him. Rochelle, I'm putting you in charge of calling her every night to remind her but," she leveled a fierce glare at Nell, "again, nobody can do this for you. You have to do it for yourself, all the rest of us can do is to guide your way and lend you what strength we can but *you have to do the work*. Do you understand?"

"Yes, ma'am."

"Very well then. I'll see you in a few days. And Nell, in both of these ceremonies we will open ourselves to the Other Side. Make sure, very sure, you come here with a happy heart and if you can, while we're in the Sacred Circle, try to focus your memories about your father in the positive; on the good things about him rather than the pain of the loss of him. Do you have any questions?"

"No, ma'am." Nell said meekly.

"Very well," said Laura. Here's my card. Call me if you do have questions or if you need anything but, by all means, make sure you keep our appointment at the full moon."

Nell glanced at the card. It said:

☽ Laura Rose

Witch

She turned it over. On the back, over her phone number it said:

Practice Limited to White Magic

The drive home was quiet. Uncharacteristically, the friends didn't even turn on any music. Nell sat with her hands in her lap, staring off into space while Ro, pensive, said nothing.

§

The days passed quickly. Dutifully, Ro called every night at first, but Nell needed little prodding to think of her Dad and what she wanted to say to him. Just the process of forming her thoughts for the ritual helped her think of her Dad without wanting to vomit up that hairball for the first time since she'd lost him. It was the first time she'd been able to think of him without her thoughts being first for herself; without feeling martyred and abandoned.

She told Ro to quit bothering her after the third night, told her that she'd thought of little else than the witch's instructions, and that she'd be ready.

Ro picked Nell up on the appointed night at precisely a quarter to five. That would place them at the witch's house at just about 5 p.m. they figured.

"Perfect!" said the witch, beaming, as she opened the door. She had on a flowing black robe with long, pointed sleeves that made Nell smile. "You girls are here in perfect time. Ro, there are tea and cookies on the table for you. Luna will keep you company while Nell and I get ready."

She led Nell to the tiny, immaculate bathroom at the back of the funky little cabin, and handed her a small jar of fragrant bath salts. Laura turned on the water. "How hot do you like your bath?" she asked.

"Uh, my bath?"

"Yes, your bath. But not just any bath, your ritual bath. We are going to approach the Sacred tonight, my girl, and ask the Goddess herself to shoulder some of the pain with which you are burdened. I've had my purification, but you must approach the work we do tonight clean in mind, body and spirit. You must clear your body of pollutants and your mind of negative thoughts."

"Uh, warm but not too hot, I guess."

"Fine, then," Laura said, as she tested the water temperature and adjusted the faucets. "Here are towels and a robe to put on when you're done. You can add more hot water if you want." Laura waved to a stack of towels folded on the seat of a chair with a plain, white shift and a belt rope neatly draped over the back. She lit a small white candle and turned back to Nell, saying "This candle is for more than just soft light. Focus on it, Nell. It is a meditation. You are going to go out into the Sacred Circle with me tonight and we will bare our souls to Death. It is not something to be taken lightly. The bath is to make you clean, to purify you body and soul and make you worthy of such a dangerous and bold undertaking. You must ask the flame to give you the courage to do this. Fire is warrior, ask for protection. Fire is transformation, ask to heal."

Nell gulped as Laura dumped the jar of salts under the hot running water and the room filled with the pungent fragrances of juniper and sage.

Half an hour later the candle was burning low and starting to gutter. Nell had prayed to it with an earnestness that belied her outwardly flippant attitude. She could use an ally who was a warrior. She realized she was starting to suspect maybe this stuff was real and although she hadn't been scared in those days since she and Ro were here last, she had filled the days with greedy, selfish thoughts of seeing her father again and all she wanted to say to him. But when the witch put it that way, that she was going to bare her own soul to Death, it put a very different light on things.

She emerged from the steaming bathroom with pink, flushed skin, feeling a little woozy. Half scared and half sleepy. "That's all right," said the witch when she told her about the bath, "you should be a little scared. We are going to open ourselves up to the Sacred and that is no small thing. But your bath was supposed to make you relaxed, too. There's a difference between being scared enough to be respectful which," she winked at Nell, "is what we're going for, and being so terrified you miss the blessings of the ritual, which is what we're trying to avoid.

"Rochelle and I have been discussing the role she will play." Laura handed Ro a sword, a real sword, like a knight would carry, and it looked to be sharp, too. Nell's eyes widened in surprise.

"The sword is forged in, and symbolic of, Element of Fire. Rochelle will be our warrior tonight and guard our circle while we do our work. She will keep watch and keep us safe. Now, are you ready?"

Both younger women nodded their assent as Laura draped warm, woolen green cloaks around their shoulders against the chill of the autumn night, taking care to tuck Nell's damp hair under the hood. "Follow me," she said, picking up a candle lantern.

Laura went out the door of the cabin and a short way out into the darkling woods. The full moon was just cresting over the tall trees and gave plenty of light for them to find their way to a place Laura had obviously prepared for the ceremony. There were four large posts set upright, with a fire ring in the middle.

"Now, ladies," she said, "we enter and Cast the Circle. This is my Sacred Circle and I keep it clean and protected, I invite you to enter, but only if you can do so with a clean conscience and a happy heart. If you cannot leave any negative thoughts or emotions behind, I beg you, say so now and we will try for this another night." She waited, but both younger women were looking at her with serious, eager eyes. "Very well, then," she said, picking up an abalone shell that had been sitting on the ground and lighting the sage wand it held with the candle. She washed herself in the smoke and then held it out to Nell and Ro, "purify yourselves in the smoke and enter. Ritual is the enactment of myth. It is the manifestation of Sacred time, space and story. In the Circle powers that have run down are regenerated. When we enter we leave the world as it is and enter the world of what may be. Enter with open minds and open hearts. Please take great care what you ask for while you're in the Circle, and ask for it in a pure, clean, positive and beneficial manner bearing in mind that whatever you Cast will come back to you threefold. You must try to leave behind any fear, negativity, misgivings, or dark encounters as you enter."

Ro and Nell looked at each other and nodded, both washed off in the smoke and stepped hesitantly into the circle of posts. The witch left the sage wand smoldering in the abalone shell which she had returned to the ground near the altar in the north of the circle. They stepped to the altar, on which a large crystal gleamed in the full moonlight, and turned outward to face North. The witch held her candle high and said in a loud voice that startled the still night, "We gather to celebrate the great Cosmic Spiral which is both whence we came and our ultimate destination in this lifetime. We welcome the coming season of Death as a time of renewal and await joyous rebirth at the Winter Solstice. It is now, when Nature dies back to slumber through the winter that the boundary between this world and the next is most porous. It is tenuous now, passable. It is time to recognize the importance of Death as an essential part of life's rhythm and know it as integral to the turning of the wheel in time. We draw together tonight, humbly, in ways both ancient and new to celebrate the eternal cycle of birth, death, and rebirth. We gather in Circle tonight to honor our ancestors and look to our future. We come here for introspection and healing. Ours is a celebration of kinship and continuance. We ask all we ask in a pure, clean, positive and beneficial way, harming none. We know that the purpose of Casting a Circle is ultimately to set it in motion, to leave it turning. We Cast our Circle in the pure, white light of the full moon, and will release our Circle into the cosmos toward a greater good at the end of our evening's work. We ask these things in perfect love and in perfect trust. If you are not of the light, be gone!"

Laura held both hands high and turned in a circle, three times sunwise, and walked slowly toward the altar in the East. Ro and Nell trailed behind.

She held her candle high again and shouted "We begin in the East, in the direction of the rising sun. We recognize and celebrate the Element of Air and welcome its projective power to our Circle tonight. In the East is born the essence of light, of laughter and cheer. We welcome Air's forces of intelligence, power of suspension, instruction, freedom and recovery. We invite freshness, thought, creativity and movement. May the gentle winds of faith stir our souls to seek the Sacred. May we share laughter and wisdom."

She lowered her candle and nodded to Ro, who stepped up to the altar and rang the little silver bell there as she passed it three times around the top of the altar sunwise.

They walked to the altar in the South and the witch held her candle high and shouted "We recognize and celebrate the Element of Fire in the South, and welcome its purifying, transformative power. We ask for its heat, its protection, courage, energy, and strength. We pray our Circle might be blessed by the forces of transformation, love and passion. We bask in the recognition that it is the fire of the stars in the burning turning universe that bring light and animation to the black darkness of the cosmos in time."

The witch picked up a short, blunt two-sided knife and drew a figure over the altar with it before passing it sunwise around the top of the altar three times.

The three continued around the circle to the altar in the West. The witch raised her candle and chanted "We recognize, celebrate and welcome the Element of Water in the West. We understand Water as the stuff of life itself for us and welcome its receptive, restorative, generative power to our Circle tonight. We look to the sunset with respect and longing for our dead. We wish them Godspeed on their journey and would not have them tarry here on account of our love for them or on account of any unfinished business. We know we will meet them again in the fullness of god's own time. We invite the forces of love, purification, healing, growth and friendship to our Circle with Element of Water." The witch lowered her candle and Ro stepped forward to take up the full silver goblet on the altar, lift it to the moon, and then pass it around the top of the altar three times sunwise.

They walked past the abalone shell and returned to the altar in the North. The witch raised her candle and said, "We recognize, celebrate and welcome the Element of Earth in the North. We invite the powers of stability, foundation, prosperity and the Mother's timeless fertility to our Circle tonight. We understand ourselves as infinitesimally small, yet integral parts of the living cosmos and ask that we may make our way through this life harming none. We ask that we may learn without unnecessary pain." The witch took the crystal from the altar, knelt, pressing it to her forehead, and was still for a moment or two. Nell's heart was hammering so loudly she thought surely it would break the spell. The witch rose, passed the crystal three times sunwise around the top of the altar and replaced it. She turned and nodded to Ro, who nodded back at her and walked to stand in a warrior's pose—her back to the interior of the circle, feet planted wide, hands resting on the pommel of the sword that was resting on its tip—just behind the abalone shell. She was on full alert, but not tense, weight on the balls of her feet.

Laura turned her back to the Element of Earth altar and raised both hands to the full moon. "It is done!" she intoned, "The Circle is Cast! Let no harm come to any within or by its workings!"

She paused for a moment, looking into Nell's eyes with kindness, to let her last ringing declaration fade away into the night. She took Nell's hand and led her around the Circle, deosil, once again to the altar of Fire in the South. Both women stepped forward and knelt by the fire ring. Laura held her candle to a small pyramid of kindling there and said, not to the world, but to Nell, in a small voice "As we set spark to our sacred fire tonight, we do so with profound respect for the power and importance of the Element of Fire. We recall it was Fire which drew our distant ancestors together as cultural and social creatures, it was Fire made us who we are. Fire cooks our food and keeps us warm against the cold of loneliness and danger. It gives us light to learn by. We are humbled by the enormity of its power and have not forgotten that Fire can also be destructive. We approach the Element of Fire with respect, tonight, asking it to carry our wishes for transformation to Spirit, our greetings to our Ancestors, and our greater purpose into Time. We ask these things in a pure, positive and beneficial way and trust Fire will warm and sustain us and our purpose this night. We recognize Fire tonight as the center of our Circle, and welcome its blessings as a primal source of balanced energy, within and without."

And then, in the loud, ringing voice meant for the wider world, for the cosmos as a whole, that voice that made Nell's heart pound, Laura chanted:

By the fire within our hearts

We call you forth, O Sacred Flame

From first creation's light you came.

Arise bright Fire into the world!

Arise bright fire, this moonlit night!

§

183

Laura spoke to the Fire, now gaining strength, in a more intimate voice, saying "We ask the Fire to carry our greetings to our ancestors, and to bring its destructive power to bear in helping us eliminate the negativity of unresolved issues with our dead with the waning of this moon. We ask that we may be left with only our love for them to warm us through the cold, lonely nights of our lives."

Laura rose and drew Nell to her feet. Nell was staring into the fire, transfixed. Laura gently let go Nell's hand and placed her candle lantern on the Element of Fire altar in the South, walking deosil to pick up the full chalice of water from the altar in the West.

Laura approached Nell with the cup. Nell started as though from a reverie. Laura handed Nell the chalice and said "Now, tell of your father, and of yourself. Walk around the circle sunwise with each telling and hand me the cup. Tonight the moon is full. Tonight is the night to ask for the waning of unwelcome influences. Tonight is the night to tell him what you wanted to tell him but didn't get a chance to. Tonight is the night to unburden yourself."

Nell took the cup, gingerly, like she was afraid it might bite her. Tears started coursing down her face as she began to speak. She told of her father; stories of untarnished love from her childhood, stories of tarnished love from her adolescence, stories of the full, rich love between them as adults. Sometimes she spoke to the chalice, sometimes she spoke to him directly, telling him all the things she wished she had told him before he died. She told him about that hairball of grief in the back of her throat that she could neither swallow nor vomit up. She told him how lost they were without him.

Every time she finished a story or a prayer she would walk around the Circle and hand the cup to Laura. Laura would raise it to the full moon, walk around the Circle and hand it back to her, round and round, until Nell's voice was cracked and rusty with exhaustion, she was out of tears, and the earth was packed beneath their feet. At last, when Laura handed her the cup, Nell gently shook her head. She was emptied of tales; her shoulders were sagging and her collar was wet with tears. Laura smiled warmly and hugged the shaking, exhausted woman as she took the chalice from her hand.

Laura spoke, her ringing voice filling the night where Nell's spent voice had dwindled. "Into the dying Fire we Cast our wishes for healing and peace for Nell and her Father." And she poured the water from the chalice into the fire, now weak and old.

The steam hissed and rose from the embers. Nell gasped in astonishment as her father appeared across the fire from her. He was smiling, and his hand was reaching out for her. He was wearing that beat-up old hat he had always worn when they were out in the woods, the one she'd seen him in so many times across so many campfires. His lips were moving but his words were more etched into Nell's heart than they were heard by her ears. He smiled at her once more, sadly, and disappeared with the steam.

"Laura!" Nell cried, her voice loud, but still harsh from overuse. "Did you see? Did you hear?!"

"I saw," said Laura, but I did not hear."

"He said . . . "

Laura put her finger to Nell's lips. "Yes, I saw but no, don't tell me. Don't tell anyone. Those words were for you alone."

Nell fell to her knees at the side of the smoldering fire, sobbing in earnest, gasping for breath. The tears were different now. The tears felt healing now, rather than bitter.

She cried herself out again and when she came to the fire was almost dead. Laura and Ro stood by quietly, attentively. Nell got to her feet. The silence spoke eloquently. Nell's smile was one of gratitude, genuine and natural. Both Laura and Ro could tell something had snapped, something brittle and bitter had broken in Nell this night. They helped Nell to her feet and Laura walked around the Circle once, widdershins, to close it, thanking the Elements for their blessings and protective, healing presence in a low voice; thanking Nell's father for his presence and kindness, and Ro for her steadfast protection. Laura raised her arms and voice rose once more. "We Cast our Circle of white light and positive energy into this confluence of time and space, as if a woven circlet of supple willow Cast into flowing water, in perfect love and perfect trust."

Ro and Nell were clinging to each other, trembling with cold and exhaustion and feeling tapped out as they left the Circle. Nell stood mute as Laura and Ro made sure the fire was out, she could hardly remember getting back to the witch's cabin and changing clothes. The witch put a small pumpkin in her hand and told her she could either carve a jack o' lantern with it or make her Dad a pie. Nell vaguely recalled their warm, but perfunctory leave taking and the drive home. She remembered Ro taking her home and putting her in bed, but she fell into into a deep, healing restorative sleep as soon as her head hit the pillow,

§

She dreamed of her father, but rather than waking to a pillow wet with tears as she had for so many long months, she woke refreshed and happy, ready to greet the day. She had a bounce in her step and went through the motions of her life; of going to work and keeping her house and all the millions of mundane things that the living do, with a song in her heart again. She was still sad, but she was no longer in free fall, hurtling toward the bottom of a bottomless abyss.

A number of people remarked over the next two weeks that Nell was a changed woman. Although she wasn't the bright light she had been before the tragedy, she was overheard humming under her breath on occasion again; she did her job without resentment; greeted people she knew when she ran into them at the post office or the grocery store with genuine warmth; and she even attended some small social gatherings without Ro badgering her. People said it was a magical transformation.

Nell felt that hairball of grief gradually dissolving in the back of her throat. She didn't walk around terrified she'd vomit rage and grief up on some unsuspecting somebody any more. She discovered she didn't have to throw it up or swallow it either one. The witch had told her to be careful what she asked for, and that the full moon was the time to ask for the waning of unwelcome and destructive feelings in her life. She had considered it carefully. She didn't want to be heartless, and not be touched at all by grief from the tragedy. She asked only that the grief not cripple her and the people, still living, who loved her.

The witch had told her to give thought to what influences she would like to grow in her life during the coming waxing of the moon, ways she would like to enrich her life, what she would want to fill the void left by the crippling grief with. Nell knew at the New Moon ritual she would ask that the grief allow her to be happy for her father and to honor his memory.

§

By springtime Nell was again able to feel the joyous resurrection of the world as she had done in springtime before the tragedy. By the thaw of that winter she realized she felt her father's presence, not his absence, in each one of her days. Nell smiled to herself when she finally noticed that his presence was often accompanied by a raucous, scolding raven that sat atop the street light across the street from the shop. It was there most of the time and kept an eye on her through the work day. Although her father's absence was a hole in her life and always would be, she rarely fell in it unawares anymore. She could go there now, with purpose, to sit on the edge and honor his memory

Nell got a fresh pumpkin every year from a local organic farmer at Halloween and made a pie with it. Pumpkin had been one of her Dad's favorites. She would take a piece of the pie to the cemetery for her father and sit awhile by the headstone to honor the living man he had once been and wish him well in whatever great adventure he was on now. The rest of the pie she took to the witch, and they had pie and tea and the warmth of shared healing together.

A Sensual Season

Laud and lust if you will after the lighter seasons, but for the truly sensual among us, nothing could possibly be more satisfying, or more fulfilling, than darkest, deepest winter. Nay! I beg you, speak not of it in harsh and unforgiving terms! Granted there are some unhappy words associated with the cold and dark of the year (frostbite and stuck leap immediately to mind), but linger rather, if you will, on the merriment and wonder of the sensual spells Cast by much of winter's language.

Jingle, for instance. Yes, it is a term that has been co-opted by the advertising industry but what, in these cynical times, has not? Even tarnished as it is, jingle is a difficult word to encounter without evoking childhood dreams of winter's longest night, and the ancient, generous elf who roams it. Just speaking the word makes your mouth taste like Christmas. Now, really, which of your neighbors, drinking beer around the barbeque on a sweltering summer solstice night, are going to come over and sing an inspirational song on your doorstep?

We can hardly bear the thought of hot food in summer, diets are brisk and businesslike. It's far too hot to simmer anything for long and we're all outside till far too late to do so anyway. Simmering is a gradual and subtle process to infuse food with flavor, and one that is ill-suited to summer fare. We toss together a salad, throw something on the barbecue and call it good enough. Bake? In summer? I don't think so. Who can think of generating hours of heat in the house to rise dough and then bake it, when you're already sweating and miserable and peeled down to your skivvies to begin with? But take that same warmth, that very selfsame yeasty savor, and place it on the table, still steaming, when they've been out in winter's crispy cold, right next to a cauldron of stew that's been simmering and bubbling all day, and watch the care and feeding of the human being raised to an art form. They fall under your spell the moment they walk through the door and the aroma hits them; their rosy faces are rapt and their mouths are watering before they can kick off their boots and tuck in. Your table is transformed into their heaven on Earth, and serving a simple meal into an epiphany.

Maintenance, too, is a perfunctory business in summer. You stay in the shower just long enough to scrub off the grease and the stink, seeking, but somehow never quite finding, that optimal water temperature that's hot enough to get you clean, but cool enough to stop your roasting. But a long, luxurious soak in a steaming, fragrant tub on a howling winter's night, before crawling into bed so warm and relaxed you can hardly keep your eyes open? Well, when God said "let there be bathing," that's what She was talking about. Sleep aids are neither necessary nor welcome.

Here are some more wonderful winter words: cuddle and snuggle. Think of your lover, and how much nicer it is to snuggle into his (or her) armpit in the winter than it is in the summer, to curl up next to the warmth of him and just linger there, basking like a cat in a sunny spot. If he's truly wonderful, he'll even be kind enough to cuddle with you like spoons in the silverware drawer, to melt the blocks of ice that are your feet. It is a delightful thaw.

And how about those bulky, layered winter clothes in all their vibrant colors!? Aspirin white, I never looked very good in the pastels of spring and summer (they tend to turn me pale yellow, or violet, or pastel green as the case may be), and the breezy, fragile, insubstantial fabrics of summer always seemed almost too delicate to get out and do any real living in. I loved snuggling down into the comfortable, baggy, warm, richly-hued clothes of winter—garments that have heft and substance—even before middle age bequeathed to me the tire I now wear around my waist.

Seems we're more generous with our cuddle time in winter, too. Summertime keeps us out on the frenetic race track of modern life until almost bedtime—it's still light, after all, and there's always so much needs done. But in the winter it's dark before you even get home from work, and the darkness somehow lends permission to cuddle in with an enticing book or a good movie, a sweet someone, and maybe even a toasty, purring cat for your lap. To spend some high-quality quiet, intimate time before a nice long winter's sleep.

But beyond mere hedonistic creature comforts, think on the sensory experiences of winter. The sights and the sounds! The sights sparkle and shimmer with frost. Hardly anything can dazzle quite so brilliantly, nor call forth a sky quite so deep blue, as the sun on new-fallen snow. Sometimes the winter reflects, in uncounted rainbows from infinite miniscule crystalline surfaces. Sometimes the winter refracts, the light is flat, drawing horizons in close. Boring old mundane walking, not generally acoustically interesting in and of itself, becomes squeaky and crunchy, musical even. Those of us who are of an age no longer really walk when winter is slick outside, we mince and pick. It's worth it not to bust our asses, and as a bonus, provides entertainment to the sure-footed. Don't worry about the kids, even if they do fall, they've got so many clothes on they bounce.

Sound can be muffled by winter, when it's soft and still out, drawing auditory horizons in close as well, or winter can fling sounds extra far, echoing in the brittle, frigid air. Winter weather can bawl and complain with its windy voice, and icy winter air can cackle, eerily, even when it is stone cold still. Plop is a great winter sound, too. There is that magical, single degree of warmth when the tree branches surrender their load to the inevitability of gravity. I swear I can hear the tree people tittering in mischievous delight if they can somehow dump it on my head, or even better, down my collar, just as I'm skiing past or, foolishly, shoveling underneath. I don't even mind the work of winter that much. Shoveling is a great cardio workout, and can become a Zen meditation after a fashion. Scrape, pitch, repeat. Make a hole, clean it out. It's not bad as chores go, it beats the hell out of scrubbing the shower.

Even trudge isn't such a terrible wintertime word. Trudge out to the end of your driveway with a steaming cuppa for your plow driver and watch your small act of kindness light up his or her morning.

Perhaps the weather outside is frightful, so recall another wonderful winter word—hunker. Stock up, and stay in. Treat yourself to a snow day. Go ahead! Do it! Enjoy a cup of hot chocolate with whipped cream! You just burned off a few extra calories shoveling, and that baggy sweatshirt forgives a multitude of sins anyway. Dress in enough clothing to bounce like a ball if you should crash, find you some tall shoes, and go outside and play in the deep weather! Romp and frolic! Or stay in! Bake and simmer! And if you're too responsible to play hooky, or maybe don't have a kid around with whom to have a snowball fight, at least sneak a snow angel in while you're rolling around on the ground anyway putting on the tire chains.

⋆⊙⊙⋆

THE SWEET SPOT: EQUINOX

"Our lives might become a protracted mourning for, or an endless tantrum about, the lives we were unable to live. But the exemptions we suffer, whether forced or chosen, make us who we are."

Adam Phillips, Psychoanalyst

Maat is a goddess of ancient Egypt. She is the goddess of justice, of balance and fairness. Maat is depicted mummiform, which tells us she is a goddess of the afterlife, that great beyond whence we are all ultimately bound. She's always seen with a long, elegant peacock feather in her hair. Her mythology holds that in order to cross the river into that great beyond, a human soul must first pass a test on the riverbank. The deceased person's heart, the seat of their soul, is placed in one brightly polished pan of a balancing scale by the scribe Thoth. Thoth then places the peacock feather from Maat's hair on the other side. If the lightness of heart balances out against Maat's feather of justice, the person is allowed to pass on and into the great beyond. If they should fail this test, with eyes watering and the acrid stink of burning feathers in their nostrils, they are turned back.

§

The world is peopled with many mythological creatures and, as mythological creatures are wont to do, they have epic capabilities lesser mortals cannot hope for. By many reliable accounts, among these mythological creatures are otherwise normal human beings to whom balance comes naturally. Easily. It is said balance is inherent to their physical, emotional and spiritual makeup to such an extent that they are able to maintain equilibrium for long periods of time. I wouldn't know anything about that.

These magical creatures must, I suppose, be closely attuned to Element of Earth. They would have to be grounded to be so well balanced and so steady on their feet, wouldn't they? Me, I'm more closely attuned to Element of Air and, disconnected from the ground. As it is, there is not much that will contain Air save balloons and kites, and both are wont to float away in any case. Balloons are thin-skinned and burst easily, so it is that I am naturally vulnerable to chaos, disorder and rupture. It's my nature; balance is a fleeting, ethereal experience for me. On the bright side, Element of Air is curious; ranges far and samples broadly so it's not like I'm unhappy living in this thin skin. Element of Air struggles with too much information, more than can be synthesized into a coherent worldview.

I could bellow and bloviate the day long about imbalance, but that's not the spark I'm trying to get to catch here. What I really want to celebrate is the Equinox, that elusive moment in time where things even out. The sweet spot. Even those of us who are comfortable in our imbalance breathe the equality of the blessed Equinox, where day and night meet and embrace as partners; where summer and winter meet in truce, kiss in fairness and share a moment of cooperation in the turning of the wheel of the year.

Those of you who live in balance might not be able to fully appreciate the sweet calm of this momentary equilibrium for those of us who don't. It is peace we are unaccustomed to. It wafts past us like a beautiful scent on a gusty day. We get one delicious, blissful breath of it at the equinox, and then it's gone. We don't pine for it the rest of the year, we are generally happy in our chaos. Equinox is a brief moment of respite, an exquisite rest, perfectly timed, in a beautiful peace of music. Do you live with such harmony all the time, or is it so stunningly singular for us, the imbalanced, because of the contrast?

§

You might not think it, but remarkably, you can actually balance a peacock feather standing up longways on the quill, on the end of your finger. Now, a balancing feather is a truly extraordinary thing. Every Equinox I pray fervently and humbly for balance; that I might remember the taste of that magical, momentary stillness. Every Equinox I seek out a little something special of Element of Earth to leave on the altar as an offering to Thoth and Maat. A shiny crystal or maybe a rock with a hole in it; something small that Thoth may, if he's willing, palm for me and slip onto the scales on my behalf when my time comes. It's not cheating, it's propitiation.

৩৩ ৩৩

BLUSH

Absence makes the heart grow fonder. If the Spring Equinox is the subtle stirring of an initial thaw, Beltane (May Day or May Eve) is a luscious, tumescent awakening. Beltane cherishes the power of the Sun as it warms the Earth into Her season of fertility. This is no fleeting, adolescent crush. This is that heart-pounding, ecstatic moment you first find true love; the moment you know this is The One (capital T, capital O); the moment the flirtation quickens and grows into the kind of life-affirming love you can trust enough to build your life around. Love that we all share with Goddess and God in this season of reincarnation and generation; a tidal pull far too delicious and compelling to resist. This is a time for lovers in the most Sacred sense.

The lessons now are gentle ones. This is the arousal of love everlasting. The Goddess stirs and awakens fully to her lover's touch. Pink and white abound, naturally, in the world. Trees burst into flower and deciduous trees are achingly vivid, bright, new green. The green that neon tries, but fails, to capture.

A potent and widely recognized symbol of Beltane is the Green Man, the primal consciousness of the plant kingdom. He is a seed who starts out as an undefined character and, with a kiss from Element of Water, jumps up from Element of Earth at Beltane to join and influence the world of the living, his face hidden in leafy camouflage. He is the resurrected god, reincarnated after death to bring salvation and hope of life after death. Guardian spirits (think Fairy Godmother) in the other world and in this one safeguard the newborn life that it may strengthen and grow.

Element of Air stirs us to rise to the season in small ways at first; with gentle butterflies and raucous hummingbirds. The scents are sweet and wet. We gasp as they waft past. Although appeased through the winter by the savory smells of soups, roasts and wet wool, our sense of smell by the time spring stirs is starved for tastes of the living, resurrected, outside world. We gulp the fragrant Beltane Air deeply with its savor of mud, compost, pollen and flowers. It is a time of opening up. A time for spirited and effervescent conversation; a time for opening ourselves to possibility; a time for allowing fresh air to clear away impeding doubts and gust change into our lives. It is a time to rekindle energy and realize connections. A time to see the missing parts of ourselves and connect with that special someone who completes us. It is a time to let our hidden selves out to play in the moonlight; to invite the child within us to adult wakefulness.

As celebrated by the ancients, Beltane was a fire festival when Element of Fire was propitiated with passion. The blessings of the Sacred fire's light and warmth were fertility and safety for people, animals and fields alike (over which the ashes from the sacred fire were scattered). Beltane is the season to court, to write love letters and seal them with a kiss. To let our lusty hearts (as Sir Thomas Malory called them) blossom and bring forth fruit.

Although Beltane celebrates the intimate, its blessings are also wide. We throw ourselves single into the circle of time at Beltane and come out multiple. After being cooped up all winter it's finally warm enough to get outside; get in the garden and get some dirt under your fingernails. It's time to open the windows and reconnect with the wider community, human and nonhuman alike, who have likewise been cooped up all winter. It is a time to celebrate by leaving your neighbors anonymous baskets of flowers, and lean over the fence to catch up on all the news with them. It's time to move; to put aside winter's sedentary enjoyments and dance.

§

Beltane and Samhain separate the pagan year into summer and winter, into the seasons of the living and of the dead. Beltane is a time to focus on life and renewal as Samhain is a time to focus on the death that must needs precede Beltane's glorious rebirth and resurrection.

෴

A SUMMER SOLSTICE SERENITY SPELL

In the Key of Blue

The powers of Nature reach their peak at Midsummer. The fecund potential of Goddess and God at Beltane is now in full flame and flower. It is a time to ask undesirable influences to wane under the withering power of the Sun. It is time for work. A time for magic. While the Winter Solstice is a time to hunker down and draw your horizons in close, at the Summer Solstice our horizons are as broad as they will be for this turn. At the Winter Solstice we will be reborn, as if into a new lifetime, one free of the negativity and bitterness from which we have asked to be freed here in the fullness of Summer. We lay the groundwork here and now for that Winter rebirth filled with peace and happiness.

§

The color of this Solstice Casting is Blue. Light blue opens us to tranquility, healing, patience and happiness. Dark blue opens us to change and flexibility.

§

Privacy and quiet are essential to Cast into the spiral of time with a happy, peaceful heart. Ever remember that we're Casting into a circle —if we Cast with anger or bitterness in our hearts, that is what we will get back. If, however, we Cast with peace and joy in our hearts, that, too is what we shall reap from today's work under the auspices of the Summer Solstice. So gather your tools carefully and place them in your setting with a happy, hopeful heart. Purify yourself with humility to create space in which the positive improvements you want to make in yourself and your life can grow.

§

THE TOOLS

Element of Earth:
> One flat rock for the candles and
> another, say, fist-sized one for the jar.

Element of Air:
> A small bell with a sweet voice.

Element of Fire:
> Three small candles, one white, one black, one pink, tied together with a light blue ribbon. A single clove.

Element of Water:
> Fragrant, herbal bath salts.

§

A small, clean, empty glass jar.

A large-ish piece of blue cloth.

A sparkling clean bathroom and bathtub.

A special, secret spot outside where you feel most akin to Element of Earth.

§

THE CASTING

The beginning and end of this and all Castings, is the Element of Earth. Her symbol is the five pointed star of Earth, Air, Fire, Water and Spirit, enclosed in the circle which relates us, one to all. Untie the candles and stick them to the piece of rock, making sure they are secure and well-centered. Although they may last longer than your bath, let them burn completely down.

Mother Earth is that on which we stand, that which holds us up and sustains us—She is solidity, the law-principle, and Her virtues are endurance, responsibility, thoroughness, practicality and peace.

§

Cleanse your space of all lingering negativity with the sweet voice of the little bell, Element of Air, walking the circuit of both your bathroom and chosen space outside three times deosil. Feel gloom lift and dissipate. Air is the element of intellect, of the life-principle. Air is the instructor, the traveler, the healer of wounds. The virtues of Air are diligence, dexterity, optimism, and the joy of living. You may revisit these virtues and this Casting at any time in the voice of the bell.

§

Fill your space with magic by lighting the candles. Element of Fire. Light the white candle first, to purify and strengthen your sacred circle. Remember to ask for your freedom in a pure, clean, positive and beneficial way, harming none. Light the pink candle second, to protect your circle with friendship, the friendship and trust with which I offer you this Casting, and the circle of your own friends (both human and nonhuman) that surround and support you. Feel the healing, safe, pink warmth of friendship surround you like a bubble. May no harm come to any within this circle or by its workings. Light the black candle last and as you contemplate the candles while you're in your bath, pour what you would banish from your life, along with its attendant negativity, into the black candle as you watch it burn down. So mote it be.

Fire is the element of action, of the light-principle. Element of Fire is warrior, the victor over injustice and ignorance. The power of fire is transformation. The virtues of fire are courage, daring, enthusiasm, and valor against evil. In ancient times the Midsummer bonfire was leapt to encourage fertility, purification, health and love. It was fire and the sacred herbs thrown in it that sanctified the longest day in a wild, anarchic, joyous festival.

§

Draw a ritual bath in your sparkling tub and add the salts. Watch as the tub fills with the powerfully purifying Element of Water. Bring the candles and bell to the side of the bath. Water is the element of fertility, of the love-principle. It is Element of Water which turns force into form. The virtues of water are compassion, tenderness, receptivity, forgiveness and creativity. Toss a single clove into the water, for the courage to change what you can.

Ease into the tub and soak mindfully as long as you want to. Trust, feel, know that the negativity of bitterness is soaking out of you as you bathe and that you are becoming infused with positive healing vigor in its stead.

§

When you drain your bath, you also drain away that which you would banish; it is out of your life and down the drain. As the tub is emptying, fill the jar with some of the bath water and, as the black candle burns out completely, take the water outside and pour it onto bare earth in your secret, chosen spot. The Power of the Mother Goddess and Element of Water is dissipation—infinite dilution. Earth and Water will take what you have banished and turn it into something positive. Wrap the jar well in the large-ish blue cloth and smash it with the fist-sized rock. (Be careful!! Make sure the jar is wrapped well in the cloth —a couple of times around in all directions—so you don't cut yourself or get any shards). Throw the cloth with the broken glass (hard) into the recycling barrel. There is no vessel left in you now to hold what you have banished.

Sit in meditation for as long as you need when all is said and done to consider what you will fill the emptiness left by what you have banished with. Take care what you ask for, both in what you ask to banish, and what you hope to gain.

Offer gratitude to all the elements who have brought their influence to bear on your behalf.

'TIS THE SEASON: LUGHNASADH

Lughnasadh (loo-na-sa) is an understated change, more a sweet little tug on the heartstrings than a fully-formed thought. It doesn't so much spur us to actually put another blanket on the bed as it imparts nostalgic fondness for the cedar chest safeguarding those extra blankets we were so glad to be rid of last spring; a vague recollection of the warm, welcome weight of that wintertime nest. This first undefined awareness surprises a bit because it's not chilly, not yet, it's only a mild, nearly subconscious impression early in August. This trifling surprise triggers the sudden recognition that the vibrant yellow of the clover has faded a bit gray now and the bees are no longer very much interested in it; recognition accompanied by a prayer that the season has been kind to them and that they have enough put up and put by for winter. The spider people start their insistent efforts to move into the house. The season hasn't turned, not yet, but we can see it from here for the first time. We realize it's time to start thinking of putting up and putting by for winter for ourselves. Apples litter the sidewalk and it's time to make cider. Lughnasadh is the subtlest touch, presaging fall's more adamant caress.

As summer gives forth these first delicate hints of farewell, the air in quiet rural neighborhoods comes alive early of a weekend morning. It starts early because it's still summer enough to make what is a pleasant job early in the morning too miserably hot to enjoy later in the day. The stillness is banished before full light by the baritone buzz of chainsaws, harmonized with the tenor voices of weed eaters. Few run mowers here, there are too many rocks. When we open the storage shed to get the saw, the ski equipment, which has of course, worked its way to the bottom and back of the shed over the course of the summer, begins to whisper its siren song.

The cut weeds of the mountain Southwest fill the air with the tangy perfume of sage mingled with sweet, cloying clover, and the harmony of these two voices make each breath taste like the purification ritual it is—we're just more aware of it than usual this particular early morning because we can taste it and smell it. Scent and taste invoke powerfully.

Like all of us, plants have magical, spiritual and physical presences and power. Plants and trees create aromas by means of the essential oils they make. These oils are the plant's immune system, the perfumes attract or repel in the plant's best interest. The bright colors and aromas of flowers attract pollinators, and resins are anti-microbial and anti-fungal to keep plants and trees safe from predation. Spiritually these powerful aromas and bright colors are what make the plant people engaging and welcome neighbors. Sage is a balancing aroma used in purification rituals since ancient times, and it's the terpene alcohols in the cedar wood we line our linen chests with that smell so good to us and so bad to the moth people. Sweet flower smells like clover act as gentle nervines, they make us breathe deeply, relax, and smile dreamily.

Chainsaws may add the vocal bass note to the sounds of this early August morning, but their work adds the aromatic treble of heady cedar to the attar in the air. It's a species of juniper, actually, but people around here call the fragrant shaggy-barked trees just off the rim cedars. We can't help ourselves, they smell like cedars and scent invokes powerfully. Just a short drop in elevation from here lives a diverse Pinon-Juniper forest and beloved aromatic cedar is so plentiful there we burn it in our stoves and fireplaces in winter. We only take the ones that have already died a natural death, of course. No hard work ever smelled so good as going out to get a load of cedar to warm your bones through the dark of the year and, for a bonus, the squirrels love to peel the strands of shaggy bark to make their nests with. Their comical antics trying to bundle more than they can realistically carry make us laugh out loud while we pray that they, too, have a nice, warm nest for the winter. Oak here is rare—solid gold—and we'll take it if we can find it of course, but the majority of the woodpile is fragrant, beautiful cedar. The dark red body of the perfumed wood is shot through with brilliant yellow streaks. It looks like it's on fire already and smells more fragrant than any burning incense ever could. Although it makes a lot of ash, it burns hot and long. We burn it preferentially to the closer and more plentiful pine because pine has more resin and doesn't burn as hot, so it makes more creosote to gum up the stovepipe. You want to have a little pitchy pine on hand, though, (fatwood) to splinter down for kindling. One match, no paper is a worthy goal for the family fire starter and if you have some nice fatwood under some small-ish pieces of cedar, it is an eminently attainable and satisfying goal—lighting the fire in this way becomes a ritual of thanks to the tree people who capture the light and warmth of the sun and bring it in to warm our homes in the dark, cold of the year.

§

The subtlety of the season is most eloquently spoken by a miniscule shift in light, and the first taste of it each summer at Lughnasadh is a miracle *du jour* that makes hearts sing with anticipation of the coming turn. The light somehow tastes slightly different. We know on a rational level the arc of the sun has slipped a fraction lower toward the horizon with the noticeable shortening of the days, but oh, the magic in that fraction! The microcoating of resiny sap on the pine needles makes the trees shimmer in a way they didn't just a few days ago. The blue of the sky is somehow more deeply blue, anticipating the black, black nights to come that will ultimately embrace longest night at Winter Solstice.

Gossamer spider webs, invisible only yesterday, float lazily in the breeze animating and illuminating what was darkly inanimate. The spider people spin two sorts of webs. One is fixed, a home to live and work and make babies in. The other is a means of transportation; they anchor one end and jump off. Kowabunga. Arachnoid repelling. They spin their way to their destination, tie off, and continue on their merry way. The tethers they leave behind are as beautiful in the Lughnasadh light as tinsel hanging from a Christmas tree. From close up they float and wave in the breeze and rainbows play up and down along their ethereal lengths. From afar, the entire forest glitters and dances with waving beauty, each tree meticulously and individually decorated by uncounted industrious tiny elves.

Ancient pagan folk celebrated Lughnasadh (after the god Lugh, The Shining One, skilled in the arts) at the beginning of August as the first of three harvest festivals. It marked the time to start putting up and putting by for winter. This holiday was also called Lammas, the Feast of the Bread.

If you should happen to see a beautiful, garnet-colored, sun-kissed raspberry as you walk past the bush you've been carefully tending all spring and summer, you are well-advised to grab it and revel in its sweet magic right then and there. This isn't the Pacific Northwest, where people have to hack and hew to defend their personal space from the encroachment of the wild berry people. Nor is it the Midwest with the agricultural abundance of its black soil. This is the desert southwest, and aside from the odd Mesquite pod or Prickly Pear fruit we are not accustomed to chancing across fresh fruit here. The Stellar's jays have a sharp eye and a bold manner. They are no respecters of other people's berries and there are a handful of them who apparently have nothing better to do all day than lurk in the adjacent pine tree waiting for those raspberries to achieve the perfect color that proclaims ripeness. The berry will not be there later if you pass it up now.

The family of Cassin's Kingbirds, of the Flycatcher clan, who have miraculously survived the cat to raise their family in the eaves of the house all summer, have fledged their young and are starting their long journey to winter in warmer climes. Their cheerful chee-wheet! calls are missed, as are their complicated and spectacular banking, hovering aerial acrobatics in front of the dining room window to gain entrance to their sequestered nest.

§

The great, pulsing artery of life in the desert southwest is the Rio Grande. Its magical presence touches vast stretches of Southwestern barrenness with Element of Water; the life-giving miracle here in the drylands. This is the time of year our mouths start watering in anticipation of the Hatch chili harvest. Mother Earth has blessed the Rio Grande valley in the vicinity of the village of Hatch, New Mexico, with a symphony of miracles that include the Water of the Rio, the Earth of the Hatch Valley, and generations of the expertise and passions of People who are deeply connected to both. Working in concert they grow the best chili peppers known to human kind.

Communities throughout the Southwest begin to buzz about this miracle *du jour* as soon as the roasters are set up. We know the harvest will not be far behind and we couldn't be more excited if Santa Claus had parked his sled in front of the Farmer's Market. The day the trucks rumble in with their brightly colored boxes the assessment begins. The bravest among us taste first. "How hot are they this year?"

Darn right we tip the young farm hands who come to work the roasters, and we tip them well. We get to enjoy the delicious fruits of their labor all year long. Theirs is heavy work next to a large fire in the

August heat. You can buy the chilies raw, but that means you get to spend time in the company of your own oven or BBQ for long periods of time during the hottest part of the year, too, getting chili juice in the myriad little cuts, cracks and hangnails you didn't even know you had on your hands till you got chili juice in them. Do NOT rub your eyes for any reason. Try as you might though, you'll never get them roasted as perfectly as the big rotating drum with its propane burners. When the pros do it every surface is done to a turn so the blackened skin slips off easily leaving only the fragrant, delicious chili underneath.

These are the miracles *du jour* my plant, animal, and human neighbors share with me at Lughnasadh. You have neighbors who will do the same, wherever you are. If we look to find the small miracles in our lives, the local folk, both human and nonhuman, will share them willingly if only we will listen to them, watch them, smell them and see them.

§

Fall is in the air, you can taste it.

๑๑ ๑

BARBARIANS AND THE POLITICS OF PLACE

Pray for Balance

Landscapes are living, dynamic. They are not merely a slate for the enactment of human history, but protagonists themselves.

Amitav Ghosh, "Writing the Unimaginable," The American Scholar (Autumn 02016)

While the Vernal Equinox is a slow stir, a sluggish, yawning awakening that doesn't want to get out of a warm bed into the cold, slumbering world, the Autumnal Equinox, when the abundance of nature is at its zenith, leaps up in boisterous, exuberant tribal waves.

Humans aren't the only ones for whom this is a busy, busy season. Everyone is bustling in anticipation of winter. As we are dashing madly about to get our firewood in, harvest our crops, swarm the orchard to make applesauce, gather herbs to make medicine, get back to school, and winterize our homes, the squirrels are busy squirreling away. My neighbors leave peanuts out for them and the squirrel tribe is busy as can be, hiding and hoarding them. The ravens attend this process closely. They land overhead to supervise, carefully making sure their shadows are behind them when they do. The raven generally pilfers the peanut soon after the squirrel leaves. Although perplexed about the missing peanut when they come back for it later, the squirrels seem to take this petty thievery in stride and with good humor. Hopefully there were peanuts enough for all and they have put by plenty to get them through.

If we're going to have a lush season here in the high alpine desert, (lush being a very relative sort of term, of course) it will be now, in the late summer/early fall. As the sun continues to slip ever so subtly toward the horizon and I, too, start to be less than enthusiastic about stirring from my warm bed of a chilly morning, the insect, plant and avian tribes are in full throat and full flower. The world is predominantly yellow here; its shimmering brilliance is astonishing, inflaming endless fields. The season is piquant with Penstemon red, Mallow orange, Yarrow white and Lupine purple but it is glorious, cheerful yellow that blankets the world as far as the eye can see. The lesser goldfinch tribe knows this and comes dressed appropriately, in yellow and green, to work the sunflower seed harvest.

Just as the first sad thought that the achingly bright splendor of the yellow blanket might be starting to dim a little, the goldfinch army descends with joyous abandon. This wave of small-g gods and goddesses vanish against the sunflowers. The only way to know they're busy from first light till last is to watch for plants that bob in a way not quite in sync with Element of Air. The tiny goldfinches land on the stem and, unruffled as the plant flails even in a strong wind, hang on with exquisite balance and tenacity to pick seeds from the face of the flower. What at first glance might be mistaken for a breeze ruffling the field of sunflowers can really be a bazillion industrious little birds, working their harvest.

When the monsoon rains have been kind to us, there's a puddle at the north end of the yard both big enough and long-lasting enough to generate an impressively intimidating cloud of mosquitoes. They make playing in the yard very unpleasant but fortunately, their arrival is followed closely by that of the bat tribe, who love playing in the yard with them.

The bat people can get into the darnedest, tiniest little places, and one of those darnedest tiniest little places is a gap in the rafters just over the laundry room door out on the front porch. It's less than a half-inch wide, but bats like it. They camp there for the mosquito harvest year after year and ask nothing in return but a safe little spot in the rafters and all the mosquitoes they can eat. Welcome to them.

We are inclined to think the world exists for our use and convenience, but this is hubris. It's not really all about us. The shaggy bark cedar trees don't make their terpene alcohols so we can line our cedar chests with the fragrant wood to protect our wool blankets. That is a secondary benefit, they make the terpene alcohols to keep themselves strong.

The terpene alcohols are the tree's immune system. It's only as a bonus that this makes their wood—in addition to superb firewood and blanket protector—perfect for fence posts because it doesn't readily rot. Only steel t-posts last longer. It's hard to find pieces of the cedar long and straight enough for fence posts though because the shaggy bark people are inclined to grow in wonderful, twisted, curving and swirling ways. So the pile of 12-foot long, straight, shaggy bark cedar fence posts that was here when I moved in so long ago, was an added bonus this property offered. Treasure stacked beside the driveway. A goodly pile of them was left when the fence was completed and since it seemed a sacrilege to cut them up for firewood, I left them for the squirrels. I thought they might make a good hiding spot for peanuts. The squirrels did love the fence post pile but, Buddhas that they are, taught me it was all about nesting.

Turns out the shaggy bark, in addition to all the other manifest blessings of the cedar wood it grows to surround and protect, is premium nesting material. The squirrel people prefer the long strips of bark they can pull off the fence posts to the shorter pieces I pull off the bucked up firewood for them. I imagine the longer strips must coil better to make a more airtight and warmer nest. The long strips do present transportation problems for the squirrel tribe though. I have lost many delighted hours (when I should have been attending to my applesauce) watching the squirrels try to bundle and coil the long, pliant strips of bark tightly enough to carry home in their mouths. Sometimes the bundle becomes too big to see over so the squirrel has to stop frequently to adjust course and load. Sometimes they lose control of the wad completely and—sproing!—it comes apart and has to be put back together again. Once a squirrel thought she had a such good grip on her load she was running with it—bouncing along in that charming, lighthearted way squirrels do—and it tripped her. Sproing! The squirrel did an endo as her bark bundle flew apart. I laughed until I cried. But the squirrel folk are as unfazed by the difficulty of their cumbersome bark bundles as they are by raven pickpockets. They patiently put their bark packages back together and persevere until they can eventually get them home. Shaggy bark is treasure for them, too.

§

Bats are a ghostly, otherworldly presence. Their survival depends on stealth. Human awareness of them is fleeting and ephemeral. They are incredibly silent, more often guessed at in the periphery of human vision, as they drop out of the rafters of the porch, than they are really seen. Perhaps it is this stealth, coupled with their (largely undeserved) connection with rabies and horror movies that makes people so afraid of them. This is not to suggest bats never carry rabies, they do. So do dogs and skunks and many other tribes. Neither is it to suggest you seek out a bat to handle it intentionally; they are fragile and elusive and not much interested in being pawed by humans. It is, however, to share with you that although I have lived in close proximity to the bat tribe for decades now, and have taken them in my hands many times in the spirit of rescue, never once has one tried to bite me.

When the kids were little and visiting one summer, my Momcat, Morgan le Fey, had a litter of four kittens. The kittens and kids were all at that adorable age when all the world is a wide wonder to them; wonder that likewise enchants all around them. It was one of those delicious late summer evenings to hang around in the warm night, raucous with cricket commentary, and play or read or just sit on the porch listening to the commentary. We were curled up in our respective chairs with our respective books with all the windows and doors open when Morgana came in with a live bat and, casual as you please, dropped it into the box of kittens.

The bedlam was explosive. The bat and both shrieking kids and all four kittens bounced instantaneously from the quiet repose of the lazy evening to full-volume bank shots off ceiling, walls and windows. After the first time we developed a plan. Because I wasn't afraid, I went after the bat. The kids went after the kittens. Morgan le Fey, in the indifferent way of her people, took a bath, bemused as she watched her training exercise unfold.

The kids are grown now and the kittens long gone, but I am still called upon to rescue a bat or two every year. My cat thinks they make great cat toys. Poor little things. Their terror, their tiny, heaving chests and hammering hearts against my palm, bring tears to my eyes. Ghosts that they are, I never see them again so I'll never know if I've actually ever saved one or not. I may have only prolonged their suffering, but there is gratitude in their eyes when I snatch them from the jaws of death, and I know with certainty they trust my intent. When we reach safe distance I open my hand to let them rest in my palm until they feel strong enough to take flight. Sometimes they prefer I hang them from a safe spot, a tree limb or rock overhang. They wrap their wings around themselves and tuck in to hide from the world and recover from the trauma.

I am far more irritated by the mosquitoes than I am afraid of rabies. As steward of this place, it's a sweet deal for me; there is no need for pesticides that kill bat and mosquito indiscriminately, and when the impressively intimidating cloud of mosquitoes is gone, so are the bats. I know neither whence they came nor whither they are bound, but they are a blessing and I'm grateful to them for showing up for the mosquito harvest.

Maybe all we humans need to do to successfully mediate and balance relationships in and with the natural world is to leave them alone. If I should ever be bitten by a bat know it was me, and not the bat, who did something stupid and inappropriate. I try to live in peace and harmony with neighboring tribes to the greatest extent I can. It's not all about me. We need bats more than bats need us. The bat people are unfairly maligned, social, intelligent, beneficial, and misunderstood. I offer a prayer for them:

May you live a long, happy, rich, full bat life

May you die a quick, merciful death in your great old age

And may all your children live

Bats, like horny toads and prairie dogs and manatees and krill and octopuses and so many other of Gaia's most benign creatures are poorly understood and viciously ill-treated by humans, but they are also among the many millions of tiny threads that weave the world together into a coherent whole.

§

The English language is as interesting as it is, and capable of such subtleties because it is such a diverse patois. England was the northernmost reach of Rome, the westernmost reach of the Teutons, and a southern port for Norse language speakers, so the language that developed there is a hybrid of many Romance, Norse and Germanic tongues. The word and concept of barbarianism comes down to our tongue through the Latin lineage of Western Civilization—that is, the cultures downstream from the western half of the Roman Empire when it crumbled. The Romans, fierce conquerors and colonists they were, had never encountered cultures as fundamentally alien to their own as the Germanic people they ran into by the time their conquest of the known world reached northern Europe. The languages the Teutons spoke were so different from their own Latin the Romans characterized it gibberish, unintelligible—barbaric.

Latin borrowed the word "barbarian" from ancient Greece. It was coined to describe all (unintelligible) non-Greek speaking people although it is a term that has taken on a more sinister connotation in the ensuing centuries. Now barbarianism also incorporates notions of crudeness and cruelty, but I use it here without any attendant negative value judgments, only to identify "others" who are so fundamentally alien as to be incomprehensible.

Barbarians, no matter their species, are difficult to understand by nature, by definition. They are *fundamentally* alien. Even the hardest of hard sciences—physics—now corroborates what intuitive people have been positive of for a very long time: that consciousness creates reality. Physicists, with quantum mechanics, have proven with scientific certainty that the person observing the phenomenon defines the phenomenon, in a very real, very physical sense. This is a gross oversimplification of course, but the germane point as applies to the bat people is that each of us views the world—and our neighbors— from a particular subjective standpoint. Someone who is biophobic and perceives bats as scary, plague-infested vermin will encounter them as such, and those encounters will undoubtedly be frightening at best, violent at worst. Biophiles, on the other hand, will be delighted. The bats in my belfry are an encounter with the Sacred for me.

Biophiles and biophobes can't seem to understand each other and generally view each other with suspicion of barbarism; the relationship is characterized by mistrust and confusion.

Thomas Nagel, a philosopher whose work focuses on the distinction between subjective and objective points of view, famously argued—presuming to speak for us all—that as consciousness is essentially subjective, we cannot know what it is like to be a bat, as a bat. He says "anyone who has spent some time in an enclosed space with an excited bat knows what it is to encounter a *fundamentally* alien form of life." That is, he finds the bat people barbaric and says we can only know what it is like to be a bat from a human perspective. Fair enough, we are, after all, contingent, limited and finite creatures. We're stuck in our own skin and culture and consciousness and, from the bat perspective, deaf (=blind) as well.

Perhaps the most enriching and rewarding work we can do as human beings is to try and understand barbarians, be they human or nonhuman. Puppies, for example, are not barbarian, they are not difficult to understand, and most of us speak their language fluently. Perhaps for the rest, for those fundamentally different from ourselves, the most enriching and rewarding thing we can ask is the oh, so important question "what is it like to be you?" The response is not likely to be easy to understand. They are, after all, barbarian and we do not share language, so we must rely on our considerable powers of intellect, compassion and spiritual intuition to imagine the answer.

Imagine. Imagine you are a bat. You're not malevolent. You're not out to hurt anyone, you just want to live your life and raise your kids in peace. You're flying around one fine, warm, cacophonous summer night feasting on a blessedly abundant mosquito harvest (a human comparison would be strolling through Eden, feasting among trees heavy with low-hanging fruit), when a sharp-eyed, blindingly fast carnivore the size of an elephant swats you out of the sky with a blow like a sledge hammer. She then takes you in her mouth, gently, because she wants you healthy for her young to kill. Casual as you please, she drops you into a nest the size of a house, which is full of her sharp-eyed, blindingly fast carnivorous young. You bolt for it. You start to think it can't get any worse when an even larger creature yet, Godzilla-size, the size of a ten-story building, starts chasing you around with a broom the size of a mature tree, trying to swat you out of the sky again. Your chest heaves and your heart hammers. This is the fiery, terrible expulsion from Eden. Your carefree, abundant life is over, your best and only hope now is just to live through the night to make it home to your kids.

This is the stuff of which nightmares are made and yet we're afraid of them?! The tribes only want to get ready for winter. There is no malice at work here and it's not all about us. Maybe Nagel is right and I can't know what it is like to be a bat but I can know what it is like to live with neighbors who want nothing more than to live a peaceful, prosperous life, like me. For them a dry, warm, safe, dark space above a laundry room door and a field full of unlimited mosquitoes is living large. A haven in which to hide from predators, eat well, and raise their babies. The only time I ever actually hear the bats is, very occasionally, during the daylight hours, when they're in their little rafter haven. Sometimes they squabble. Bitch and shove. It gives me a smile because it sounds for all the world like my family around the holiday table, grousing about politics or the price of tea in China or whatever the gripe *du jour* is.

Horny toads are also among Mother Earth's most benign and endangered. They are slow-moving local lizard folk who, while enchanting for little children to play with—they will stay and be the dragon in your dirt castle moat the day long—are, along with the bats, easy prey. They are an ancient and honorable race. They have triangular-shaped, plated heads that make me think they might be distantly related to the triceratops people of the extreme past. If so their family has known cataclysm we can only guess at. They have already survived the environmental catastrophe that killed off most of their kind, and I can't help but wonder if our family will be able to say the same in turn. The meteorite that hit Earth with such disastrous consequences for the dinosaurs was 65 million years ago. I wonder if our tribe, the human tribe, will still be a presence on Planet Earth 65 million years from now and if so, in what way? Perhaps we will be some diminutive, benign endangered barbarian "other" to the ascendant species then. We might pray they treat us with greater kindness.

§

None of this is to say that boundaries are inappropriate. Nothing shows us quite how difficult our extended families can be than the holidays. I try to take guidance from those contentious holiday tables and choose my battles carefully. During the Autumn Equinox holiday some of the nonhuman tribes I am so very blessed to have as neighbors seek to move in and share my creature comforts for the coming cold turn. The skunks dig their way under the outbuildings to nest and some nocturnal creature—a fox I think—loves the cushions on the front porch chairs for taking a bath and pulling off hairballs. They force me to re-craft the inviting and welcoming spirit of my home to be a little less accommodating. It makes me as sad to set barriers for certain of my nonhuman neighbors as it makes me happy to sweep the bat poop off the front porch every morning. But if I am diligent and firm in setting these boundaries my neighbors seem to respect them for the most part. It's a matter of breaking habits and coming to mutually acceptable agreements.

I have surrendered the underneath of the shed to the skunk family; they may nest there in the winter and raise their young in the spring so long as they, in turn, remain willing to let me get the weedeater and chainsaw out of the shed unmolested. They may not nest under the house. That I will not surrender. This peace treaty is reinforced by a rag soaked in ammonia. They don't like the smell of it and I don't like the smell of them. So far it's worked out and we have accepted each other's boundaries.

I stake out my claim and surrender the rest. When I am polite but firm, lethal measures are not necessary. I try to maintain decency and manners during these negotiations. I use a bottle of cheap perfume to mark my non-negotiable space outside; essential oil of peppermint does much to make the cupboard under the stairs inhospitable to the mice people who seem to gain access to it at the Fall Equinox despite my best summer efforts (the peppermint smells as bad to them as it smells good to me); and a nice, long drink from a boiling tea kettle will bid farewell to unwanted plants (aka weeds) just as well as any poison and with more discriminating precision. Although the boundaries are necessary, it makes me a little sad to set them because I understand it is I who am the intruder here. I am the barbarian. It is my people who have invaded, colonized and compromised the homeland of the other tribes who lived here before my arrival. Are my measures 100 percent effective? No. Absolutely guaranteed? No. They are polite dis-invitations that say I prefer you not sit on my porch and pull your hairballs, but I'm hardly going to kill you over it. Dis-invitations that say I am a member of this community, not in charge of it. I know I have neither the wisdom nor the power to play God here and I am blessed and freed in the knowing.

§

And if you will indulge me a few more paragraphs in the pulpit, the Autumn Equinox is also the time to seek out ethical food. It's time to go to the county fair, if you're a carnivore, and spend savings scrimped over the course of the year to buy (or buy-into) a 4-H animal. The unspeakable cruelty and horrific suffering of meat raised by the agrimonsters is unimaginable. 4-H meat is wildly expensive and worth every penny. It is healthier for us to eat, and most people don't live as well as 4-H animals do. You get to promote your own health, support a future farmer, sleep at night with a clear conscience, and reinforce humane husbandry for a bonus. It's a win/win/win/win situation. Food activists are working hard to democratize local, healthy, ethical food, and strides have been made, but meantime the tiniest gestures on our part make a huge difference. Yes, suffering-free eggs cost a buck or two more, but they're worth it. Ethical food is worth saving for.

Cheap food comes at a huge cost to others and to the planet. The agrimonsters and their monstrous allies—the advertising agencies—have conditioned us to believe that cheaper is always better. I disagree with that on lots of levels, but as concerns food, cheaper is what empowers the agrimonsters to visit untold suffering on living beings at the same time they convince us it's in our own best interest simply because it is cheaper. I am not a wealthy person by any stretch of the imagination, so I get that there's no such thing as extra money, but I save my pennies and dollars toward this season. A freezer full of cruelty-free food sees me through the winter in far better stead than a weekend at a swanky spa or an expensive new handbag. I connect with the community of people who believe in the ethical treatment of animals, plants and ecosystems, and all of us are happier and healthier for it.

The abundance of the season is accessible even in cities where local farmer's markets and community supported agriculture (CSA) offer opportunities to support ethical farmers and—bonus!—another opportunity to fill the freezer with ethical, wholesome food.

The agrimonsters will never do the right thing just because its the right thing to do. It doesn't work that way. The only way to defeat the agrimonsters, to *make* them do the right thing, is to deny them their paychecks.

§

We are intellectually inclined to work out our definitions of reality in terms of what it is not. The five-dollar university word for this is dialectic; white is defined by its contrast to black, biophilic is defined by its contrast to biophobic, hard is defined by its contrast to soft, etc. And while this is a handy mental tool for sorting things out in their simplest sense, experience of the living, breathing, complicated world goes much further than this simplistic either/or way of looking at things. One scholar's articulation of the Sacred is useful here. Rudolph Otto wrote that the Sacred is numinous, and that an encounter with it is a non-rational, non-sensory experience or feeling of something outside the self. He said that the Sacred is a mystery both terrifying and fascinating at the same time. It is "wholly other" (fundamentally alien), an irreducible, unknowable reality underlying all things. That thrill of fear you might feel when you encounter the bat people or whomever of your neighbors you find barbaric, so different that you can't begin to fathom them, might be your body's way of telling you that you have encountered something—someone—Sacred. It will do your heart good to seek out and connect on a spiritual, perhaps even a conversational level, with the misunderstood and ill-treated people in your neighborhood, be they human or otherwise. We can, if we put the effort into it, learn how to live with others in peace, how to consider them, not as resources or enemies, but as neighbors. The spider people taught me this.

I am no big fan of spiders. They were utterly barbaric to me. Fundamentally alien. The way spiders move is just creepy to me, it always has been. I have had to work hard to overcome that thrill of fear and revulsion I still experience when I encounter one in the house. I catch them now, and take them outside. It makes my hands shake. As a reward for my hard work, one spider showed me she wasn't so alien after all. I just had to get over being scared of her before I could see it, before I could see her as a neighbor rather than as a barbarian. I trapped her in a glass and slid a piece of paper underneath to take her outside. It was a windy day, and when I slid the piece of paper out, she attached a line to the lip of the glass and began to rappel down in the way of her people. The remarkable thing was that she pulled her legs together in such a way as to fashion wings, rudders, and angled them so that she could make the ride down in the strong wind safely, so she could control and direct her blustery descent. It was awesome! Think of a swimmer swimming inefficiently with fingers splayed versus swimming with fingers pulled together in a fin to command their speed and direction with hydrodynamics.

The spider's aerodynamics were brilliant! A miracle *du jour*. A tiny little breakthrough. The cleverness of my spider friend lifted my heart that day and (as I was a swimmer) they have never seemed quite so fundamentally alien to me since. These are the politics of this place. I live with the spider tribe and would prefer to learn to live with them in peace.

§

Perhaps most unintelligible to me, among the human tribes, are city dwellers. I am a hick, from a long line of hicks. Big cities are fundamentally alien to me; strange and vaguely threatening. I don't go to the city much, and when I do go I do little but stop in to visit and wonder; go to the museum, go shopping, and get out. I am acutely aware of how very blessed I am to live in a landscape I find so beautiful, so enchanted, and so miraculous. I am also aware, though, that many of my city-dwelling friends think I live fifteen miles past the exact middle of nowhere, and they can't begin to imagine why or how I'm so happy living out here in the quiet and the dirt and the dark with the skunks and the bats and the pullers of hairballs. I'd be very interested to hear from you about the miracles *du jour* where you live, and the politics of place where you thrive, wherever that is. My contact information is at the end of this book and I invite collaboration, to collect another volume of miracles, especially one for city folk.

Our diversity is our strength. The company of diverse "others," human or nonhuman, can offer much in the way of enlightenment; they enlarge and enrich the world for us. These are the politics of landscape. It is a worthy effort, to learn to live in peace and harmony with neighbors when possible, when the harried, hectic, sometimes hateful modern lives we lead leave us little time and opportunity for consideration of much beyond the rat race we run everyday. It is a gift, to be aware of neighboring tribes. So when you next encounter a barbarian, someone human or otherwise who is utterly incomprehensible and unintelligible to you, try to respond to them with curiosity and kindness rather than fear or violence. Kindness is its own reward.

؎؏ ؏؎

ON SHADOWS: A HALLOWEEN

BLESSING

November Eve

The word *hallow* means to sanctify, to make holy. Halloween (Samhain, for pagan folk) in America is a caricature of something that might be, perhaps once was, much more meaningful: a night to honor the dead in recognition of their significance to the living, to honor their contribution to immortality.

Inspired by and dedicated to:
Kari Ann Allrich, Goddess of the Hearth

Everything has a shadow. Night is the shadow of day. Winter is the shadow of summer. Sickness is the shadow of health. Old age is the shadow of youth. Last year is a shadow of this year, and death is the shadow of life. A world without shadows would seem flat and stagnant, one-dimensional. Indeed if it were not for the shadows we might not much appreciate the light at all—it is the contrast that illuminates. Our world grows deep with shadows now; another cycle is completing its course. The days are shortening and the nights are filling with whispers.

It is the shadow of death which offers us the insight to comprehend the continuum of life; it is what empowers us to understand our own place in the eternal procession of the ages. The living and the dead are linked together in one unbroken chain —we feast our dead tonight to honor that connection and keep it intact.

Samhain exposes a crease in time; it is a fissure between summer and winter, between the old year and the new, between this world and the next. We bid the God farewell until Solstice and wish Him well on his sojourn to the Other Side. Our sorrow at His passing is balanced by the sustenance and comfort the Goddess provides, and the joyful anticipation of His return we all share. As it wanes, now is the time to take the years' lessons to heart and to face our inner world alone. The coming winter season brings a turn inward. We descend to the underworld to confront our fears and to hallow our wisdom. The Goddess feeds our intuition and, waning, deepens our secrecy. Let us give in to our true passions, develop our instinctive natures, and explore the mysteries that call to us. Pray honor your complexity and your value. Trust your heart.

Let us feast, then, on the fruits of the harvest to support our bodies and deepen our connection to the Goddess's supple guise. We do so in joyful gratitude for the abundance of love and kinship around this table tonight, wholly understanding that contemplating death is neither morbid nor scary. Tonight we celebrate the blessing and liberation in the lesson that the greatest gift of the shadow of death is the challenge to live with full consciousness and conscience. To those who have traveled this way before, we toast our thanks.

MERRY MEET AND MERRY PART, UNTIL WE MEET AGAIN.

꧁ ꧂

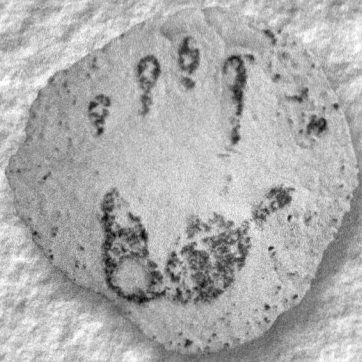

Conclusion

RETURNING HOME

"Imagination is a rational faculty."

Ursula K. LeGuin, *The Wave in the Mind* in the essay "The Question I Get Asked Most Often."

Conclusions are thought of as an end point removed from the original point of departure in a straight, logical line. They're supposed to tie things up; gather all the points together and come up with an Answer, a tidy, deductively sound end. *The Miracle du jour* doesn't have a conclusion. It just returns from whence it came as pilgrimages do. It returns home, footsore and tired, after a long and deliberate journey. Home. Where we belong. Where we fit. Where we thrive. Where Mother Earth knows us best.

Pilgrimages are journeys with intent, undertaken to visit a shrine, a place where something important to the pilgrim's religious understanding has occurred. I have shared some of my shrines with you here in *The Miracle du jour*. But the experience of the shrine itself is not the primary point of the pilgrimage. The shrine is a momentary and fleeting experience in the journey; the purpose, but not the point of the trip. We take pictures and memories of the shrine, retaining it in photographs and souvenirs. What a meaningful pilgrimage cannot shelve in a scrapbook are the changes the journey has wrought in the traveler. This *Miracle du jour* has hoped only to articulate the joy and blessings of understanding the world as a Sacred place, inhabited by holy people. It has tried to impart the happiness and peace that can be experienced living in an enchanted and mysterious world.

In our exhaustingly complex world the simplicity of a capital-A Answer—a neat, strong conclusion—will always have appeal. It is an easy way out. And because we long for an easy Answer to complex problems, there will always be charlatans out there who will gladly provide one for us in return for some or all of our savings accounts and/or our emotional well being. Please take care. Putting a bandage over that hole in us will not heal it all better.

Fortunately the answer (small a) lies within each of us as does the means of reaching it, of synthesizing a conclusion from information readily available to us all: local, contextualized, authentic information and inspiration from the small-m miracles we can encounter every day if we look for them. The kind of information and inspiration that can be found from talking to a neighbor, from being part of a community, from lingering in the company of the wild. A butterfly might give you a big part of that small-a answer, or you might discover it for yourself in conversation with a local tree. These are imaginative, intuitive and contextualized ways of knowing and means of discovery.

I am not disparaging traditional forms of education and ways of knowing. Far from it. School is wonderful and I recommend as much education as you can possibly get. More, I heartily encourage you to read everything you can get your hands on (go broad and deep) but by all means, read with a discriminating eye and study with a critical mind.

For myself, the more I learn the more I realize how ignorant I am. So, in addition to all of the traditional education and good books you can get your hands on, for real and meaningful information, for news that's really important, go down to Rita's Burrito Wagon in the next block. Avoid the fast food place and the zombies enslaved there like the plague. Rita takes time to talk to her customers. Find out what she knows about the world; about the curious and the miraculous. It's a lot. She might even teach you new ways of seeing things by introducing you to another language and culture in the bargain. Find out what that tree on the corner and the squirrel who lives in it know about the neighborhood. It is the nature of trees to stand and watch and wait. They have a lot of carefully considered information. Consciousness is a community of minds.

As you converse with these people, you may find your world a little less lonely. You may find that you are full and satisfied. Replete and at peace, rather than aching and empty. Wanting. Here and now is really the only time and place we have an opportunity to do anything meaningful to save those whales choking on plastic or to win the fight for social justice. It will be the small-p pagans, those who hold the world and all the people in it Sacred, who will help us save ourselves.

I am a witch. I have tried to be courageous and gentle in Crafting my spell and Casting it your way. Contrary to Hollywood and popular opinion, a spell is not an overwhelming or powerful thing. A spell is naught but a seed, one that will only germinate if watered with the intuition, imagination and actions of the person it's been Cast for. It must be carefully tended to grow and manifest into something meaningful, something of substance. I have Cast these small-m miracles into the world as an act of kindness and an imaginative prayer for shared healing and kinship.

§

We live in strange and disconcerting times. Maybe Chicken Little is right. Maybe the sky really is falling. Maybe this really is the end of the world as we know it. Maybe these really are the worst of times. If so, then the resurrected world is ours to Craft as we see fit. Let us give very careful thought as to what kind of world we will build from the ashes. If consciousness does create reality (which I am convinced it does), we can choose to understand our ecosphere as Sacred, inviolate space in our reincarnated world. We can Craft a world where we recognize our neighbors as friends and allies, as our safety net. We can reincarnate a world where power is in the hands of ethical people, a world that resonates with kindness and fairness. A world where we recognize that our diversity is our strength and our reintegration with the natural world our hope for survival.

Imagine.

Imagine having enough. Imagine what even a few more people who were happy and fulfilled—contented with the stuff they have and the neighbors they live with—might mean for Planet Earth. For our Home. It would substantially reduce the consumerism and greed that has us collectively committing ecocide. Imagine not spending ourselves individually or politically into squalorous debt trying to fill that awful hole in us of "want" and "power" and "money" and "want of power and money."

Imagine living a mindful and spiritual life. Imagine being at peace with ourselves and with others. Imagine what that might mean for healing the oppositional polarity which so divides and fractures the human community into the fearful and the hateful now. Imagine talking to other people about what we love, rather than about what we hate.

Imagine if we became comfortable in our bodies as we are; as we were crafted by Mother Nature, that ineffable, mysterious absolute beyond full human comprehension or manipulation. Imagine the disappearance of anorexia and the cosmetics industry. Imagine if we lived on healthy, ethical food. Imagine the Westernized world spending its incredible wealth and brains on food and health care for the world, on education, on sustainable ways of living, and on repairing the damage we've done to our biosphere, rather than on teeth whiteners and plastic surgery.

§

Nobody can hold up the whole sky if it is falling by themselves. None of us goes it alone. Resurrecting the world will start with the little stuff, with small-m miracles and small acts of kindness and reconciliation. These small acts may not change the whole world but they can and will and do change our world, yours and mine. It can start with something so small as a single phone call to get off one junk mailing list. By the end of the year that's a tree that didn't have to die. Go down the street and tell that tree on the corner you did it, that you made the phone call. Wait until the dust settles in your hair and you will be able to hear the faint whisper of her gratitude for her people. Maybe she'll give you a pretty leaf in thanks, or send her squirrel friend to play with you for your troubles. That one phone call, that one insignificant little thing, lights a single candle in the deep dark disaster that is junk mail. It's enough because it's a start.

The most important of what we lost when the world rent us asunder are relationships. What has been lost is community. Our previous and now, some might say, outdated mythologies, were exclusionary. They served to cohere homogenous communities that divided us into "us" and "them," whoever the "us" and "them" might be. One survival strategy to consider for resurrecting and reincarnating our world might be to craft new, inclusive mythology, with aforethought, that allows room for egalitarian pluralism as I have intentionally tried to do here. *The Miracle du jour* has explored encounters between fellow subjects, not between subjects and objects; intentionally muddying exclusionary boundaries and blurring deep lines of distinction. Rounding off injuriously sharp corners.

The capital-S Sacred surrounds us all the time. Whether you are a polytheist like me and see it as multitudes of small-g gods and goddesses, or whether you see it as multitudinous manifestations of one capital-G god is immaterial. What matters is that you see it. What matters is letting the in-sight in.

I trust my people. I trust my community. *Mitakuye Oyasin.* I know that most people are fey enough and open-minded enough to have mystical, gnostic, personally transformative, ecstatic "religious experiences," that neither discount nor negate their analytical and logical ways of knowing or their ability to think critically. I trust that we can escape the stranglehold of the cynicism and negativity we are choking on. I trust that we can grow beyond the either/or ways of thinking we're so trapped in now and into both/and ways of thinking.

§

Just imagine. All it takes is one little miracle.

∿

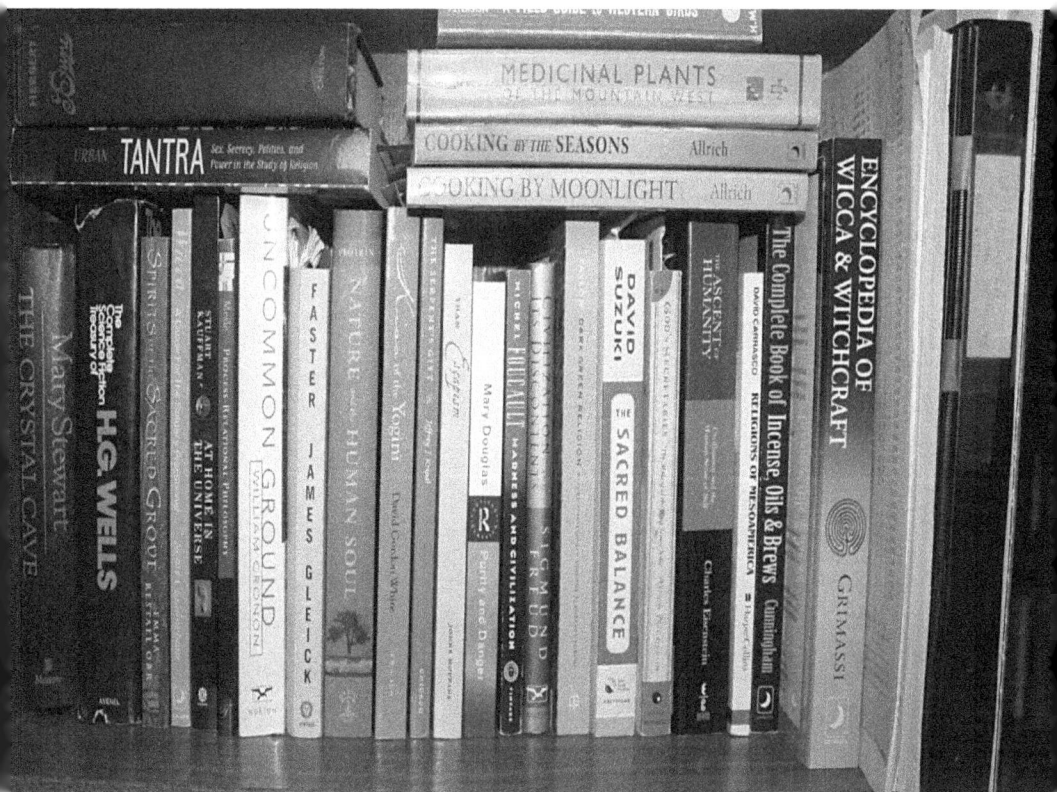

For the Interested Reader

These miracles *du jour* are only an appetizer; they skim the surface and offer merely a prelude, I hope, to your own discoveries. My experience is additionally enriched by the many small-m literary miracles that surround me. It has been difficult to put the books of my teachers down to write one of my own. I offer you my work with deep humility.

More Interesting Titles

A scholar of religion might consider *The Miracle du jour* a folk expression of reverence for nature as Sacred. If you'd like a brilliant academic work on this topic, *Dark Green Religion: Nature Spirituality and the Planetary Future* by Bron Taylor (University of California Press, Berkeley, 2010) is an excellent expression of the global groundswell that is gradually turning into a new pantheistic, pluralistic, inclusive religion. A religion which, if it can become a powerful enough social force, may just help us save ourselves and our planet as we have known it.

It's a tricky business, writing about a religion (a supra-rational phenomenon) from a rational standpoint. That euphoric, oceanic feeling of religious ecstasy (which, you should know, some deem madness) can rob a person of their rational capacity and ability to think critically. Scholars of religion have traditionally been expected to check their own stuff at the door. This, theoretically, was to empower them to engage with the religion of others as objectively and as non-judgmentally as was humanly possible. There is a growing awareness that there is no such thing as purely objective understanding of anything, especially, scholar of religion Jeffrey Kripal notes, of something so inherently and integrally *subjective* as religion. Kripal encourages those of us who find the study of religion such a fascinating insight into humanity not to try so hard to leave ourselves behind that we come to the table artificially hollowed out. He encourages the respectful student of religion to engage in thought experiments that "transcend the failure of imagination that defines the thought of those who can only reason or believe" (pg. 24) in his excellent *The Serpent's Gift: Gnostic Reflections on the Study of Religion* (University of Chicago Press, 2007). *The Miracle du jour* is just such a thought experiment and Kripal's superb bibliography (itself worth buying the book for) inspired the one you're reading now.

Dr. Kripal says that gnosis is a triple-edged word implying at once a privileging of knowing over believing, an affirmation of altered states of consciousness, and psychic functioning as valuable, legitimate modes of cognition. He reassures us that as students of religion we can be mystical and rigorous without contradiction, that we can engage critically and intuitively with the faith traditions themselves. If Foucault (more about him later) noticed intellectual and academic culpability in the subject/object split, Kripal has set out to mend the break and that's not a bad thing. The subject/object split is what tore us apart in the first place.

§

Another broad homage I would like to offer as a backdrop to *The Miracle du jour*, is Charles Eisenstein's *The Ascent of Humanity: Civilization and the Human Sense of Self* (Evolver Editions, 2013). It is an inspired, accessible history of human civilization. The story is told with both passion and compassion. It clarified for me how we came to be the way we are, but it's not one of those books that just stabs you in the heart by exposing all of humanity's missteps and wrong turns. There are plenty of books that accomplish nothing further than that. Eisenstein does not flinch from telling us what went wrong, but he also offers thoughtful, gentle guidance as to where we might go from here to build a better world for ourselves and our children and our fellow travelers on this tiny blue dot hurtling thorough space. He argues, in part, for an animist worldview. *The Miracle du jour* tries to whisper, barely begin to articulate, an animist worldview.

§

If, recalling a class in high school, you thought all biology books were dry and boring, you owe it to yourself to read David Suzuki's excellent *Sacred Balance: Rediscovering Our Place in Nature* (Greystone Books, 2007) It is passionate, intelligent and easy to read. You do not need a scientific background to apprehend the science in this book, which is what makes it the very best kind of science book. Science for scientists can be intimidating tending, typically, to fragment rather than synthesize understanding. Suzuki's work is science enhanced with both spirituality and beautiful writing. It helps the world cohere into a better and more sacred place, rather than splitting it apart into so many tiny pieces it becomes incoherent and meaningless.

§

For an excellent exploration of how humanity has trapped itself in eternal, irresponsible adolescence and, more importantly, how we can grow out of it, read Bill Plotkin's *Nature and the Human Soul: Cultivating Wholeness and Community in a Fragmented World*, (New World Library, 2008).

§

Those of us who enjoy reading science fiction are wont to let our imaginations wander to other worlds. The looming apparition of global climate change is such an enormous, and enormously complicated, problem that many simplistic and far-fetched solutions are finding purchase now that I'm certain, were we thinking clearly, we would never consider. Among them is the idea that we can get away with ignoring the cultural and spiritual shortcomings in us that brought us to this brink, abandon all hope of survival here on the planet that raised us, and migrate elsewhere. Look for another place to live, a new home planet to colonize.

This way of thinking might be dangerously delusional and very possibly scientifically naïve as well, don't you think? If we were to colonize (which, ahem, we would do well to remember has been an unmitigated horror show on our own planet) a planet that had an active biosphere, we might find ourselves in the same pickle as the Martians were in H. G. Wells's *The War of the Worlds* (which is available in many different formats and places—I read it in a compilation of Wells's works, *The Complete Science Fiction Treasury of H. G. Wells* [Avenel Books, 1978] but there are several internet sites offering the full text).

Wells wrote (emphasis mine): "At the sound of a cawing overhead, I looked up at the huge fighting machine that would fight no more forever, at the tattered red shreds of flesh that dripped down upon the overturned seats on the summit of Primrose Hill . . . [The] germs of disease have taken toll of humanity since life began here. Directly the invaders arrived, our microscopic allies began to work their overthrow. . . *By the toll of a billion deaths man has bought his birthright of the earth and it is his against all comers; it would still be his were the Martians ten times as mighty as they are. For neither do men live nor die in vain.*"

To my read, Wells's tale cautions against the kind of escapism that might have us thinking we can run away from our problems here taking our self-destructive habits with us. We have paid our debt to Mother Earth and purchased our right to live here with the toll of our "billion deaths." We may very well have to pay the same toll elsewhere in order to purchase an immune system that would allow us to survive there with bacteria we didn't coevolve with.

Stuart Kauffman, in his exploration of the tendency of life to self-organize titled *At Home in the Universe: The Search for the Laws of Self-Organization and Complexity* (Oxford University Press, 1995) reiterates.

He observes evolution and the biochemical tendency to self-organize and says of bacteria that they perfected their molecular wisdom for three billion years, flourished in trillions of pools, cracks, hot vents, and crannies, blossoming across the globe. Early life-forms *linked their metabolisms;* traded their molecular products, toxins, nutrients, and simple waste; eventually creating a supracritical wave of molecular diversity that spread throughout the biosphere.

Life on this planet, including us, is a product of those diverse, linked metabolisms and the three billion years of design perfection that developed them. We should consider carefully before dropping ourselves into an alien biosphere. Adapting to the biosphere of another planet might just be a long and brutal process. It might not, of course, given that the same essential chemical building blocks are likely be found elsewhere. But in what ratio? Consider the enormous trouble we've caused ourselves and our biosphere by skewing the percentage CO_2 in our atmosphere. Our range of biological tolerances in the grand scheme of things is breathtakingly small.

This planet is built into the very DNA of us. Far better that we mend our ways and make peace with our own home, our own kin, and our own biosphere. Evolution is typically neither quick nor kind.

If, on the other hand, we were to run away to another planet that didn't have an active biosphere, one we had to terraform, the imaginative reader could do no better than the prescient divination of Kim Stanley Robinson's fictional *Red Mars* (Spectra, 1993). The whole trilogy is outstanding, but the first book in particular imagines the future of humans—both of those left behind and of those who strike out—who terraform and colonize Mars. The darkest and most nightmarish aspect of *Red Mars* is the social dynamic; the isolation of the colonists for months on the journey; the terror of the landing; the insecurity of being utterly cut off from Earth and everyone they ever knew; the desperation of being left behind in the cesspool as Earth degrades into a barbaric, heartless corporate kleptocracy (yes, it could get even worse than it is now). It's a nightmare for everyone and for a very long time. The larger message for me here was that we need to hold the planet that birthed us Sacred and inviolate. I wouldn't go so far as to say I'm against colonizing Mars. I only want to advocate running *to* Mars, not *away* from Earth.

Introduction:

I'd like to clarify my interchangeable use of the words magic and miracle to characterize encounters with the Sacred throughout *The Miracle du jour*. There was no ambiguity for me in the experiences I've shared with you here. They were both magical and miraculous. Wondrous. Experiences of and with the Sacred, capital S. But uncertainty about the word "magic" accounts for a good deal of that confusion I see on the faces of my friends when they ask me about my religion and I tell them I believe in magic; the confusion that prompted me to share *The Miracle du jour* with you in the first place.

How to write about such wonders in a manner meaningful for non-pagans has been a quandary; one I settled in *The Miracle du jour*, by using both magic and miracle interchangeably when neither, as they are generally understood in common use, is really quite adequate.

The word magic is often used to describe a trick; a deception perpetrated by a huckster on the unwitting; sleight-of-hand; illusion. Because the experiences I've shared with you here are as real as real gets for me, the word magic, with this baggage of the unreal and untruthful, is woefully inadequate. Mary Douglas, a social anthropologist interested in symbolism, suggested that if the word magic brings to mind this kind of petty dishonesty, substitute instead the world miracle for it in *Purity and Danger* (Routledge, 1966). Douglas respected the indigenous wisdom (characterized dismissively as magical by her colleagues) of the native cultures she was studying more than that, as do I. She understood the magic of indigenous cultures as sympathetic, as touching the very life force of the cosmos itself in kinship. She thought using the word miracle might lend more respect to a very real, very mystical connection.

But "miracle" doesn't quite do it here either because the miraculous, against the backdrop of the monotheistic paradigm that so significantly shapes the ways we think and feel, is generally understood to be something super-natural. Monotheistic religions typically view the miraculous as occurring outside of this, the profane material world. The miraculous lies in Otherworldly realms—in heaven and after death—in virgin births, the parting of seas, and in walking on water. The miracles I've shared with you here stand firmly in this, the natural world where they occurred and were encountered. They do not break the laws of nature, but obey them.

Although I think Freud himself should be taken with a grain of salt on the whole, the words "magic" and "miracle" as I have used them here are more akin to what a friend of Freud's called an "oceanic" feeling: that is "a feeling which he would like to call a sensation of 'eternity', a feeling as of something limitless, unbounded—'oceanic'. This feeling," Freud's friend adds, "is a purely *subjective fact* not an article of faith; it brings with it no assurance of personal immortality, but it is the source of the religious energy which is seized upon by various religious systems. . . One may, rightly call oneself religious on the ground of this oceanic feeling alone, even if one rejects every belief and every illusion." Sigmund Freud, *Civilization and Its Discontents* (W.W.Norton Co, reprinted 2005 © Louis Menand, pages 36-38).

Although Freud laments that he himself never discovered this oceanic feeling, I am certain it is the very feeling I encountered in the experiences I have shared with you here, inadequate terms to describe it notwithstanding. *Civilization and Its Discontents* is an excellent book, even with salt.

§

Some system of recording time is essential to all higher cultures; to fix critical events, to record celestial motions, and to guide the agricultural year. If you're interested in a truly fascinating journey into ideas about the essentially circular nature of time, you could do much worse than to look at the phenomenal intellectual undertaking of the most sophisticated calendar keepers our species has ever known; the Pre-Columbian cultures of Mesoamerica, the Mayans particularly.

The native cultures of Mesoamerica were among the most highly ritualized ever seen on Planet Earth; religion permeated every facet of the culture, including the calendar. The calendar, in turn, influenced every facet of life. There was no distinction between religion, astronomy, astrology, mathematics and religious observance. Mesoamericans understood their culture—and their bodies—as an extension of the cosmos, which was in a constant state of regeneration. But it went beyond that; the cosmic regeneration venerated by Mesoamerican cultures was not something they stood outside of and observed, as we stand outside of our calendars or timepieces and watch time and seasons pass. Mesoamerica did not *measure* time by the calendar as we do so much as their religious and ritual observances *made* time. Keeping the religious calendar was what *caused* the cosmic regeneration. Close religious attention to the demands of each day was necessary to preserve the parallel relationships between humans and the sacred, people were active and necessary participants and intermediaries in the great drama wherein the past and present were carefully woven together in order to maintain the cosmos.

We're most familiar visually with the Aztec calendar, that iconic round stone with the concentric circles, but all Mesoamerican cultures used the basic ritual 52-year Calendar Round.

The Calendar Round consists of two concentric circles, one with 13 numbers, the other with 20 named days. All of the day signs have a meaning and are influenced by a deity. The numbers have meaning too, depending on what day sign they are coupled with. The two circles rotate in different directions. The numbers rotate clockwise (deosil) while the names rotate counterclockwise (widdershins). Every day had its own omens and associations (many Elemental). Meshing with this 260-day count is another circle yet, but one that coupled with the first two levels of the Calendar Round from the outside, turning against it like the meshing of gears, again one turning sunwise the other, opposite. Addition of this third circle yields a 52-year bundle which was an extremely important period of time in the Mesoamerican cosmos. At the end of a bundle all fires throughout the empire had to be ritually extinguished and re-lit in a ceremony of cosmic renewal.

The Mayans added another circle, yet another layer of calendar complexity to keep the Long Count, which accounted for time since the beginning of time, and allowed for the intricacies and scale of astronomical measurement. One cycle in the Long Count is 3,766 years. The corpus of work about Mesoamerican calendar keeping is as broad as the scope of the calendar itself, but Davíd Carrasco gives a good overview in his *Religions of Mesoamerica* (Harper-Collins, 1990).

§

Although this *Miracle du jour* does not intend or claim to speak for contemporary paganism, if you're interested in looking into it further, there are several excellent primers. My personal favorites are: *Wicca: A Guide for the Solitary Practitioner*, by Scott Cunningham (Llewellyn, 1990); *Encyclopedia of Wicca and Witchcraft*, by Raven Grimassi (Lewellyn, 2000); and at the very top of the list, Emma Restall Orr's beautiful and brilliant *Spirits of the Sacred Grove: The World of a Druid Priestess* (Thorsons, 1998).

§

There is hardly any dearth of literary vitriol between science and religion, but an excellent and succinct examination of how and why the scientific worldview came to be so divorced from moral considerations can be found in Lewis Mumford's 1940 essay "The Corruption of Liberalism" in *Insurrections of the Mind: 100 Years of Politics and Culture in America*; Franklin Foer, Ed., (Harper Perennial, 2014).

§

The magic of herbalism and the uncounted miracles that manifest in the plant world exceed both the scope of this book and my very limited understanding. If you seek that oceanic feeling Freud's friend had, embark on a journey to study the subtle sophistication and magic of the plant world. I have studied it only enough to grasp the scope of my ignorance. The knowledge of plants and their powers and resonances is local and contextualized and the source of more miracles *du jour* than can be counted. The work of Michael Moore (the herbalist, not the film maker) are a good place to start. I refer constantly to my now dog-eared copy of Moore's *Medicinal Plants of the Mountain West*

(Museum of New Mexico Press, 2003), but a teacher-in-person is far better.

We are blessed, here in Northern Arizona, with the wisdom of a number of herbal sages. My own teacher is Mike Masek at The Forager's Path School of Botanical Studies (http://www.theforagerspath.com/) and I'm very lucky to have someone so knowledgeable live so near. People travel from all over the world to study with him. If you want a truly magical (miraculous) experience, come to Northern Arizona and take a weekend course from him. Barring that, Mike might be able to suggest ways to find an herbal teacher in your area.

Earth, Air, Fire, Water and Spirit

Both David Suzuki, in *Sacred Balance*, and Bron Taylor in *Dark Green Religion*, reassure us that environmental concern has always been overtly religious. The very existence of these books from such esteemed scholars in their respective fields assures us that there is nothing "wrong" with those of us who hold nature sacred and are possessed of both spiritual and rational characters. So if you, too, were "born" green, please don't dismiss it as unscientific. It is only natural (Natural) to have a spiritual affinity for the living world of which you are a part.

Element of Earth: Home

It should be reiterated that *The Miracle du jour* hopes to inspire people to find and Craft their *own* spiritual connection with the natural world. Cultural appropriation of bits and snippets of Native American cultures, in particular, on the part of well-intentioned "wannabes" is both inappropriate and distasteful. The nature of culture is it's something you immerse yourself in for life. You don't sweep in for the weekend. Stealing it is bad karma. Us melting pot folk sometimes feel we have no culture of our own and, because culture is such a complex, far-ranging and multivalent thing, we are lost without it, tempted to take the easy way out and rob from the richness of the diverse cultures around us.

Generally you will find little in the way of Native American Earth-based spirituality in *The Miracle du jour*. I have made an exception in use of the term *Mitakuye Oyasin*, "all my relations" because my own culture (or want thereof, if you will) lacks a term for family that includes people and nonhumans not in my direct human line of kinship My people's tribal and clan connections were boiled away long ago in the melting pot. *Mitakuye Oyasin* insists that we *are* all related to each other, biologically and otherwise. It is a phrase that is elegant in its simplicity and beauty, forging meaningful and enduring connections between each of us and every other element in and of our living world. I pray I may be forgiven the cultural appropriation of using it.

§

The Rock People: If you have never read Mary Stewart's *The Crystal Cave* (William Morrow and Company, 1979) you owe yourself a treat. It is historical fiction (some would say fantasy) *par excellence*. Stewart's vividly imaginative story is told with elegant, evocative language.

§

The philosophy and model of the machine has been with us for a very, very long time. So long in fact that it is a deeply metastasized way of thinking about the world we are a part of. We inherited a worldview wherein we think of ourselves as *discreet* pieces of a greater machine, as humans in the West have done since Plato (reinforced through time by Newton, Galileo and the Enlightenment).

Alfred North Whitehead was a brilliant philosopher who tried to articulate the benefits of thinking of ourselves as an organism, a philosophy and worldview wherein we understand ourselves as integral and interconnected (as opposed to discreet) parts of the greater whole. It is such an alien concept here in late modernity (or early postmodernity if you prefer) in the West that Whitehead was hard-pressed to find essential vocabulary with which to communicate his ideas (the same struggle I have had here with "miracle" and "magic"). Whitehead made up new words and laboriously defined them. It's a wonderful way to opt out of all the very powerful (typically inadequate) symbolism inherent in the words we already use, but it can make him a little difficult to apprehend in the first person. He is trying to get across wildly different philosophical notions than those shaping the mechanistic world we live in as defined by the scientific model and radical individualism.

Process-Relational Philosophy: An Introduction to Alfred North Whitehead (Templeton Foundation Press, 2008) by C. Robert Mesle is a good secondary source. Mesle interprets Whitehead into language we can all understand. The mechanistic worldview draws lines of differentiation between "self" and "other." Mesle and Whitehead notice that these lines tend to be arbitrary and artificial in general and that they contribute inordinately to our incoherent worldview; the worldview based in the suppositions that a) humanity is superior to the rest of the natural world and b) that our actions have consequences only for ourselves.

These delusions of superiority have resulted in the culture of narcissism we currently find ourselves immersed in. Drowning in.

Poisoning ourselves and our planet in. Humanity's psychosis, writ large, is that of the rapist, where valuation of anything outside of the self is instrumental, rather than intrinsic. This fractured way of thinking separates body from soul and intellect from the Sacred.

Element of Air: Spirit

If you've never heard the song of a canyon wren in the first person, come for a hike in the desert southwest's canyon country or, better yet, take a river trip. If you can't do that listen to this as a poor second: https://www.youtube.com/watch?v=If6whwtbaCs

§

Roadside Puddles: You'd be hard-pressed to find an essay that ties us together with our feathered kin any better or more articulately than George Sibley's "Still Cranish After All These Years" (*High Country News*, September 13, 2010, Vol 42, No. 16).

§

Mary the Yogini: The Bible is a book. An artifact of human language. In the ancient world (as now), the language of record keeping was that of the conquerors. Alexander the Great, a Greek, was the first to conquer most of the known world after the advent of writing (that's why and how we know about him). His conquest spread Hellenic Greek culture and language throughout the empire so the story of Jesus was initially committed to writing in Greek, but little of it by people who actually knew him.

Sixteen hundred years after the sacrifice of Jesus, the Bible was first translated into English and other vernacular languages after passing through Latin. The story of the history and preservation of the English version of the Bible is a fascinating one. If you want to know more about the King James version in particular *God's Secretaries: The Making of the King James Bible* by Adam Nicolson (Harper Perennial, 2003) is an excellent read. The point here is that God didn't dictate the Bible verbatim in English to King James. Erasmus, for example, edited the New Testament four times (and badly, by many accounts), publishing it in both Greek and Latin. The Bible is a document, one that has passed through the hands and minds of many human beings (some competent scholars, some not) over the course of many centuries. It is not, cannot be, an inerrant document.

The contribution to modern scholarship made by Michel Foucault can hardly be overestimated. Foucault was curious about those somewhat arbitrary lines in the sand we draw, like the one between truth and fact we have already lingered with. He was interested in the history of mental health among other things. Foucault studied the line between madness and sanity during the Enlightenment in *Madness and Civilization: A History of Insanity in the Age of Reason*, (Vintage Book, 1988). Were certain kinds of madness treated more severely than others, he wondered? The madness of love, for instance. Was that one to be forgiven? Hospitalize the patient only when the sufferer became dangerous to himself? What about the madness of religious fervor?

What Foucault came up with in the greater scheme of things, brilliantly, is that words count. It matters how we write about things. Foucault, in examining "modern" medicine, saw that the subject creates an object in the effort to identify and understand itself. In English, that it matters how we categorize people. Writing it down, in stone or otherwise, makes the words enduring. He saw that historically the West really didn't have insanity, as a condition that required segregation (read incarceration), until we put such a fine point on our definition of reason. Once we draw those lines as mutually exclusive as, say, between sanity and madness, between homosexual and heterosexual, between religious and scientific, we create an impasse between the two.

This in relation to *Mary the Yogini* is only to suggest that the words we speak and revere as Sacred count, and count a great deal. The Sacred words Cast a spell that define the world. We should be exceedingly careful what we ask for and how. Is the Bible the word of God? Yes, absolutely, but it is the word of God as filtered by fallible human minds and hands.

Finally, as concerns this rather long-winded caveat to *Mary the Yogini*, the term Yogini comes from the ancient Hindu religious tradition of Tantra. Tantra understood Sacred power to be a terrible and frightening thing, not to be approached by the meek of heart or the uninitiated and unprepared. Yoginis were terrifying and fierce agents of the Mother Goddess. Like angels, they were intermediaries between the Sacred and the profane, but there the similarity ends. Yoginis eliminated those who were unworthy of approaching the Sacred and it was no peaceful, merciful death. There are a number of good overviews of this interesting and complex religious thought, among which is David Gordon White's *Kiss of the Yogini: "Tantric Sex" in its South Asian Contexts* (University of Chicago Press, 2003). For a thorough examination of the West's cultural appropriation of Tantra see Hugh B. Urban's *Tantra: Sex, Secrecy, Politics and Power in the Study of Religion* (University of California Press, 2003)

Element of Fire: Passion

If you don't have a favorite geographer, may I recommend Yi Fu Tuan? This isn't that boring old geography from high school, either. Tuan mulls how and why we orient ourselves in space as we do. Axis mundi is the center of the world. Our world, however we perceive it, is defined around this sacred, mythological center. I don't think you could probably find a bad book by Yi Fu Tuan, but my favorite is *Escapism* (Johns Hopkins University Press, 1998). Its primary focus is not axis mundi *per se*, but it does look at how we shrink and expand in relation to this center place. Escape is a response to both push and pull. He thinks about how and why we're connected to (and disconnected from) certain places. We escape home for work, and work for home. We escape our animal nature by immersing ourselves in culture and artifice, then go on a camping trip to get back to our animal nature. A person could fill several books just with just cool Yi Fu Tuan quotes but I'll limit myself to one, here, from *Escapism*. He's discussing disciplinary myopia (bane of the academy) and says "The narrower the field in which a man must tell the truth, the wider the areas in which he is free to lie." (139) Yi Fu Tuan is a broad thinker gifted with drawing horizons in close enough to pertain to us all.

§

Icky Neighbors: One of the most thought-provoking and illuminating explorations of what we consider "nature," how arbitrarily we construct it, and how the appeal (or lack thereof) of "nature" has changed over time, is William Cronon's excellent essay "The Trouble with Wilderness; or, Getting Back to the Wrong Nature." It appears in a collection of essays he edited titled *Uncommon Ground: Rethinking the Human Place in Nature* (W.W. Norton and Company, 1995). Cronon considers the idea of "wilderness" and follows its changing fortunes through the course of American history. He notices that when the invaders first landed in what to them was a new world, the wilderness was savage, untamed and chaotic—terrifying. Its only value was instrumental, that is, in the extractable resources it contained. It was to be tamed and subdued, stripped of its resources. Now we think of wilderness as sacred space, to be cherished and saved, set apart. It has intrinsic value now. Its resource is itself. Cronon notices (*a la* Foucault) that the idea of wilderness is a "profoundly human creation." Every essay in this wonderful collection is worthy of your time and attention. We need to think carefully about what Cronon and his collaborators have to say about the ways in which we will value the natural world, especially now our home planet stands in such peril.

§

How to Tell if You Were Born Pagan: I confess I never quite understood why pagan folk see salamanders as Element of Fire. As a desert rat, any amphibian people around here are necessarily Element of Water. Raven Grimassi equates salamanders with St. Elmo's Fire (a nautical phenomenon) and says that the Elemental nature of salamanders often appears to humans in the shape of small, lizard-like flames. They do rise from the dead and self-regenerate as fires do, so I submit to the wisdom of the pagan elders in this matter.

Element of Water: Rebirth

Frank Herbert's *Dune* (Chilton, 1965) is a fantastic story, spanning huge areas of intellectual and spiritual territory. There is an avatar and a holy war. But the most interesting thing about *Dune* is its setting. Herbert places his story on a desert planet where it never rains and there is no open water anywhere. The native people there, the notoriously fey Fremen, survive in the deep desert where no one else can by conserving every drop of precious water. The war over limited resources that rages around them is, ironically, not about water, which is what they value, but about the money and political power that surrounds a rare drug.

Planet Earth, unlike Herbert's Arrakis, is a water planet. Perhaps because water is so abundant here we take it for granted. It is becoming so widely polluted, squandered for making plastic and fracking, that there will be wars over drinking water in our future as there are wars over oil now. We need to consider our priorities. Read *Dune* and give some thought as to whether or not we want to get to the point we have to render the bodies of our sacred dead for the clean water they carry in their flesh.

The Spiral of the Year

Writing can be elusive work. Often I know what I want to say but can't quite catch the scent of it. I anticipate a feast, but can't seem to get the seasoning right. The dish is lacking a little something. These are the times to turn to Kari Ann Allrich and her *wonderful* cookbooks. There is nothing quite like good food, prepared with local, seasonal ingredients, to connect with the Sacred and to the Spiral of the Year. Kari Ann Allrich's menus and recipes stimulate and resurrect. *On Shadows* was inspired by one of her table blessings. *Cooking by the Seasons: Simple Vegetarian Feasts*, and *Cooking by Moonlight: A Witch's Guide to Culinary Magic* (Llewellyn Publications, 2004) are precious resources on any bookshelf in the house.

§

Few of us running the rat race follow the rhythm of the seasons with anything more than vague awareness of the holidays. If it's 4th of July it must be time for a parade and a barbecue. If it's Christmas it must be time for presents and carols. We don't know where or when or how our food comes, it just appears in the grocery store by magic. James Gleick's *Faster: The Acceleration of Just About Everything* (Vintage, 1999) is an engaging exploration of how we've lost track of time at the same time it has enslaved us more and more narrowly and we're more acutely aware of it than ever. Time has become disconnected from the spinning of our planet and our home's annual trip around its star.

Gleick's is a fascinating and disturbing story, one we're all caught up in whether we're aware of it or not.

§

Practice Limited to White Magic: As mentioned before, Raven Grimassi's *Encyclopedia of Wicca and Witchcraft* (Llewellyn Publications, 2000) is a delightful and accessible "Pagan 101" book. It's another one to just wander through as opposed to reading front-to-back. While it is not necessary by any stretch of the imagination to follow the pagan calendar (Celtic, primarily, for me) or speak pagan words to notice and appreciate the miracles *du jour* that surround each of us every day, Grimassi's book is a helpful insight into the calendar and vocabulary of pagan folk who do follow that calendar and use that vocabulary. I referred to Grimassi liberally throughout *The Miracle du jour* as to, for example, the proper spelling of "Lughnasadh," (although there are a number of valid spellings in play, the notion and word came from an oral, not a written, culture).

§

'Tis the Season: Pagan author Marcie Telander (http://www.marcietelander.com/) whose work is beautiful and eminently worthy, calls Lughnasadh "the yeasty time, the glorious moment of gratitude for the bounty that surrounds us and dwells within us. This is the beginning of the farewell—the long slow leavetaking of the Sun as He begins to release his Beloved, Mother Earth. At the Autumn Equinox, day and night will be equal and the depth of winter will not be far behind. But for now, the Earth Mother and the Sky Father are joined at the supreme point of their summer love affair." Lovely.

§

Barbarians and the Politics of Place: Although I'm generally to be found at the back of the Philosophy class Thomas Nagel's excellent essay "What is it like to be a bat?" http://philosophyintroduction.weebly.com/uploads/4/4/6/2/4462460 7/nagel_whats_it_like_to_be_a_bat.pdf is worth the effort in the first person. There are also a number of worthy secondary sources out there, interpretations by people who do speak philosophy. They are too numerous to mention here, a Google search will unearth many options.

Gratitude List

The comprehensive list of people and places I am grateful to for their help and inspiration in writing this book and (finally) publishing it would far exceed the volume of the book itself. The whole book is a gratitude list, really, it is the wellspring of a happy heart for which I am so very thankful with every step I take on the marvelous and beautiful path of this lifetime.

Any errors or gaffes that remain in *The Miracle du jour* are mine and mine alone.

I want to especially and specifically thank the following people for their encouragement, guidance and support:

Special thanks to Al Brown and WebDust Technology at the ATR. This book would never have come to see the light of day without Al. I'm grateful for his infinite patience and fabulous design, of course, but also most especially for his kindness and friendship through what has been a stressful and, at times, baffling process.

I am grateful beyond my ability to say for my family; both my family of birth and my family of choice. *Mitakuye Oyasin.* It can't have been easy to put up with me and my chaotic ways. Thank you for letting me live.

It's important in many spiritual and scholarly traditions for the student to acknowledge their intellectual lineage. Among my family of choice I am happy and privileged to count teachers who are really teachers. They put on their armor and wade into the muck that is the educational system and do their best to educate the resistant they find there. Among these many gurus thanks especially to Peter van der Loo, for introducing me to the academic love of my life, Religious Studies;

Paul Donnelly, Luminary, for all the interesting rabbit holes (and books!), especially for the consciousness rabbit hole, over lo, these many years, and to Sandra Lubarsky, Arne Hassing and Janine Schipper, Professors of Compassion.

Thanks to Eric Eliason. Not only is Eric a talented photographer who, with minimal whining, let me use the beautiful hummingbird picture that graces the cover of this book, he is also a brilliant (hard-headed) scientist too; one who is persistently good-natured and willing to talk about science and religion (and science versus religion).

Gratitude to Mike Masek for introducing me to the Capital-M Miracle that is the world of herbalism and to the Anarchists book club for keeping me from the complete social isolation I tend to seek if left to my own devices.

My happiness and gratitude always has and always will rest with Helen, Gayle and Jane because life without girlfriends is not worth living.

Thanks to Lynn Natal Hartman, editor extraordinaire, who magically appeared in my life *just* when I needed her, like all good Fairy Godmothers do.

There are friends, and then there are friends indeed. Friends who are allies, people you can call on when you need help. Deepest thanks to the allies who cast a critical eye at an early draft of this manuscript: Pamela El Baz and Sue O'Farrell.

And thanks especially and always to Bob Moore, Element of Earth, Element of Fire. He has been my anchor for more years than I can count now, and is the kind of advocate you want in your corner not on some opposing team. He is also a rare friend to a fledgling writer. He has read every word of drivel I've written for 20 years now, and that's a heckuva lot of drivel by now.

Colophon

To counteract and subvert the culture of fundamental corruption inherent in the overly politicized and coporatized early 21st-century calls for public organizations dedicated to protecting human rights. FLOSS, Free/Libre Open Source Software, is a concept, a movement, and a business structure. FLOSS is the Internet equivalent of free speech; it is synonymous with the right to freedom of expression in the high tech world.

To exercise freedom of speech in any meaningful way requires both the legal right to expression and the tacit *ability* to speak freely. Many of the people and organizations protecting the right to free speech are those who supply the digital tools with which to do so, and they support FLOSS principles. These people and organizations labor under a moral responsibility to humanity and ask only for attribution in return when their work is used.

MoonLit Press supports these contemporary freedom fighters and offers attribution to their work with gratitude:

The ability to have and use Free Software is supported and defended by the Free Software Foundation; [http://fsf.org/] among others.

Many FLOSS applications were used in the preparation of this book. Most of them are licensed using the GNU Public License of equivalent FLOSS licenses.

The text of this book was prepared using LibreOfficeWriter; [https://www.libreoffice.org/].

The graphics were prepared using GIMP; [http://www.gimp.org/], and Inkscape; [http://inkscape.org/]. Gimp is a high quality continuous tone image editing package, and Inkscape is a sophisticated scalable vector graphics editing package.

All of the standard fonts used in the creation of this book are licensed under the Open Font License (OFL). [http://www.sil.org/about]. The main body of this book was typeset using Gentium typeface. Gentium is a typeface family, from the SIL International Organization, designed to enable diverse ethnic groups around the world who use the Latin, Cyrillic and Greek alphabets to produce readable, high-quality publications.

The font used for headings throughout the book is Tillana, first published by the Indian Type Foundry as an open source project in 2014. It has all the characters necessary to set a variety of European and Indian languages. https://www.indiantypefoundry.com/

Libre Baskerville was used on the legal page. It is a revival of a classic old newspaper font, based on specimens from 1941. http://www.impallari.com/

Kingthing Petrock is the font used for the poetry in this book. It is based on a labeling hand its creator found in a tiny city church in central Exeter, England, in a display case regarding bell ringing. http://www.kingthingsfonts.co.uk/

The cover and title font is Qumpellka No. 12, by gluk (Luck), who designed it with Opentype Features: Ligatures and Contextual Alternates. http://www.glukfonts.pl/font.php?font=QumpellkaNo12

We offer our humble and sincere thanks to all the hard working, unnamed, and under-appreciated people around the world who build the tools we need to keep freedom and integrity alive in the high-tech world. MoonLit Press supports these dedicated champions of social and technological justice in their quest to ensure technological advances do not erode our rights. Our children will thank them.

MoonLit Press

About the Author

Terryl Warnock lives and works with a happy heart in rural Northern Arizona. She's had a handful of disparate careers by now and is settling in with delight to write out the twilight of this lifetime. She is deeply rooted in Northern Arizona, loves to read, and is a curious sort; Element of Air keeps her mind and imagination moving.

Terryl is proud to be affiliated with MoonLit Press and will welcome your correspondence at:

mailto:terryl@moonlitpress.com

www.ingramcontent.com/pod-product-compliance
Lightning Source LLC
Chambersburg PA
CBHW030004290326
41934CB00005B/220